SMILE, YOU'RE TRAVELING

Other titles in the series

BLACK COFFEE BLUES
DO I COME HERE OFTEN?

SMILE, YOU'RE TRAVELING

BLACK COFFEE BLUES PT 3

Henry Rollins

Virgin BOOKS

First published in Great Britain in 2006 by
Virgin Books Ltd
Thames Wharf Studios
Rainville Road
London W6 9HA

Published in USA 2000 by 2.13.61 Publications

A catalogue record for this book is available from the British Library.

ISBN 0 7535 1030 8
ISBN 9 780753 510308

Typeset by TW Typesetting, Plymouth, Devon
Printed and bound in Great Britain by Mackays of Chatham

ACKNOWLEDGMENTS

Thank you: Carol Bua for her long hours
put in on this book's behalf, Eugene Gant,
all of you for checking this out and
Mitch Bury of Adams Mass.

Joe Cole
4.10.61–12.19.91

1997

11-24-97 LA CA: 0213 hrs. Sitting at my desk, a couple of days away from what could be a great adventure. I came back from tour on November 03. I was burnt from the shows and the year in general. Management called and informed me that I had collected 550 thousand frequent flier miles over the year and suggested I take a trip somewhere.

I booked a trip, which I will now detail.

A couple of months ago I interviewed Ozzy Osbourne for a video press kit to promote his best of 'The Ozzman Cometh' at Sony. As always, it was cool to hang out with the man. After the interview was done, his wife and manager, Sharon, told me that the original line up of Black Sabbath were reuniting for two shows in their home town of Birmingham, England, on December 4th and 5th. I told her that I would be there without fail. There was no way I was going to miss that. Geezer Butler, Tony Iommi, Bill Ward and Ozzy all on one stage? I was already there.

I called Sharon last week and asked her who was documenting this legendary event and if she didn't have anyone, could I do it? She gave me the green light. I managed to get permission to hang out at band practice for a couple of days to check that out.

I leave in a couple of days to go to London. I go from there to Monmouth, Wales, for a couple of days to check out Sabbath practice and then down Birmingham, UK, to the Birmingham NEC for two days of pre-production and the gigs. I will be interviewing the band and anyone else Sharon wants me to. I will be coordinating all the other video crews who will be there to cover the event. I will be busy but it will be a blast. After that, I fly from London to Nairobi, Kenya, and from there out to a camp site in Maasai country to check out the animals and the locals. From there, I go to Madagascar to check out the

Indian Ocean and see what it's like there. From there I will stop over in Johannesburg and then back to LA via London. Should be intense.

The other day, I went to a travel doctor and he briefed me on all the things that I have to look out for and shot me full of vaccines. He said some intense stuff. I should be out of the range of Ebola, always good to be out of the way of that stuff. So much shit in Africa can kill you.

I have wanted to go to Africa for years. I have wanted to go to a Maasai village since I saw pictures of them in *National Geographic* as a kid. This will be intense as hell. SABBATH!!!

How unbelievably cool is this going to be. It's only my favorite bass player and drummer of all time. I have been playing Sabbath nonstop for the last few days, getting psyched for the trip. Black Sabbath and Africa. This is going to be so cool.

I never get tired of listening to Sabbath. It's timeless music. I remember listening to the *Paranoid* album in the back of the school bus in the mid-70s. Ozzy's voice didn't sound like the other bands of the day. He sounded like some guy off the street. They felt more real than other bands at the time.

11-27-97 Monmouth Wales: Got into Heathrow a while ago and then got a ride here.

I am now in my little room in this little town and it's cool. I discovered that I left my itinerary in LA on my desk most likely and don't know what to do about that for the time being as it is a holiday back there.

11-28-97 Monmouth Wales: It's a little past midnight. One of those *Hellraiser* films is on the television, I have the sound off. It's really bad but it keeps the room alive. I have the typical jet-lagged depression I always get. I wish I had stayed awake more but I needed the sleep. I am looking forward to getting into the Sabbath thing.

In my daydream I see myself as a decorated road veteran of many tours and many intense records who now has stepped aside to let others take their turn up there. Isn't that hilarious? On the other hand there's the guy who never really ces back all the way who writes all kinds of tripped out shit from different places all over the world and gets off living in fucked up rooms all over the place and no one really knows him all that well. I think that one works for me better.

I am where I should be right now. It is early. I am alone and Thin Lizzy is on the headphones. I am in a small room in the middle of nowhere chasing one of my dreams. I think that is about as good as it gets for a guy like me.

11-29-97 Monmouth Wales: Yesterday will definitely go down in the annals of my life as one great day.

I got picked up by Ozzy's assistant, Tony, and we went over to the studio where the band has been living and working. It's the place they have written and recorded on and off for years. I think it's called The Mill.

Tony says that the guys will be waking up and coming downstairs at some point and until then, I can just hang out and wait. I wander around the place, wondering what the rest of the guys in the band are like. I have never met any of them besides Ozzy. I hope that they're cool. You always run the risk of meeting your heroes and having them disappoint you.

I walked into the living room and there's Ozzy watching a movie. He's happy to see me and we hang out and watch television and it's so damn cool just to hang out with the man. From my right, I hear someone call my name, I look up and it's Tony Iommi. He's cool as hell and it starts to occur to me that this is the coolest adventure in awhile. This is so great for me. I have been into that guy's playing since I was twelve or something and now we're hanging out. I know, I am a spazz. Fuck it. Black Sabbath rules.

One of their roadies came in and took me on a tour through the house. It's also serving as their practice place. I check that out and we go into the kitchen. I'm in there with Iommi and we're hanging out and Geezer Butler walks in. My favorite bass player. Of course, I don't tell him that. I imagine that would be too weird for the guy to come down from his room and have this maniac fan boy telling how great he is first thing in the morning. I just played it cool but the whole time I am thinking that this is easily the coolest part of the year so far.

I wander back into the practice room because I saw a set list in there and wanted to check it out. What a set list. It's all there and then some. Tony comes in and we're talking about the set and Bill Ward walks into the room. Tony says, 'This guy keeps showing up to play drums!' Bill told me that he thought that the guys were kidding him that I was coming. He is a very soft-spoken man and very cool. Fuckin' Bill Ward, how cool is this? My favorite drummer.

Within a half an hour, the band got ready to run through the set. Geezer warmed up by playing 'Fluff'. So cool. I sat near the keyboard player Jeff's set up. Ozzy was in front of me and the band guys were to my right. They set up the same as the Rollins Band did. I sat still not wanting to be in the way or distracting but I felt like jumping up and down. They laid into the first song which was 'War Pigs' and it was insane. Then it hit me – I am in a small practice room with Black Sabbath and a couple of other people and I am having my own Sabbath concert. I figure this is as about as good as it gets.

I rocked out so hard in my little perch over the next two hours of solid bone-breaking shit. I sang myself hoarse. I thought about Joe Cole and how he would have been so into this.

After they finished playing we hung out in the kitchen. They asked me if I wanted to stay for dinner. Of course. One thing that really got me about those guys is the level of kidding around that they do. They really seem to get off on each other big time and they don't take themselves too seriously. The music was played with bruising malice but they were having a great time doing it. I can't remember which song it was, maybe 'Snow Blind' or 'Sabbath Bloody Sabbath' where they were all grinning and rocking out.

Tony asked me if I wanted to hear riffs he had on tape for his next solo album. I listened to some of it and it was pretty great and he asked me if I would like to sing on a track. I heard this one track that was intense as hell and asked him if I could work out on that one. He's doing the record in LA in January so that will be a snap. We ended up sitting in Bill Ward's room talking about shows and all kinds of stuff for well over an hour. He didn't know that *Live at Last* was re-issued. If I see it in B'ham, I'll get it for him. We went downstairs because dinner was almost ready. We sat around the table and shot the shit. Geezer had already left so it was band and crew minus him. Bill Ward sat on my left and Ozzy on my right. They start telling stories and it was hard to eat they were all so funny. They fuck with Bill relentlessly. Every time the phone rings, they told him it was for him. They start detailing all the things that they have done to Bill over the years. Like the time Tony set him on fire with lighter fluid. Apparently he did it all the time when they were recording and one time Tony put too much on and Bill was rolling on the ground screaming and Tony thought he was laughing so he put more on and Bill started screaming more because it had gone through his clothes and was burning the shit out of him. Poor Bill went to the hospital with third-degree burns.

Bill left to go do some errands and as soon as he left, Ozzy started telling these stories about Bill back in the days that were hilarious. Ozzy is running around the room yelling and telling these stories. Hilarious shit. We were all dying at the table. If there was ever a time to have a video camera on, it was then. There's no way to describe how funny he was and how great it looked to see everyone laughing into their dinner plates.

Tony took off and came back a few minutes later saying that he couldn't get his truck out of the mud. Ozzy and I went out and pushed him out of the ditch. There's me and Ozzy pushing the dark lord of metal out of a ditch. I'll remember that one for the rest of my life. Tony gave me a lift back here.

I got back here just tripping on the awesomeness of the day. I know for them it was just another day of practice with this nutcase hanging around asking too many questions. I am sure I wore them out on the info scan but they were so cool to me.

Maybe they see how much their work means to me. I must say, I was a little intimidated by the idea of meeting the mighty Black Sabbath but they are all cool as hell.

1.43 p.m. B'Ham UK: Made the move and got to the other hotel. It's another small room but it's a little better than the one I was in. Anyway, it's good to get the travel over with. I don't like having it hanging over my head. I was curious as to what the town here was going to have anyway. Monmouth was not the most interesting place I have ever been to.

11-30-97 Birmingham UK: It's a bit before seven in the morning. I fucked up big time yesterday. I gave in to jet lag around three in the afternoon and kept sleeping and dozing until midnight. Have been up ever since. It's fucked. Today will be hard.

I watched INXS man's funeral proceedings on the news. I saw Nick Cave sitting two seats away from Paula Yates and her kid. The singer's brother did some kind of eulogy thing. He was wearing a really loud jacket, I imagine the sentiment was INXS man would have wanted it that way. So lame. One of the band guys said that no one should try to go the same route that the singer went as if there will be people killing themselves because Michael Hutchence is no longer with us. Please. I remember Paula Yates. I had to endure her when I was on a television show in England. At that point she was fucking the idiot from the Boomtown Rats. She was a mouthy moron. She is all broken up now that her about-to-be hubby hanged himself. They managed to breed before INXS man fell off. I feel sorry for the little girl. She'll have to deal with the fact that her father was a past it fuck up and that her mother is some stretched out groupie.

Next up was Courtney Love being covered in one of those Hollywood shows as one of the four women that we will all be looking to as far as upcoming fashion trends. They showed the other four, like Halle Berry who is a knockout and then there's Courtney. The women on the show are calling her a movie star and talking about her like she's this staggering beauty. Now you can rest easy knowing that the media is totally full of it and can't be taken seriously.

9.54 a.m.: Back from breakfast. I am watching this thing about Princess Diana's brother's divorce. It's insane to get married. Look at the divorce thing. It's so lame. I can't see getting married.

7.12 p.m.: I went into the city today and walked around and it was cool. I found a few good records that Ian turned me onto when I was out at his place. I am playing one right now

I barely got into the grocery store right before closing. I got there at four right when the place closes. Luckily the guard recognized me and let me slide in to get some food. The guy was cool but fuck these places. Closing at four in the afternoon. If that guy wasn't cool enough to let me in, I would have no groceries tonight. England is a pain in the ass sometimes.

12-01-97 Birmingham UK: It's about noon. I stayed up late last night and I think I am doing alright. I have nothing to do today so I'll do stretches and pushups and stuff in the room.

I talked to Tony, Ozzy's assistant, and he said that things are going as planned for tomorrow. I will get down to the NEC around five or so and watch the photo sessions, practice and whatever else there is to take in.

7.03 p.m.: Back from dinner. It was fairly good Indian food. I heard Gladys Knight and the Pips on the radio: 'Midnight Train to Georgia'.

I was walking down the street back from the restaurant, thinking how much I like to be alone. I like to feel like I am a soldier who comes home to no one. I come home to nothing. I feel like this and am glad. I think it's great to come home to no one. I like to know things that cannot be translated to others. I am at that point in my life where I don't feel the need to communicate like I used to. I did have a lot to prove but I don't any more. I needed to do all the things I did in order to define myself. Now I feel alright and like to be alone. It's really the only way I can be. I am not a people person. the only time I feel real is when I'm alone. People are cool, but you have to keep up appearances for them. I think everyone acts out a little when they're in public to a certain extent, or is it just me?

12-02-97 Birmingham UK: Screwed up on the sleep again. Passed out for a little while and spent the rest of the night awake.

Tonight is the start of the four nights of Black Sabbath, the reason I came all the way out here. I still think it was worth it to see band practice. I will never forget that as long as I live. It was worth it big time but the last few days have been brutal. I have been cooped up in this room. To add insult, I found out today that the Fall has been playing on all the nights I have been here. I could have seen the Fall at least two nights. How about that? I was sitting here burning out when Mark E Smith was being mean to a bunch of Fall fans somewhere. I could have been there.

From now on my next few days have a bit more schedule happening. I will go to the venue at five for a few hours and then that's it. Same for the next day. Wednesday might be interesting because it is Ozzy's birthday and there will be a party for him that I will get to go to. Should be cool.

The fire alarm went off and I went out of the room to see if it was just me or if the whole building was sounding off. It was the whole building. I passed a couple of firemen on the stairs and that was about all the excitement I have had today. Birmingham.

12-03-97 Birmingham UK: It's around eleven. I am leaving in a couple of hours. Have work at the NEC, doing the EPK for the live Sabbath album that the band will be recording over the two shows. I was watching them practice at the NEC last night and I was thinking about Joe. How cool would it have been if he was here for this. If he saw them jamming like I did, I know the exact look he would have given me too. He would have looked at me with that 'This is us, this is what we're all about' look. I was thinking about you Joe. Sometimes I still don't believe that I have to settle on the fact that he's dead. I still sometimes think that there is something that could be worked out. Strange to be in denial over something so absolute.

12-04-97 Birmingham UK: It's almost nine on the morning. I wish I could sleep for more than a few hours at a time. I was dying yesterday. I got to my room after midnight and still only slept for a few hours. I will be out of this place tomorrow and I can't wait to get on to the next adventure.

12-05-97 Birmingham UK: I check out of here today. I will go from here to the NEC and get ready for the shows and do more interviews and whatever else Sharon can think of.

All day long, everyone from the crew to the catering staff were getting more and more amped as the hour drew closer. It was so cool to be around all these people who were all stoked to be in on this. It was as if we were all going to be up there with the band. Everyone is here because they are Sabbath fans. Everyone is excited as hell. Everyone is hanging out. It's like Team Sabbath 1997. I had lunch with Bill Ward and we talked about all kinds of stuff. He told me about what happened to him in the 80s after he split from Sabbath. He's got one hell of a story.

By nightfall the people were coming into the venue. The train stop next to the NEC was full of metal kids in various states of black and denim. Backstage, everyone was getting excited. The band types were keeping a low profile, the rest of us congregated in the catering area and waited. Everyone I looked at looked back at me with a huge grin. We knew that we were in for two amazing nights of the ultimate shit. Think about it, as far as bands from back in the day go, hardly anyone could play with their original line up. It's amazing that the Sabbath guys survived themselves.

Soon enough it was Sabbath time. I went out to the soundboard and waited. The pre-show video started playing and the place started going off. It was wall to wall maniacs. Sabbath walks on and promptly steps on 'War Pigs'. Ozzy sang every other line and the crowd sang the following line back at him. It was so cool. The show was awesome. I could see Bill up there working hard. He rocked it. Tony, Geezer, all of them kicked ass. It was so cool to see Geezer and Bill playing together. They are the ultimate rock rhythm section for me. The crowd was with the band every step of the way. They sang along with all the songs and never let the energy drop. On 'Sabbath, Bloody Sabbath' people even screamed back 'You bastards!' Rockin'. I knew I was in the right place.

At the end of the set, the band came to the edge of the stage to say good night to the crowd. Bill's waving to people and smiling. Ozzy sneaks up behind him and grabs the sides of Bill's pants to try to pull them down. Bill barely made the save. It was great. I went to Bill's room after the show to tell him he had played great and told him that it was a close call on the pants coming off. He said that Ozzy used to do that to him all the time.

I got back here and just tripped on the whole thing for awhile and tried to sleep. Can't wait for tonight.

12-06-97 London UK: At the airport, about six in the morning. I have to hit it soon. I will go to Frankfurt and then on to Kenya. Very nice but nothing as awesome as the show last night. The first one was cool but last night was the item. I knew it was going to be one of those nights as soon as the first song started. I have had enough of those nights myself and can see it with other bands. It was definitely going to be one of those nights. It was the best show I saw this year and one of the best shows I have ever seen period. Bill settled in way better than the night before and played with a lot of confidence. Ozzy's voice was better and he was having such a good time. Geezer and Tony never seem to miss so they were perfect as far as I could tell. The crowd was so into it. The way everyone sang along with 'Sabbath, Bloody Sabbath' was insane. They swallowed the earth whole.

It was a long day for me. I ended up interviewing everyone in the band twice. I was wandering around backstage with my camera crew and Sharon tells me that she wants me to interview Brian May, who's a few feet away. I told her that I was too intimidated to approach the guy after a show and bug him for an interview but she told me to get on with it and it's my job so I went up to him, expecting to be politely blown off. Before I can introduce myself he says, 'Henry! What an honor to meet you, I'm a huge fan.' Whoa. I asked if he would do an interview. I felt like I was asking some guy in a band to 'do an interview for my 'zine'. He said yes and we went into Ozzy's dressing room and did it and he was cool as hell! He's a long time fan and friend of the band. Top man.

Oh yeah, I met Cozy Powell. Yeah, Cozy fuckin' Powell. How awesome is that guy?! Can drum his ass off or what?! He was in Tony's dressing room and I asked Tony to introduce me and he did and it was so cool. I live for this stuff! I know that people probably think I'm too nuts about this stuff but life is short and I have to get my kicks before it's all over. The last few days have been so great. To hang out with the mighty Sabbath is a once in a lifetime deal. Things like this make me see that you can basically have your life any way you want it. You can have a great time or a lousy time. You can play it safe or go for something else.

I sang 'Paranoid' with the band at soundcheck on the first show day. That was one fast three minutes. It was such a trip to stand there and hit it with Bill Ward, Geezer Butler and Tony Iommi. That was large. What a week! What a stone cold honor. I am tripping from the energy of last night. I was getting off big time. I was rockin' hard all the way through the show. Met a lot of really great people. It was a like a tribe backstage. We were there all day hanging out and working. I'm sad it's over. Nothing I would like more than to see them play again tonight. I had a great time with everyone from the band and crew. Everyone was so cool to me and made it even better.

Now I am on some other shit. I am doing this African adventure now. Glad I am finally getting to see something different but on the other hand there's part of me who would like nothing more than to just go to LA with my stories and my chores and be in my room by nightfall. But no! The road must go on. It will be a great one to come back from. I could go back right now. I could be back by nightfall and it would be a nice little story but that is so lightweight. I would rather die out here tomorrow than have the endless stillness of the home scene. It's time to get on to Frankfurt. HAIL BLACK SABBATH!!

11.40 p.m. Kenya Africa: Hassle getting in. Lots of standing in line. I think I probably added about forty minutes by not having a visa. It was a mass of people pushing and shoving to get to the counter. No lines, no order, just low level bedlam. Finally got out of there and a fake cab driver tried to hustle me into his car just like in NYC. I imagined getting taken to a corner of the city, shot in the head and left so I told him no thanks. He kept following me and he was getting aggressive. I turned around and started walking towards him and started telling him to step away from me like I've heard cops do. It worked. Cute.

I got in a proper cab and told the guy where we were going. We drove over the worst roads I have ever been on in my life. At every corner there were intense men hanging out under the street lights. If there was no traffic, the driver went right through the red light. It was like driving around in Brazil. You don't want to stand still if you can avoid it.

I saw intense poverty all the way to the hotel. People in fucked up shacks on the side of the road. People who seemed to live nowhere. There were stretches where there didn't seem to be any houses at all but there were people just hanging out on the roadside. I wonder how they get by.

We pulled up to a gate with a retaining wall topped by a fence on either side. There was a uniformed guard with a side-arm and a machine gun who came forward and flashed a light in our eyes. I thought the driver had taken me to some army installation or police station to register my passport or something so I asked him where we were and he told me that we were at the hotel and the guard was there to help keep down burglary and rape on the hotel grounds. Even at the late hour and the seeming remote location of the hotel, there were people walking aimlessly out in front of the place like they were waiting for something.

Now I am in my room. The view from my patio is awesome. I sat out there for a while and checked out the rain hitting the palm trees and the water. I am in Africa! On my own. Pretty damn cool.

The drive into town was interesting. I liked the little kiosks with only a lamp burning. The men standing huddled in the darkness. It's broken down and poverty stricken but it's beautiful. I hate that contradiction. I am not poor so it has a romance to it. I can leave it. If I lived in it all the time I don't know how I would deal with it.

I have an 08.30 call. I have an opportunity to get some sleep here so I am going to go for it. If I had not been so incompetent at the airport I would have had more time to write. Live and learn.

12-07-97 Siana Springs Africa: I flew here from Nairobi this morning.

My mind is in a state of overload. I took a cab to a small airport and this pilot and I took off for Siana Springs. We flew through overcast sky and medium turbulence for about an hour. He just flies his plane. Doesn't say a word to me. I just sit in my seat looking at clouds and riding out the bumps. I have no idea what I am in for. I'm just going for it in Africa. The plane descended and the first thing I saw was a herd of zebra scattering from the engine noise. Seeing their stripes and the sheer number of them was amazing. I saw two elephants eating leaves off the top branches of a tree. I saw impala racing across the fields. The sudden explosion of color and motion was amazing.

The pilot lands the plane on a clay airstrip like we're drug dealers going to a remote location to make the drop. I get out of the plane and look around. I am stunned. The pilot is laughing at me. I ask him what's so funny and he tells me that almost everyone he lets off the plane has that look when they see this place. I tell him that it's the most beautiful place I have ever seen and he tells me that many people tell him exactly that. Standing by the runway are two Maasai men. They are an amazing sight. Tall and coal black. Wrapped in red, beads on their wrists, each holding a stick. I don't know what to say to them so I walk up and stick my hand out and say, 'What's happening?!' I know, not the greatest line but my mind was blown. They shake my hand and both say, 'Jambo'. The pilot tells me it means hello. So I say it back to them and they smile. They got on either side of me and lifted up my sleeves. They checked out my tattoos and started laughing their asses off. I have been out of the plane for less than a minute and I am being ripped on by two Maasai.

While they're having their good time with me, a jeep drives up and a man steps out and says, 'Jambo, Henry Rollins. My name is Francis. Come, let me take you to your new home.' I say goodbye to the pilot and the two Maasai laughing boys and head off to the camp.

Francis drove me here to this camp site and took me to the tent that I am now sitting in front of. When we entered the tent, I quickly surveyed my new home. Small bed, sink, table and a lamp, toilet and shower stall. First thing I thought of was Hemingway in Africa.

On the cot there's a pamphlet that talks about the camp site. At the top of the list is the suggestion that you keep your tent flaps tied down when you are not in the tent because the monkeys are very curious to see what you have brought them. I asked Francis about this and he says, 'Oh yes, Henry Rollins, the monkeys are very naughty.' Images of naughty monkeys filled my mind. Apparently, they come into your tent and throw all your stuff everywhere. I can just see a bunch of screaming monkeys throwing stuff all over the place and wreaking havoc. Cool. Francis tells me that he'll be back in awhile to take me up to the mess tent for lunch.

I take my chair out in front of my tent and stare out into the territory. It is the most fiercely blue sky I have ever seen. There is no pollution. I can see for miles. I don't think I have ever been able to see that far in front of me while on the ground.

I was looking around and noticed that I was being observed by three monkeys in a tree to the left of my tent. I started talking to them and it really tripped them out. I said, 'Don't even think of trying to get into my tent and stealing my stuff!' The funny thing is that they looked like they understood what I was saying. Their faces are very animated and they were looking at me like they were tripping on me as hard as I was on them. It must be strange to be a monkey in a tree and all of a sudden, this strange guy below you is giving you shit. They had bright blue ball sacks which I thought looked quite cool. That might be a way to go.

While I was checking them out, I heard a faint flapping next to my right ear. An insect the size of a small mouse landed on my neck. I slammed my hand on it and it fell on the ground and tried to crawl away. I stomped on it and felt kind of bad because I didn't need to kill it but it scared the hell out of me. Then I realized that I am pretty weak out here. It was a bug. If I can't handle the local insects, what am I going to do about the rest of the critters?

Right around that time, I see something moving in the bushes. I can't tell what it is but whatever it is, it's coming closer. 'It' is a bunch of baboons. I don't know what to do about this development. Primordial bells and whistles of alarm that I have never heard before are ringing in my head. My mind rapidly scrolls through all the documentaries I have ever seen on Africa and can remember nothing about baboons. I get up slowly and walk backwards, staring down over a dozen baboons that are staring right at me. Their asses are red. The babies are riding on the backs of the bigger ones. I can't believe what I am seeing. I run into the tent and close the flaps. I sit on my bed wondering what it is I should do. They have surrounded my tent. I have grunting baboons in quad. This a first.

I wonder how long I will be tent-bound because of the baboons. I look over my provisions. I have some mineral water, some protein bars and some dried peanuts. I am good for several hours. After about half and hour, they leave. I run from my tent to the mess tent and find Francis and tell him about what I have seen. I try to play it off like I wasn't scared. He tells some of the staffers that are sitting at a nearby table my story and they all start laughing. First I crack up two Maasai and now I am breaking up the staff. I am a hit in Africa. Francis tells me that the baboons are only interested in the vegetation that surrounds my tent and I need not be afraid. I walk back to my tent with my cheeks burning.

So here I am now, taking in the enormity of the place. The one thought going through my mind over and over is that I am alone in Africa, sitting in front of a tent, taking it all in and how totally amazing it all is.

I have never heard birds make these sounds before. The insects are at work. They're all over the place. The air is alive with them. I am going out on a drive in a few hours. I cannot wait for this place to get dark. Daytime is cool but nighttime is the deal. Everything here is here because it survives. It earns its own way. Including the people. I saw a Maasai tribesman with a stick walking along the road today. I have a discman. I have motion detectors in my home. I have a manager. I have an accountant. I have a Visa card and a body full of vaccines. He has a stick and some cows. He deals with lions and leopards. I deal with canceled flights, soundcheck and lawyers. I know who's in charge around here. I should have come here a long time ago.

6.57 p.m.: Back from the wildlife tour. It was pretty damn cool. We saw lions, elephants, impalas, baboons, buffalo, antelope. can't remember what else. It is the most beautiful place I have ever seen. It's wild and raw. The only thing wrong with the picture is all the tourists.

We were out there for about three hours. Dinner is in a little while. We lose electricity at midnight. I will see if my candle allows me enough light to read by. The weather got chilly quickly. It's hard to write.

Not a lot on my mind. Was getting a little distracted from hunger. Luckily I brought a lot of MET-Rx bars with me. I left my peanut butter in Wales and I didn't have the good sense to get more nuts at the store when I had the chance. I am kicking myself now. I could have been living large. Food here is a little hard to come by. Glad I took the bottles of water out of

Sabbath's dressing rooms after they had left. I am using all of it now.

8.56 p.m.: Back from dinner. It was good but it could have been better if the family had not sat down across from me and talked loudly and it would have been great if I didn't have to listen to the bratty kid. I will start bringing my ear plugs with me all the time.

Have been thinking about the band and the last shows we did in Japan and if we'll ever play together again. All the bad press and the failure of the last record has made me withdrawn and has shaken me as much as I hate to admit it. Sometimes I just don't want to make music anymore. I was watching Sabbath the other night and not once did it make me want to be up there. I was happy not to be on the bill. It was great to be at a gig and not have to think about being the gig.

I wonder if I have lost my taste for playing live with the band. I am not a major label thing any more. Never was really. Just one freak single and the rest of the time I have been hanging on by my teeth. None of that means anything if you're not making the masters enough money.

After seeing all the bands I did over the year and how people react to them, I think it's over for real music. I won't be one of those people hanging around for the rest of my life trying to prove a point. People aren't worth it. What a let down people can be. You do all you can to do your best and all they do is fuck you up. When they do that, you deserve it. You should not have trusted them with all you had. Should not have made it mean that much to you when you know that you will always be met with bullshit mediocrity from others. I have been thinking about the mainstream and their ways and it means nothing to me. It's country club music to me. It's meaningless and their magazines are meaningless as well. I don't read them anymore. I picked up a music magazine for the first time in months recently because it had an article on Black Sabbath in there but otherwise, why bother? Spin? Are you kidding? I would not look forward to being on festivals next summer. All those shitty lightweight bands. All that apathy. What they're calling a live show these days would have gotten your ass pulled off stage and beaten when I started. I guess that's the way of things. Sometimes I feel the other way about it and I want to do all kinds of things musically. I'm not burned out on music or playing live. I am burned out by the scene and the machine that you have to deal with to put it across. So many fakes. You work hard for years and then all of a sudden there's all these lightweight people from out of nowhere telling you how it's going to be and you think to yourself that it can't be and lo and behold, they're right. The day is theirs. All you can do is hope to be part of their dream so you can do your thing that you have been doing while these people were learning how to read. You open for bands who have made one record, who have never gone on the road for months at a time and lived it. Their first record was on a major label, even in their first shows, they're already doing all the affected stage moves and it's so hard to watch. Shouldn't take it too seriously. Just do your thing and get on with it. What else is there to do besides quit? That's it isn't it? Do or don't. Simple. Life doesn't care either way. And in that way, you're free.

Things are going pretty well for me right now, even though it is sometimes hard to come to that conclusion. Music still sounds good. I can still lift weights and still get off on it. Coffee still tastes good. I can still have a good time by myself and I am not lonely in the conventional sense of the word. I go without some things but I still get to see the beautiful nights. I see it this way now and it allows me to deal with things. At the end of the day, you don't need much to get by. I am always interested in the minimum, I try to get by with that.

I don't want people to matter to me too much. Sometimes it hurts too much to think about them. Ones you love who don't love you, ones who are dead or hate you, ones who you think about but never get to be with. I like people OK but when I get too close, it fucks me up and I can't get things done. Every time I have tried to have a relationship with a woman, I have regretted it. On that front, I admit total defeat and am happy to have all my fingers still on my hands. I like them but I can't handle them.

10.33 p.m.: Took my chair out and sat under the stars and spaced out for a good hour before I even bothered to check my watch.

The stars are great out there. I am in Africa on my own, in a tent with no one around me. I was sitting out there and all I could hear were animals and insects. No cars, no people. I don't remember feeling that far away from people. There's nothing like Africa. So glad I came here. I hope I feel this way at this time next week.

12-08-97 Kenya Africa: Been hanging out in my tent watching the clouds and listening to the birds and insects. Soft wind passing through the trees. In the distance I can hear cowbells and Maasai herdsmen calling to their cattle.

A little while ago I went into the woods and stood in a clearing. I watched some insect almost the size of a damn humming bird chase a butterfly. Most of the interaction I have seen between species has been in some degree of conflict, sometimes amongst themselves. Everything that's here is here because it continually struggles to be so. Every living thing I see seems to be eating, looking for food, or trying not to be something else's meal. About an hour ago I swatted a wasp-like insect that landed on my leg. I looked down a few minutes ago and it was being ripped apart by ants.

Everything around me is green. The sky is now grey with storm clouds. Rain has started to fall. My tent is a sounding board for the pelting raindrops. I am alone looking out at low trees and scrub in Kenya Africa. This is amazing to me. The humidity is making the page moist.

At this moment I feel unburdened. I have a simple task; sit and watch the rain falling on the trees out here in the middle of this beautiful nowhere. I am in conflict with no man. I want for nothing or no one. I am content with my chair and the rain. This day, like every day, is a blessing. I am fortunate to be alive to take this in.

Seeing the animals in the park yesterday taught me a lot. I saw a pride of lions sleeping in the scrub. About two hundred yards away, three elephants were picking leaves off trees. One of the lions got up and looked at the elephants. A moment later, all the lions got up and looked at the elephants and started smelling the air. At this point, the guide Francis started laughing, 'They're thinking about trying to make a kill on one of the elephants. No way. The elephant is too big for the kings and queens of the jungle.' The lions looked at each other and back at the elephants. A few of them yawned distractedly and they all lay back down and closed their eyes. I wondered how often those lions look at the elephants and contemplate the kill and then shrug it off. Made me wonder if anyone has ever seen me somewhere and sized me up, thinking about taking me out and then deciding that the location wasn't right and that he would go somewhere else and wait.

Up the road there was a large group of impala grazing around a tree. Up in the branches, hidden in the leaves, was a very well-fed leopard. Its bloated stomach was hanging grotesquely over the branch, its paws were hanging down limply and it was fast asleep. All around the tree base, the leopard's future meals grazed away, not knowing what was ten feet above their heads. All at once, the impala stood perfectly still and looked up at the tree. A few of them started making coarse, bleating sounds. 'A warning to the others,' Francis said. In an instant of explosive grace, the impala dashed off, their hind legs sending them into the air seemingly before their front feet touched the ground.

The grazing animals and the predator cats are locked in a circle of death and procreation. Eat to live, live to eat. Not a second is wasted.

I see parallels in the cities I live in. It's a predator/prey relationship without the efficiency and the economy of the jungle. The animals here do things that are brutal, like when hyenas take down a zebra and literally eat it to death. What they do is brutal but not done with any malice. Man's brutality is a concentrated effort. An inner city man who has had a life of violence and brutality knows full well that when he commits an act of violence, it is indeed violent. Besides providing work for local law authorities and law firms, he has done nothing of any real use.

I visited a Maasai village yesterday. They live in circular enclosures of huts made out of sticks, grass and cow dung. An outer wall of branches circles the huts. They subsist on bone, blood and meat from cows and goats. They eat fruits and vegetables when available.

The women build the huts, do the cooking, washing and take care of the children and the elderly. The men herd the animals and protect the village.

At night, the animals are brought into the enclosure to keep them safe from predators. Besides a sentry, dogs are used to warn the villagers of attacks.

A man's power is measured in the amount of cattle he has. More cattle, more wives. I met one man with six wives. I don't know how many cows that takes or which comes first.

I sat in the hut of the village elder. The ceiling was low and I couldn't stand. We sat in almost total darkness around a pile of burning embers that is kept lit at all times so a fire can be made whenever. Slowly my eyes became adjusted and I could look around. The hut was a series of small partitioned rooms with the fire being the center space. The husband sleeps separately from the wives and children.

The Maasai village I was in had no electricity, had no running water or plumbing. Rains and wear demolish the huts after a few years. They are a nomadic tribe that have to go where it's good for their livestock.

Their life is constant work. They live a simple, low to the ground life. At night, they gather around a fire in the center of the village.

I was told that they sometimes open a vein in one of their cows, draw out some blood for food and close the vein again.

What a trip. That was cool. One older guy was checking me out hard. I think he was tripping on the tattoos. The little kids didn't know what to do about me. They would come up close and look at me and then run and hide behind the legs of the old women. A few of them threw rocks at me and then went back to throwing rocks at each other.

The campground I am staying in has an open air hut where they serve meals. In the afternoon, they serve tea and coffee for a couple of hours. I came up the path to this place to get something hot to drink because the tent was getting cold. I got there and stupidly asked for a pot of tea. There are two families of pushy Europeans and their screaming children. The entire area has been turned into a play area and the shrieking noise that these people are making is unbelievable. In their world, no one else exists. They don't see themselves for the rude, loud pieces of over moneyed Euro trash that they are. In my mind, a male baboon takes one of the children off into the bush never to be seen again. How so much cacophony can come from such a small group of people is amazing. More intense than the Jimi Hendrix Experience.

When I think of Africa, I always think of Arthur Rimbaud and how he left Europe and went to Zimbabwe, I think. I saw a book about his time in Africa when I was in Australia but it was expensive. I should have got it so I could have learned more about his time here. Africa makes me think of Ferdinand Celine and his trip here which left him with amebic dysentery that plagued him for years afterwards.

The children's noise and their parents treating the staff rudely is too much for me to take. I am out of here. My tent is much better than this shit.

Later: Came to dinner armed with earplugs and they are serving me well. A few minutes after sitting down, the double family noise unit sat down and the noise level jumped right off the scale. The meal could have been so great. The people at all the other tables are talking quietly amongst themselves. These clowns are a nightmare. Why did they bother to come here? It's not as if they have left home. Each family brought their nannies.

The night sky is cloudy and the air is moist and cold. I don't think it will be a good night for staring into the sky and spacing out like I did last night.

I like this solo journey. I like the idea of being in this land where no one knows me, where I am such an obvious outsider. I like the fact that I am doing it alone. It was amazing to sit in my chair and stare off into the bush last night. The sound of the creatures and the sight of the moon, stars and passing clouds were unforgettable and never once did I think of anyone I would want to be seeing this with me.

I think the last time I felt lonely, really lonely, as in lacking for someone in particular was a couple of years ago. Since then, I've just been going hard and dealing with a lot of work and stress. There's been a lot of disappointment and struggle over the last couple of years and the only way I have found to deal with it is on my own. I do not confide in others. It doesn't make me feel any better to 'Talk things out' or whatever. You got problems? Deal with them or don't but never weigh down others with your bullshit unless you're paying them by the hour. Companionship is nice in a song or a movie. Maybe it's good for someone else. These days, I can take non-work-related company for an evening and into the night. The next morning I am over it for about a month. Maybe one day all that will change. None of these things are written in stone. I think to make those kind of things happen in your life you have to be in the zone. You have to want that thing. When you want that, everything you do in your life will start to push you towards it.

I used to feel tremendously lonely after shows. I would be all torn up and emptied out from the night and wanted to be with a woman, not so much for the sex, more for the company. The need not to be alone. Those days are forgotten and those ideas are foreign to me. I would have to check journal entries to see how I even articulated thoughts like that.

These days my thoughts tend to run a bit harsher. My thinking is that if you can't take the march, get off the trail. Shows hurt you and make you empty? And to fill that emptiness, you're going to leech off someone else to extinguish the flames that burn on the path you have chosen? I think that's bullshit because you are using someone as a tool. If you're going to do that, you might as well go to a professional and do it right. If it's a mutual leeching session, great, but know what you are. If you can be cool with that, there you go.

The only people I asked for help this year were lawyers. Lawyers always charge, so you never have to worry about how you treat them. They're rentals. I don't mind making them sit still and listen to my little tales of woe. The man who owns a record company I was on went out of business and when I tried to go to another label he sued me. All the money I had and some I didn't went to motherfuckers. Not even the guy who sued me got any! Just the lawyers. The three-piece-suited vultures of the big city, who make their living only when there's conflict, who never get a scratch. I got deposed by some twerp who thought he was the cock of the walk. What a snappy dresser. It was corny, like a movie with Tom Cruise.

The case settled but in my mind the other guy will always be the winner. I'm fucked. He's rich. I worked my ass off and with the band, made a great record that threatened the pukey little critics and they yapped and whinged like the ants at the picnic they are. Toured hard and played great shows to partially filled halls. Now I'm sitting in a jungle in Africa breathing fragrant night air. What the fuck can you do for me that I can't do for myself? What am I supposed to do, ask someone to hold my trembling little hand? I don't think so. If you can't hack, then pack. That's the way I feel about the whole thing. So it was a rough year. So what? Next year will probably be rougher. I enjoy a good fight. These pricks can't break me. 1-1-98 we face off again and I will be ready. No matter how bad it gets, life is what you make it so you might as well make it a fucking blast.

The business I am in is brutal. Always has been. The ones who get torn apart are the performers. The managers, lawyers and label types have lunch, cluck and shake their heads when some rock idiot checks out. They're like pebbles at the seashore. Lose one, go back and get another. They worry about the investment they have made and that's about it. Now, thanks to video, the selling of music to a large degree is a visually oriented task, all you need is good-looking musicians. The rest can be taken care of. Not all these people are like that of course, I have met some great ones. But still, the business I'm in is brutal. A lot of egos getting smashed apart. It's not for the fragile, which is unfortunate, because a lot of the artists are exactly that. They get chewed up in the act of creation and they weaken themselves further with drugs and alcohol. How pathetic when you see some musicians all weak and fucked up. Walking wounded. You would think they would take better care of themselves and know that no one else really cares about them past entertainment value.

I think musicians should be like warriors. Defiant and searching, like Miles Davis. I always liked Keith Richards' playing but his habits made him less of what he could be, not more. He'll never know his true potential. He's known more for his habits than his playing. Musician types know that his playing is great. Whatever. It's not as if these people don't know what they're getting themselves into. They're all big boys and girls.

The guy from INXS, now what was that all about? Druggy fuck up died in his hotel room with a belt around his neck. Suicide or auto-erotic? Either way, it's pathetic. I wish he hadn't died. I passed him coming out of an elevator in Germany earlier this year. He said hello to me and I just nodded. I didn't know what to say to him. I liked some of his band's music. His woman, Paula Yates, she's a real piece of work. I endured this talentless groupie twice on television shows in the UK and thought she was a complete idiot. She went from one lame rockstar, Bob Geldof (a guy whose band sucked and who whined when, after promoting two Live Aid shows, he didn't get a Nobel. Bill Graham raised more money in more places than this poser ever could hope to and never asked for a fucking award. All those pictures of old Bob with natives in Third World countries was nothing but a photo op. How could he believe his own PR? Just another fake trying to get famous. What a racket!), to another. They deserve each other and the misery they bring to each other's lives. I feel bad for her because I am sure her grief is real. I feel especially bad for their daughter who will grow up never knowing her father. A least she'll be able to see the pictures of the funeral with her mother wearing a low cut dress, flexing those fake tits and sporting that great dye job.

The above is one of the many reasons I love jazz music. Many of the great beboppers were warriors of the highest pedigree.

They were black and got fucked over for their beauty and brilliance. They were hardcore and many of them went out poor and beat down. No five-car garages paid for by the royalties of one hit record for these guys. It was the hard route, the real road, poorly lit rooms, prison, insane asylums, addiction, obscurity, oblivion and cowardly whites holding them down. Amazing music from a higher level that they paid for in full. Sonny Rollins, Ahmad Jamal, Pharoa Sanders, Billy Higgins, Elvin Jones, all still out there doing it. Imagine the stories they could tell. I did a short phone interview thing once with Sonny Rollins. I asked him about his 'Bridge Period' when he dropped out of the scene for a while and worked on his chops on a bridge in New York because he thought he wasn't good enough to play in front of an audience. The resulting album, *The Bridge*, is a masterpiece. I asked him how he could think that he wasn't good enough as his albums leading up to this time were great. He said that when you have contemporaries like Duke Ellington and Coltrane you might have a tendency to think you need to work on your technique. Whoa.

It's about 11.45 p.m. and they have shut off the electricity fifteen minutes early. What is this, the Gulag? Now writing by candlelight. Rain is pounding on the tent's roof. It has been since I got back from the mess hall. I am tired. In the morning I'm heading to the Kichwa Tembo campground. It's about ten minutes from here via plane. Apparently there's a lot of elephants there. It was pretty cool seeing them yesterday. I liked watching the monkeys the most. The way they silently fade into the treeline and just vanish. OK. Tomorrow is another adventure.

12-09-97 Kenya Africa: The baboons have designated the area around my tent as the morning eating place again and their grunting woke me up. It was raining hard but they didn't seem to mind.

I go to breakfast. Same scene. Pushy, high noise level family hassling the waiter about every detail of the menu. Treating the guy like some step-and-fetch-it. I am ready this time. I came armed with headphones. I can see the little girl pointing at me and touching her head. I think she is mad that she doesn't have headphones as well. Maybe she is frustrated that she is unable to disrupt my serene sonic surroundings. Her nanny fixes me with a look. I smile at her and mouth the words 'fuck you' as I nod my head with the music. Of course it's Black Sabbath. What could possibly go better with breakfast? The child is banging her cup on the table like a convict trying to start an uprising. I can't hear it. I am deafened by the roar of genius.

1.07 p.m. Kichwa Ternbo Campground: Flight was an hour late leaving so I stood near the airstrip with a Maasai herdsman. Neither of us said a word. It was silent and beautiful and so strange standing next to this guy who said nothing and stood so tall. I guess he liked to watch the planes land and didn't mind waiting.

The plane finally came and now I'm here and it's not as cool as the place I was this morning. It's a nice place but it's crowded with people. Mostly English and American.

This place feels like summer camp. There's lots of 'activities' for us 'campers' to do. Why do I feel like hanging out at the rec. room, cadging smokes and listening to Iron Maiden? I am in a camp with a lot of senior citizens who speak the same language as I do. I don't want to understand.

The coffee in this place is pretty good. They give you the whole pot and leave you alone so you can grind your teeth and contemplate the wildebeest. It looks like it's going to be 48 hours of just me, my aging camper buddies and the wonders of nature.

I have decided that the baboons are my favorite of the animals I've seen here. Touring would be a lot more interesting with about a dozen of them in tow. Just take them everywhere. Instore appearances would be very memorable to say the least. They would add fun and excitement to any occasion. All bands could have a baboon posse to go with them. 'I'll have my baboons call your baboons.' 'Send the baboons to bail the drummer out.' 'Sir, your baboons are confirmed for business class, is there anything else I can do for you?'

I think it's that ass that does it for me. That fine baboon ass. It's up there, proud, talkin' to ya. 'Love me, love this phenomenal ass of mine. Never mind those kind of greyish monkeys with the bright aqua marine colored ball sacks who are always trying to break into your tent and fuck your shit up. The real deal is right here with my amazing baboon butt, Safari Boy.

They do things with such focus and intensity. When they eat, they eat for keeps. When they stare at you, you're being judged. They were there today as we drove from the airstrip to the camp. They were scowling at me like I was an annoyance, which to them is about all I will ever be. It hurts to know I'll never rate with the baboons.

I'm not in the mood to play favorites here, fuck it. Next tour, we'll bring the baboons and some of these geriatric campers. Imagine the backstage rider. 'Yeah, you heard me, two hundred pounds of bananas, three bushels of assorted vegetation, that's right vegetation. Two boxes XXL Depends adult diapers, one of those padded rings for the toilet seat and a hot plate to heat up the sake. Yeah that's right the sake. The baboons got a taste for that shit in Japan and now they go thermonuclear if they don't get it. Oh yeah? Then you can take it up with the baboons pal. That's better. OK, we'll be down there in an hour.'

At three thirty, a pack of camera wielding seniors and I will go out on a little jaunt to enjoy the local fauna. People near me are talking about going to Tower Records when they get back home so they can buy their grandchildren the new Spice Girls album and oh wasn't it wonderful that Elton John was able to overcome his sadness to make that beautiful tribute to Princess Diana? Pity me because the day is young. Perhaps now is the time for me to start experimenting with drugs.

8.27 p.m.: Excruciating. The animals were as beautiful as you would expect them to be. We saw giraffes, zebras, impala, buffalo, banded mongoose, wildebeest, baboons and did I say lions? There were a lot of lions. We spent two of the three hours out there looking at . . . lions. The people in the jeep couldn't get enough. First we encountered a male and a female lounging in the grass. Of course we had to take a million pictures and of course we had to make lots of cooing baby noises at the damn things for the duration of the photo op. The woman next to me, a large specimen from England was really, really into it. She was into it enough for three people. She was talking to them like they were her mischievous grandchildren. She's probably one of those creepy cat people. 'I'm the troglodyte at the end of the street. I am into watching the Queen become fossilized in her throne and talking to my naughty cats. Spank me.'

The rain started coming down so the guide had to put the top up. Now the tourists have to use the windows for their photos instead of the roof. Big elderly asses careen dangerously close to my head as the tourists scramble to take yet another roll of film of the lions who are not even looking at the cameras clicking away. Reminded me of the scene in *Caddy Shack* when Al and his assistant Wang are walking across the parking lot to the club and Wang is taking a ton of pictures and Al says something like, 'Wang, it's a parking lot for cryin' out loud!'

All at once the lioness stands up and looks off into the distance. A zebra grazes alone. The lioness starts making her move on the zebra. Our jeep and four others race after her like safari paparazzi as the male lion is engulfed in blue exhaust fumes and sheets of flying mud. The zebra, sensing danger, turns around to see a lioness running for its life as jeeps bear down on her. The zebra, seeing the look of overwhelming panic painted on the face of the lioness like a mask of roaring death realizes it's in the same boat and follows it's fellow game reserve resident and hauls ass until it's out of sight. I look at the lioness who is standing there amongst the jeeps, panting, tail twitching. Made me think of me at the grocery store trying to get a can of soup off the shelf with Richard Simmons running interference.

The jeeps turn around and make a semi-circle around the male who is staring off in the direction of where the female had gone, his visions of zebra steak going poof! The lady starts talking to the lion, asking it to yawn. Her varicose veins are changing color. It's tripping me out.

'Com'on, give us a yawn!' she sing-songs. The lion just spaces out, looking into a valley. I start thinking of all the things that I think would be funny to say at this moment:

'Here's a firecracker. Throw it at the fucker!'

'Hand me my back pack, I've got a wrist rocket in there!'

'How about I go out there and give him a kick up the ass and get some action going?'

Finally, the lion looks right at us and yawns, the massive set of teeth are exposed. The cameras' motor drives go ballistic. We get to leave. Seventy minutes to go.

We drive across a field and animals are all over the place. I am taking shallow breaths because I know if I take deep ones I will explode with laughter. I am in one of those moods where I think that everything is hilarious. Whenever an impala runs directly in front of the jeep, I want to yell, 'Ram 'em! Got a gun? Let's blast the little fuckers. Yee Haw!'

I can barely contain myself. I maintain by staring catatonically through the windshield into the distance like I am on three shots of cough syrup. I am trying to get a string of drool going.

We pull up to two female lions and six, count 'em six lion cubs. I know we're in for it now. We'll be taking pictures of these little bastards until sun up. Visions of my dinner go poof! I am biting my tongue. 'Mow the little fuckers down. They can't run yet!' The guide tells us that three lionesses had two cubs each and they all take turns taking care of them. The cubs play fight and god bless 'em if they aren't the cutest little things I've ever seen.

I start thinking that if I was that guide, I would get that three-hour tour down to a brisk, exhilarating half hour. We wouldn't stop for anything. The only photos they would get is animal asses and the occasional terrified profile shot as the poor beasts ran for their lives as I bore down on them with all speed. I would narrate the tour by screaming out the name of the animal I nearly ran over at the top of my lungs. 'Lion!' 'Zebra!' I would hit termite mounds with as much speed as I could muster and try to catch as much air as I could. I would tell them before we left, 'If any of you have weak bladders or deteriorating hip sockets, you better sit this one out. When we get airborne, you better hope the roll bar holds. Sometimes it snaps and it's all over. You do the funky chicken for a few minutes and then it's bag 'em 'n tag 'em time. We're only stopping for road kill. Alright, strap in. LET'S GET IT ON!'

Finally, at six thirty it was all over. The nice men at the camp welcomed us back. 'Jambo my friend. Welcome home.' I went to my tent, my jeep mates beelined for the bar.

I have not seen any guests here younger than fifty. I am the only one here without company. I eat alone and only talk to the staff when they say hello or ask me something. When any of the guests walk by my tent and say hello, I just wave at them but say nothing. I am the enigma! They'll never know me!

During dinner, the nice man came to my table and told me that we would be leaving at 0630 for the morning safari. I laughed at him. I told him that I would be sleeping in and there was no need to wake me. I was thinking about adding that his mother might like to go in my place as a joke but I refrained because I have heard that Kenya can be a rough room to work.

The Gun Club is on my headphones right now. 'Desire' from the *Lucky Jim* album is playing. I love this band. I miss Jeffrey Lee Pierce a lot. It's hard to listen to his music sometimes because he's dead and he was a friend of mine. When I listen to the Gun Club, I think of his mother and his sister. They're so brave. They're trying hard to deal with the fact that he's gone. I know that frustration. I hear the things they say and the way they keep him in their lives and I know what that's like. People in mourning, people who are dealing with a loss like the loss of a son or brother have a certain energy or way they carry themselves that I didn't recognize until I was in that position myself.

I put out two Gun Club records on my label. Jeffrey died right before *Mother Juno* came out. Such a great album. I put out another great one after that. *Pastoral Hide and Seek* with another record called *Divinity* on one CD. A great batch of songs, a good deal, great mastering by engineer par excellence Phil Klum, the whole works. Of course, neither record sold. I get so sick of this shit. You bust your ass to put out truly great stuff by people who are really living the music, not treating it like some little project like so many of these trite fakes are these days, and no one shows up to check it out. People make me sick. I feel like going to record stores, standing by the counter and telling these people what mediocre pieces of entry level shit they are. Look at what they buy millions of copies of. Dumb motherfuckers. That's why I never bother to care about how many records I sell. I see what they are buying and it's no wonder I don't sell as many. I played with a lot of these bands this year and some of them were the most phony wastes of time I have ever heard. Some of these 'bands' were on the covers of every magazine this year as the direction of where music is heading. What a bunch of lame white bitches. If that is the direction of music, then fuck all y'all. You guys call yourselves men?!

I should spend even more time alone. When you're alone, you're free of the millions of incredibly low-level no-vision weaklings. I put in ear plugs at dinner tonight because the sound of my own breathing was better than the alcohol fueled drivel that was spewing so freely from their flapping pie holes. Gladys Knight now on the headphones. Now that's singing. I would love to meet her. I have been into her since I was in fourth grade.

12-10-97 Kichwa Tembo Campgrounds Kenya Africa: Slept till ten in the morning and then sat on the front porch of the tent. Many people gone today. The new ones seem to be younger. About twenty per cent less seniors with their pants riding oh so high. Spent the day thinking and reading *The Ruined Map* by Kobo Abe. Abe is a tremendous writer. He reminds me of his fellow countryman Yukio Mishima. Both writers make stories with almost invisible character development and movement of story. Sometimes they remind me of a cloud moving slowly across the sky. They make the outline and kind of turn you loose inside the scene with these brilliant and intense characters. *The Ruined Map* is like a small room you have been in too long. I've been slowly lead into the lead character's mind and now his dilemma seems like mine. There's nothing over the top about the plot or the writing. Everything is seamless, sharp so brilliantly considered. His writing speaks silently like a voice inside your head. His book *The Box Man* is the same way. What a strange one that book is.

Tomorrow I will stay in a hotel in Nairobi. It will be a good break from the tent thing. I go from Nairobi to Madagascar for a few days. That should be interesting. The tourist hand-out said that if you're not into 'potential chaos and radically changing schedules, then 'Madagascar might not be for you.' Shit man, it might not be for me either. I don't know how much chaos I'm really up for at this point. On the other hand, I can always go back to LA and sit. I can always go and work at Millie's waiting on tables where the first singer of Black Flag and the singer in Thelonius Monster work. I can always get addicted to heroin and spend the rest of my life recovering and taking it 'one day at a time' or I can go to fucking Madagascar. There's always a choice. You can always quit. You can always let one of these little actors pull you off the trail. Hack or pack. Lift the fucking weight off the floor or drop it. It's all there for you to do or not do.

I have been faced with that one so many times in my life. So much daunting shit has stood before me. Never once was I sure that I could withstand the rigors of the test, but I went for it with all I had every time. Every tour, I look at the itinerary and think no way am I going to be able to pull it off. The press shitheads have accused me of being cocky. I wish. When I say that I am going to go out there and kick ass, what the fuck am I supposed to think? That I am going to go out there and try to be 'okay'?

Either kill or stay the fuck home. When I go see a band play and they don't give it up all the way, I feel ripped off.

Saw so much of that shit this summer on these festivals. Those bands. What a travesty. What a load. Doesn't matter, if that's what people want to hear, then give them truckloads of that uninspired lukewarm cute crap. I used to care but now all I want to do is perform as well and as extremely as I can and keep it real for myself. I don't care about what they do.

All the bad shows I saw this year only made the two best shows I saw this year, Jane's Addiction and Black Sabbath, all the more fantastic.

When Jane's was playing in LA, I was going to be in England checking out Sabbath. I checked Jane's tour schedule and saw that I could see their show in Miami and still make the shows I had to do a few days later on the east coast. It was such a thrill to get the tickets booked and know I was going to see Jane's for sure.

I flew into Miami on November 13 and got to the hotel just in time to drop my bag and head down to the Bay Front Amphitheater for the show.

When the cab was a few blocks away from the venue I started to see all the people heading to the gates and I got very excited. We were all going for the same reason. Fuckin' Jane's Addiction. One of the greatest bands ever was playing again after six years away like it was a dream of years past coming to life. I felt like I was going back in time.

I was met by one of the promoter reps and who gave me a laminate. I saw Goldie, who was opening for Jane's, in the back lot and called out to him. He didn't know I was coming and was surprised to see me. He picked me up and carried me around the parking lot. He is such a trip, that guy. He's a live wire, so much energy coming off him it's unbelievable. We did a song together earlier in the year for a movie soundtrack and it was so great to work with him.

I went to the dressing rooms to see if I could find the Jane's guys. They were all sitting in one room hanging out. They all looked good and they were happy to see me. It was great to see them as I had not seen some of them for a long time. Flea was playing bass since Eric Avery, for whatever reason, was not on the tour. They said that the shows had been going well and that they were having a good time playing.

After Goldie had finished playing I positioned myself on Flea's side of the stage and looked out at the crowd. There's no crowd like a Jane's Addiction crowd. The effect the band has on people, I have never seen anything like it. They just go apeshit for the entire set. I was hoping tonight was going to be more of the same. My heart was beating hard in my chest. It was great to be at a gig that I wasn't performing on so I didn't have to think about all that.

The lights went down and the crowd started cheering like crazy. The band was onstage starting 'Ocean' with the curtain still up. While the guitar intro was burning like the fuse on the ultimate stick of dynamite, like the five seconds before you come, the curtain dropped and the band dropped into the song and it was like stepping in front of an oncoming train. Like a raging torrent. I was swept away. I was consumed. I was singing along for all I was worth. Part way through the song I put my hand to my face and noticed that tears were coming out of my eyes but I wasn't aware that I was crying. The crowd was getting off in waves, like a storm of excitement, this is what I remembered about a Jane's crowd. The songs started coming one after the other. 'Stop', 'Ain't No Right', 'Then She Did', and onwards. They delivered big time. I thought Steve's arms were going to break he was doing so much beautiful damage to those drums. He has so much fluid power at his disposal. He has the ability to absolutely pummel the drums but seem like he's just loping, not even breaking sweat. Watching and hearing Dave Navarro on this night was another installment in the saga of his mind-blowing talent. The guitar is like a wild animal in his hands.

I noticed that the 'Edge' was standing to my right. I wondered what the thoughts of such a corny, overpaid undertalented guy like himself were while witnessing the real thing. I knew it was his night off and that his bogus singer and weak rhythm section collectively known as U2 were going to be partially filling the local Mega venue the next night. I decided to leave him alone. With the poor ticket sales all over the world, the guy probably needs a night off from his turgid band.

I found out later that my main man, Bono, was also at the show and that I missed him by seconds in the Jane's dressing room. 'Very bald, very short' was how a girl described him to me.

I remember at one point, some piece of shit Brit-puke writer from one of the many laughable Limey tabloid music mags was scolding me about my treatment of U2 in print over the years. Maybe that weak link in the food chain could use a little clip in the teeth to help him get his shit together. I think critics, whether they like me or hate me, have fake jobs and no guts. Some of them I like as people and have written some insightful shit but they are nothing but professional ants at the picnic. I have a card back in LA that some guy gave me, I kept it because it's so funny, it has his name and underneath it says, 'Rock Critic'. Hilarious. It's like a guy having a card with his name on it and underneath it says, 'Professional Golfer'. What a waste of mamma's good cooking. But I digress.

Jane's played brilliantly and it was moving all the way through. I didn't want it to end. When it did, I felt empty and kind of lonely. I wanted the show to start again. I know that sounds stupid.

I went backstage and said thanks to the band for being so great and for letting me come to the show and all. It was good to find out that they were all happy with the liner notes that I did for their live album. I was almost afraid to ask. I remember when I was offered the job. I almost didn't do it for fear of getting it wrong or screwing it up somehow.

Back in my room I was unable to sleep. I wanted to go out and walk around to get all the things I was feeling sorted out.

It was emotionally confusing to see the band play. It was like being transported back to 1991 – a year that had some of the best and worst times of my life. The funnest tour I was ever on was the first Lollapalooza where we were the opening band. At the end of that tour we made the *End of Silence* record. It was a great year until Joe died. I associate Jane's Addiction with Joe still being around. All these conflicting emotions were going through me. It's not as if Jane's is back to stay or anything, it's just a one-off tour. Sometimes it's painful to go back. I wonder what it has been like for the guys in the band. There's no way Perry could get a crowd that size to see Porno for Pyros play. He must have dealt with that on some level. Maybe he doesn't care. I don't know. It's only been a few years, but music has changed so much since they were around. The show seemed like an intense throwback, like it was twenty years ago.

They'll be playing the last show on the 14th in Seattle. I'll be thinking of them. I like Seattle. Whenever I am there, I always wonder if I could live there. There's a lot to like about the place. The people there, for the most part, are very kind to me. It's a very hip city and when I go into stores there and see the locals, I know that I will never be hip.

I think I fit in well in this tent here though. The tent is wet. The air is damp and cold. The cover of my notebook is curling up. I like this trip I'm on. It's putting me through some changes. The last several months have been full of change. I am almost 37. I remember 2-12-83, I was in Holland. I was going to turn 22. I quoted Iggy's line from his song '1969' in my journal. I've been out here quite a long time. I outlasted all the members of Black Flag except for Bill. He's still out here playing his ass off. He never stopped. Not like some of those guys.

I remember every time I was in my place in LA this year. After three days, I got restless and missed moving all the time. I only feel good when I am out here or about to go out. Best when moving alone like now. I like hotels and airports. I like cities when I'm only in them for a day or two and then gone to the next place. I don't think I was meant to stay put. I have been living like this for almost half my life. I don't remember the first half in as great detail, it was one town, a small part of a small town. Ever since then, it's been wide open for the most part. Out here I have to prove myself night to night. At least I feel I have to. If I don't somehow prove my existence regularly, I feel as though I don't deserve to live. Some might say that is taking life too seriously. If you're lightweight, then blow away back to your television set and your beer. The mediocre life awaits.

12-11-97 Nairobi Kenya. Back in civilization. I got a room with a door. Been awhile since I had one of those. No hot water but you don't always get it all. That was a trip landing on those airstrips with all the animals running for cover.

It's an interesting place. I have had to be careful all the time with everything I do. I can't really go anywhere. You leave the grounds of this hotel, past the armed guards, and you're on your own. You're definitely taking your chances. I had to wait for the guide to take me to wherever when I was at the camp. I feel dependent on others for too many things here. It would take me quite a while to get the streets around here wired. It's too intense in some of the parts I have seen to just walk around casually. Reminds me of some parts of Brazil I have been to where people check you out hard.

A television show just finished about a young man who was beaten to death in Somalia. Wrong place, wrong time. Time to go out and see if I can find some food around here.

12-12-97 Nairobi Airport: Waiting to fly to Antananarivo, Madagascar. Today's cab ride was an eye-opener. Intense poverty. Shacks, garbage piled high and stinking in the heat. I have never seen so many people get into a van in my life. The public transportation are vans and even when they were beyond full, they kept putting people in there. There were women walking along the road with large bundles on top of their heads. People asleep in the dirt. A man shitting on the side of the road. It was endless. The entire ride to the airport was brutal. Not one of those markets had food I would have been able to eat. Pieces of meat hanging from string, covered with flies. Many of the buildings were surrounded by walls topped with broken glass embedded in the cement. It was hellish.

I don't know what someone who lives like this thinks. How do they process the information? What to them is a good day? What is their concept of freedom? I have no idea of how to deal with their reality. I have no idea how these people deal with their surroundings. It's fucked here. People shouldn't live like this. I have written this line before: 'There are two distinct races of people – rich and poor.' Paraphrasing Celine from *Journey to the End of the Night* I think. I think squalor is obscene. Isn't that a nice little observation? That takes a lot of guts, just driving by it. What does that make me? This bugs me. I don't feel guilty for the way I live and the good life I have compared to this shit but looking at what these people are going through makes me think that humans are blowing it on a grand scale. We are the ultimate natural disaster. I am not the tree-hugging type but if you saw what I saw today and you didn't have some questions or conflict in your mind, then you have some shit to deal with.

Now in the gate lounge. A fascinating group of people. One couple are very dark but look Asian. I didn't want to annoy them by looking too long but they looked so amazing. Across from me is an Asian family. One of the children is very retarded and screaming loudly. He is flailing his hands and it looks like he is imitating a fish with the way he puckers his mouth. He is holding on tightly to the neck of another young male, I guess his brother.

Now on the plane. A woman up from me has really intricate tattooing or perhaps henna dye on her arms all the way down to the cuticles of her nails. The man across the aisle from me has an Izod shirt on, complete with Alligator, the design is a series of swastikas. I can't help but look at it. If you wore that one in the States, you would get some resistance to that particular fashion statement. I guess where he comes from, it's just a design.

The plane is packed and it's late taking off. It's a three-hour flight. All the flight attendants are exotic and insanely beautiful. I like the idea of this trip. The reason I am going to Madagascar is because I saw it on the map while on a flight in Australia a couple of months ago and I decided that I was going to go some day.

I get in late and will have to deal with the visa hassle. I will get a few hours of sleep and then an early morning flight to some coastal city, the name of which I forget. I will be staying on the Indian Ocean for a few days. There are only two flights out of this place per week so I am stuck if I don't like it. I hope it's cool. I'll have to make it cool as there is no choice. This whole trip has been about looking up the trail as far as I can and staying sharp.

12-13-97 Antananarivo Madagascar: Madagascar is some different shit. The soldier/police at immigration had their patches safety-pinned onto their uniforms. I wonder if that's so they can tear them off when the insurrection happens. The guy at the visa counter haggled with me over how much to pay. He asked me what kind of currency I had. I told him I had some Kenyan, he said he wasn't interested. He asked me what else I had. I asked him what he would take. He listed dollars, German Marks, English Pounds, etc. I asked him how much in pounds. He said twenty. I told him I had ten. He said he'd take it. I had some twenty-pound notes, I just wanted to see if I could haggle over the price of an entrance visa. I did and it worked. He pocketed the note. I can't believe I haggled my way into this place. What a scam! I went through the 'nothing to declare' line and they were searching everyone's luggage anyway. I wasn't going to stick around for this shit and have my toothpaste confiscated for further investigation so I just went for it and walked right past all the soldier/police and steamed towards the door figuring I can play the stupid tourist part if they tried to stop me. As one of them turned away to lock one of the exit doors in a feeble attempt to impede efficiency and access to the outside, I slipped by him. One of them saw me and started waving at me to come back and I ignored him. Nothing happened. Fuck those guys.

I found a guy holding a card with my name on it. It was spelled all wrong and barely legible but I made it out OK. Got swarmed by several men who wanted to carry my suitcase.

The ride to the hotel was interesting. It seemed like every home was shuttered so no light could come out. It was either that or all the places were vacant. The windows that weren't shuttered had bars on them. Hard-looking guys standing on the corners. It's an intense place. It was wild riding through the streets because with the shutters closed, it looked like the city was vacated.

I have another night in this city two nights from now. I want to walk around and check out some of the streets around here but I have to be up and out of here in about five hours.

8.11 a.m.: At the airport. What a trip. The airport is just chaos. There's no lines at check in. You just run at the desk and aggro your way up to the front. Everyone else is going for it the same way and no one seemed to notice me elbowing my way to the front. I think if I hadn't done that, I might have missed my flight. If you did this kind of thing in America, someone would just beat the hell out of you.

Yesterday was Sinatra's birthday and CNN made a big deal about it, as they should. Sinatra is the man. They interviewed owners of a few restaurants he used to go in. One place he had not been in since 1985 and they still have lots of pictures of him on the walls and the CD jukebox is filled with Sinatra CDs only. *We're still waitin' for ya Frank!* Works for me. They cut to footage of some big shindig like the American Music Awards. The footage shows Sinatra standing there and Bruce Springsteen being led up to meet him. You can tell from Springsteen's body language and the look on his face that he was nervous. The introduction is made and Sinatra kind of just 'notices' him, like, 'Yeah, what did you say your name was?' And shakes his hand like it was one of those meet and greet things and then turns away leaving Springsteen just standing there. It looked like Sinatra didn't give a fuck who The Boss was. I bet that doesn't happen to Bruce Springsteen too often. Sinatra is supreme. Then the footage switched either to a different event or later in the same one and Tony Bennett was trying to escort him by taking him by the arm and Sinatra pulls his arm away like, 'Get the fuck off me!' You see Bennett try to cover by laughing it off but you can tell it burned him. It was hilarious.

It was interesting to listen to how the restaurant guys talked about Sinatra. Like the guy who runs Mateo's. He obviously loves him and is very proud to have had Sinatra in his place but at the same time you can see the slight trace of fear as well. That was the same with all of them. Total respect and devotion and the trace of fear.

I imagine they are blown away to have come in contact with him. I speak of him highly and I'll never meet him. He is the Chairman of the Board, after all. I like reading the stories about how he fucked with journalists who gave him grief. I think that all critics and press people should get clipped in the teeth every once in awhile. All of them, even the cool ones. I think that should be part of the job. Every once in a while you get your arm broken or your teeth loosened. I get slammed around by the pressmen and the audience and I take it as part of the job so what the hell?! I think it's a beautiful thing reading about the critic who fucked with Sinatra getting his face smashed into the flusher in the men's room. Oh, did that hurt? Get a picture of that and frame it.

I like the records he did where he's all bummed out like *In the Wee Small Hours*, *No One Cares*, *Where Are You* and *Only the Lonely*. I like Sinatra because all his life he's been saying fuck all you motherfuckers with the talent to back it up. He kept coming back no matter what was thrown his way. He inspires me big time. He's like a swan, graceful but mean when confronted.

The ride to the airport was an eye-opener. I was on the road by seven in the morning and the streets were packed and everyone was hard at work. Same intense poverty level as in Nairobi. Men selling green bananas. Butchers cutting meat off fly-covered haunches hanging from string. Streets packed with people selling what looked like garbage. I wondered how all these people survive. So many people, so much filth. All the shutters that were closed up tight last night were wide open and people were leaning out on their elbows watching the action on the street. The mix of people was interesting. Lots of people who looked part Indian, African and Asian. Some really beautiful people.

Now on the plane. They changed the gate at the last minute and all the announcements were in French so I was lucky to figure out to get on this flight. I am going to a town called Maroantsetra. It's on the coast. My place will be right on the Indian Ocean. I am looking forward to this. I remember clearly the flight in Australia last month when I was looking at Madagascar on the map and thought how cool it would be to sit on the beach and look at the Indian Ocean and now I am on my way.

12-14-97 Maroantsetra Madagascar: It's a little after midnight. Hot and moist out, just rained.

I got here around 10.30 in the morning. The back of the plane had people with TB. This one woman was coughing horribly into a piece of cloth wrapped around her face. The cloth was wet with blood and mucous. My favorite!

The airport here is very small and when I landed, it was full of little kids who all gathered to watch the plane land and see the people get out. Men with no shoes loaded the luggage and mail out of the plane and dragged the carts across the tarmac into the building. Baggage claim is a two-foot-high wall of cement with these guys throwing the luggage on it. Again, people just push and grapple to get a good position.

The place looks and feels like south Florida. If I knew it was going to be this hot and humid, I might have gone somewhere else but fuck it, I am here and it's cool.

I am in a small bungalow. There's only one guest here besides myself. Sarah is a student from America. She's been in Madagascar for the last five months studying birds of prey. Last summer, she was in Costa Rica studying. How cool is that? We both got here on the same plane. I walked around today, sat outside, read and spaced out. She went to the village, bought food and found a guide and made plans to go to an island at the crack of dawn to more research. How totally impressive. The ever sturdy Air Madagascar managed to lose her luggage on this one-hour flight so I gave her a T-shirt, socks and some toothpaste.

Tonight, I went out to the ocean and sat on the sand for a while. The moon was fairly full and it was bright enough to read under. No one was around and it was like I had the entire planet to myself. Saw it on the map and now I'm here. One of the most satisfying things in my life is the ability to actualize ideas. Hear a song in your head and then make it happen, come up with an idea for a book and then execute it. The work it takes that gets me to the final product is often more meaningful than the thing itself. I usually get depressed when a tour is done. All that velocity with nowhere to go. I like it here though.

It's wide open and there's no one around to bother me. It's amazing. I want a moment to myself so I go to fucking Madagascar. Here I can open up my gills and breathe. Places like this is where I belong. Alone in a remote corner of the world. This suits me. I like staying out on the road for as long as possible. I come home and it's always a letdown. I don't want to hear about people's little trials and tribulations about their car fucking up or their bullshit job getting to them. What did they expect? How can you complain that you're bored unsatisfied when you surround yourself with mediocrity and a grind that slowly drains you of your will to live? You can have it any way you want or have a hell of an interesting time en route if you have the guts to go for it. Or you can let events run your life and determine how it will go. The concept of fate is hilarious to me. 'It was fate'. Please. That's just giving up when you can't figure out how to make the VCR record something while you're away.

Why not be an outsider? Why not ride the rails? Why not go about the whole thing differently? I think too many people get wrapped up in their idea how things should be as we all do from time to time, but they let morality and the common story of the many, the mass of city-footed flesh determine how they will live their lives. Some people let others make up their minds for them. They let others formulate their lifestyles for them from the toxins that poison them to the jobs they hate to the marriages they want to leave to the children they don't want to the culture that bores them to the media that lies to them. And they can have it all as far as I'm concerned. They can have my helping too. I'd rather go on my own ideas and fail miserably than go their way and make it. They can have all the pointless hatred, the ignorance and the fear. I'll take my chances out here, wherever that is today, any day.

As I sat on the beach tonight, I could not help but keep turning around to see if there was anyone behind me. Makes me wonder how much living in cities has fucked me up. The idea of being alone in a space this big is amazing to me. To be so far from other people and have the view that I did tonight is something that I will never forget. I would like to explore that level of isolation. I would like to live very privately. I could see living deep in the woods over the winter and having no contact with people for months. It would take some getting used to and it might be painful but I know for sure that there are things to be learned. At some point, I will do this.

Seems to me that after you got the hang of it, your mind would start to empty out and a great weight would be lifted off your shoulders. I am forced to endure a certain amount of strife brought upon me by others. Everyone does to a certain extent. No, it's not enough to just ignore them. You can't ignore everybody. You live in a city full of them. Your apartment building is crawling with them. They buy their food at the same place you do. As much as you want to ignore them or tune out and find ways to avoid them while you exist amongst them, there's nothing like geographic isolation. You can go part of the way there in your mind, but to really go you have to move yourself and get there. I escape in my mind all the time. I go to a coffee place on tour and wait for soundcheck and just space out in my mind. It's a drag when you are all wrapped up in your thoughts and someone wants to talk to you. It's kind of corny to say to someone, 'Excuse me, I was thinking.' They'll tell their friends about 'the past-it-alternative-music-notable' who was a pretentious asshole to them when they came up and tried to engage him in conversation. When you are thinking your thoughts, there's usually nothing anyone can tell you that is more interesting. My thoughts are the only thing I claim total ownership of. Doesn't matter if I came up with the idea or not. It's one thing that cannot be stolen or broken into. Everything I own is merely on loan until it gets stolen or destroyed. I have always thought this way. I got rid of the idea of ownership while I was in Black Flag. I would go on tour and when I got back, half of my thirty-record collection would be gone. It sits on my shelf for awhile and then it sits on someone else's shelf. The next time you come back, someone will have taken the shelf, and there you go. No shelf, no shelf problems.

To this day, I still think that the number one is the strongest and ultimate number. I don't believe that two people can be one. There's some corny song out there, Celine Dion or Mr Bolton, one of those types with a song called 'Two Become One'. Why don't they just call it 'Two People Fucking'? Two people can be very close but only so close. I have a few friends, I think. I think that a lot of people don't realize how few friends they have. Get ripped off and lied to by a few of these friend types and it clears the steam off the lens in a hurry.

If intimacy with another works for someone, more power to them. I think it's great when two people are happy together. I think happiness looks good on most people. I don't know if I am there yet. I have always associated happiness with being idle. If I am working, I am happy but I'm too busy to notice that I am happy so I don't think about it. When I am depressed, I don't wish for happiness. I just try to slug it out against the bastard and prevail. I don't know if I want to get there either. Doesn't really matter does it? Do what you're gonna do. Try to aim so the brains from the exit wound are easily cleaned up or SMILE, YOU'RE TRAVELING!!!

I chose to grin and bear it, no matter what. Old Fred Nietzsche said something about mixing joy and malice. I like the idea of that blend. It's like watching Bruce Lee in *Enter the Dragon*. He was kicking ass and he was having a damn good time.

1.39 p.m.: Offshore breeze is back but it's still hot and humid. I am sweating while sitting still. In front of me: waving palm trees, a canal, two women walking barefoot with a cow and the Indian Ocean.

Getting some water boiled to have a cup of bad instant coffee. It is an ordeal. The two girls who work here don't speak any English and shrink back in terror whenever I try and speak to them, no matter how much I smile and try to be nice. I don't get it. Finally, I am unable to convey boiling water and then just go into the kitchen myself and get the jar of instant and make some coffee while they look at me in fear.

I leave tomorrow morning back to Antananarivo. I will stay there for a night and then go to Johannesburg.

I finally get the hang of not doing a whole hell of a lot and now it's time to go. I don't know if I would like to get good at doing nothing or get too used to it but it's been cool. Definitely a learning experience. Can't say I am looking forward to going back to the city and it's poverty and confusion. I could see staying out here a little longer.

I know I'm fucked up in a lot of ways, can't handle people, don't like to take shit from them, feel better on my own, feel fine in the middle of nowheres like this. I know it's a mess. Sometimes I feel done with them. I feel done with them altogether. I don't want to know anything about them. I don't want to know what they listen to, what they're going through, nothing. I feel like I am from another planet and I am visiting, or I have been left behind. It doesn't make me hate them, I just don't feel part of them. Places like this make me see it clearly since there's no distraction.

12-15-97 Maroanstetra Madagascar: 12.20 at the airport. It's hot and the air is moist and unmoving. Flies are all over.

In situations like these I make all my movements small. I try to slow down my metabolism, hopefully making me feel less hot. I have a long time to wait.

The jack off who told me to come here this early is a strange one. He looks like a shaggy Euro tennis instructor to bored Hollywood wives. When we got here, he said, 'You have a long time to wait, no?' I said I did. What the fuck, it was he who told me that I had to come here this early. He asks me, 'Where will you go?' I looked around the airport, which is an airstrip in the middle of palm trees and scrub and asked him, 'Where could I possibly go?' He gave me this funny look and said, 'I don't know, don't you know?' I just turned away and sat down. Outside of the beat down I should have administered, I was done with that guy.

There's about five of us here, we're all being well attended to by hundreds of flies. It looks like it's setting up to rain.

The drive here was another eye-opener. Tin roof shacks lining the roadside. Children playing in the dirt. Men lying on the floors of the shacks looking out at us as we drove by. People wearing some of the most worn-out clothes I have ever seen. It's interesting for a few minutes and then it just sucks big time. Only saw one other vehicle during the whole thirty-minute drive.

All of a sudden, the airport is packed. I have never seen so few people make so much racket. The noise level is a formless din punctuated by a little girl's chirping shouts as she runs around. She is dressed better than most of the people in the airport, including the woman who I guess is her mother.

I am glad to be moving on. It's hard to be in one place for more than a couple of days. I can be in my place in LA for about a week and not feel too confined because there's enough to read and listen to as well as the weights. I am always relieved to be packing my case to leave. I am always a bit depressed to be unpacking.

I strive to be known and unknown at the same time. I do interviews and write songs. I do speaking dates all over and tell the story or whatever. On the other hand, I find that I keep people at a distance for the most part. When people call me and try to ask me how I am, I just reel off facts and figures and events on my calendar to keep them at arm's length. I know it's boring information and it's meant to be. Every once in awhile, one of the interviewer shitheads asks me about this contradiction. It's funny to see these weaklings try to come across like they're cross-examining the defendant.

Why? Because about 99 per cent of the things in my life are best experienced alone. I feel alone a lot of the time anyway, might as well cut out the middle man. Alone in a room, alone in a room full of people, feels the same a lot of the time. There's a lot of people I like. It was great to hang out with the guys in Black Sabbath, an all time high. A really cool group of people. An ultimate musical force in my life. But, the beauty of the experience was leaving that scene solo, going to Heathrow airport and hours later, bedding down in Kenya, Africa. Alone.

Any time I'm with someone, I feel alone anyway so fuck it. Some people were meant to go down the trail alone. I am my own point man. Most of the people I used to go down the trail with have gone soft so fuck them.

How a man can allow himself to go soft is beyond me. I think that would be the ultimate failure. Civilization breaks men. In cities, women break men. Some men listen to the wrong women and become tame as house cats. They put on that hibernation fat layer and in many ways, it's all over. I think it's disgusting. I know that I could take a lot of flak for saying this but of course, I don't care. Never mind that it's true.

I read an article in *Time* or *Newsweek* about how American white couples are getting married and 'cocooning'. The article talked about these young couples, usually pulling down a pretty good salary, who pack their apartments with nice things and stay in all the time. Kind of like the couple on the television show *Mad About You*. A tame, overweight couple insulating themselves from the world. The part of the show that bugs me most is the husband character. The guy is a good comedic actor but what he represents is lame to me.

I know that I leave myself open to attack here. I come off as some hard-ass macho American stereotype. I'm not saying that it's great to be an uncultured, tough guy with zero sensitivity, for goodness sake, drop and give me fifty real ones! But there's no reason to let yourself slip either. You have a problem with this attitude? Then get out of your home, because some hard-working, non-cocooning mother fucker built it, another one grew the leafy green salad that you will eat tonight. On the other hand, I don't give a fuck if you turn yourself into a mediocre piece of shit. It is the American way, so just go with it. I can only do what's right for me.

6.24 p.m.: Back in Tana. Another intense drive from the airport to the hotel. Tons of people, not many cars, lots of squalor. So many kids running all over the place. What made it look all the more grotesque was that the sky was so blue and clear and the sunset was so beautiful. I wonder what it's like to be one of those CNN reporter types who are out in this shit all the time but know that they have a nice place to go to when the job is over. For the ones who live here, they have no perspective like that. They might not even feel the weight of the depravity like someone who knows there's something better.

I am in the sorry lounge of the hotel drinking the not so good coffee that's at least better than the powdered stuff they were giving me out on the coast.

The sun is almost gone and I will be looking for some food soon. I was told that this hotel is a good place to get food poisoning. I looked at all the food stalls on the way here and couldn't find anything that wouldn't kill me or make me puke.

12-16-97 En route to Johannesburg: I am on the plane. I was reading an issue of *Time* magazine and it listed an obituary for Kathy Acker. It said she died at age 53 in Tiajuana Mexico. Was she that old? A girl in San Francisco had been giving me updates about her health situation, which had been declining for some time. It was a hell of a thing to read in *Time*.

I first met Kathy in Amsterdam in 1985 when I was there for a poetry festival. Also on the bill were William Burroughs and Jeffrey Lee Pierce. I still have a note JLP left me to go find him at this bar down the street from the hotel I was staying at. I sometimes pass that place and think of him.

I have been reading *Newsweek* and *Time* on the plane today. I read that Sheryl Crow has sold eleven million albums. It's intense how people will show up for that stuff. I met her this year and she seemed like a nice enough gal. I heard some of the set and it sounded alright, just like the records.

She asked me why I had been dogging her in the Australian press, something I have no memory of doing, but I absolutely believe her. I told her that I probably put her on a long list of people like Sting and Michael Bolton, whose music means nothing. She didn't have anything to say to that and walked away. When you sell that many records, nothing I can say will really hurt all that much, so go on with your bad self, girl! In the great book of music history, she is a chapter with color plates and I am a mere footnote.

I watched her perform on the Grammys and she totally sucked. The song 'All I Want to Do is Have Some Fun' sucks and when she walked out of that place with all those Grammies I knew I was going to give mine away. I did. If they're giving them away for that crap, I don't want one in my place. What an insult to real music and musicians everywhere.

I read that she is dating Eric Clapton. That works for me. I had to endure his utterly wretched 'Unplugged' performance all the way to the airport on the car's radio. That guy is pathetic. Talk about a guy who stepped off! The two of them make a perfect match. Eleven million albums sold! People can be so brutally dull. Cattle.

It's good to read figures like this. It helps me to see the truth. Reviews, good or bad don't matter. Interviewers and critics are not to be taken seriously at all. They have no credibility whatsoever to me. People's opinion of what you want to do is really irrelevant. Life is too short to listen to all of them. At some point, you have to just get up and go. I am sure that old Sheryl means well and busts her ass to make her music happen. More power to her. Nothing she does impacts on my life so she doesn't matter to me. Records like hers sell well because they are lightweight, like the people who live in the West. It is the soundtrack for a culture that is dying, still listlessly going through the motions, nourished on the last bits of their lean tissue.

That's one thing I learned on this trip. People from where I come from, me included, are getting off easy. You might think you are a badass but you probably couldn't deal with the life of the downtrodden kicking it in Nairobi. That's a reality that all the guns, rap songs, money and privilege will not prepare you for. It's like what Jello was talking about in *Holiday in Cambodia*. I'm sure there's way worse situations in Africa. I have a discman and a Visa card. I am easy to kill.

I was reading an article about the Sunderbans Bengal tiger in India which attacks and kills people all the time. People who go to this part of India to collect honey are continually being attacked and killed. The article said that in the eighties, about sixty people a year were being eaten by these tigers. Can you imagine what that would be like?

Now, what do we learn from this? Either stop complaining or move out. If you're in the jungle and a tiger has you for lunch,

53

who's out of line? The Sunderbans Tiger has never shoved me in the subway. Humans deserve to be eaten by tigers in the jungle. That works for me.

9.02 p.m.: Another damn airplane. Went to Lufthansa and asked if I could get on tonight's flight to Germany and then to London. I don't want to stay here a full day. The place is bumming me out. The vibe here sucks and I see no reason to hang out when I can go to London and get some good food and a day to myself. I will be taking a day off from my 'vacation'. There's something about the people here that puts me off. Out of here and glad of it.

I called management and told them to try to book me a show on my birthday in Chicago and bring in a crew to record it. I hope that works out. I love that town. That might make a good record.

Now everyone around me is speaking German. I am in seat number 30D, adrift in a sea of people. The pilot said we are in for a 9 hr 55 min flight. I'm used to this. I've been in a plane for five hours already. Ear plugs in, blinders on, I will go into a larval state.

12-17-97 London UK: A little past ten in the morning. I am in the happening coffee place that I always go to. It's still good too. I am starting to heal. I got into London with no problem. Flights went without incident. The weather is cold and raining. I'm going to spend most of the day outside, hitting book and record stores. Tonight will be the Indian food get down of all time. My eyes are aching and I could fall asleep right now but I'm glad I came.

8.21 p.m.: At the restaurant. Found some great stuff today. Andrew Hill, Link Wray, Johnny Cash, The Fall, Flipper, UK Subs, Joy Division and some music of Kenya and Java.

There's something about this city that has a strange effect on people. So many times I am walked into. It's not me walking into them. I am off to the side and all of a sudden someone just kind of dead ends into me. It's like they wake up from a coma and shuffle on. The city is a narcotic. Maybe the sound of the cars and the trains underneath mixed with the steady rainfall hypnotizes them. They are the blood cells running up and down the concrete veins of the city. It's different than being in New York City. NYC gets me pissed off fast. London makes me feel cocooned in gray shadow and car exhaust. There's something about the way the voices fill shops and restaurants, the way it sounds, muffled and subterranean. The table next to me has filled with American businessmen in their early thirties. I listen to the things they talk about, makes me see how differently I turned out. The food is good but these guys are laying waste to my vibe.

Later: Now in a different coffee place trying to get my world back. The radio is on and a DJ is playing this mix of several seconds of an Oasis song going into the song where the girl says, 'love me, love me, say that you love me' over and over for about ten minutes now. No one seems to notice but me. I finally got the pukey guy behind the counter to change the station. He didn't seem to notice the utter hellishness of the music, but then again, the British are subjected to bad music almost every day so they have built up a fairly amazing resistance by now.

It's very easy for me to let people go. When was the last time I saw my mother? Fourteen months ago? Something like that. I don't hate her, I think she's cool. I don't think about people like that. I figure I'll see them when I see them and that's that. I don't miss anyone at all who's alive and it allows me to work and not have to think about things that would distract me. I figure if I am not attached to people, then I stand a chance. I am alone a lot of the time – much to my relief. Somewhere along the line, I lost something. I used to keep in touch with people, now I just see them when I see them. People sometimes come up to me with a few letters that I wrote to them in the eighties. I read them and it seems like a different person who wrote them. It was back then, back there. Back there. What the fuck. For three weeks I have been traveling by myself. I have made about five phone calls in this time. All of them were business calls. That's saying something, like maybe I have no life. I think I have one of those, I think it might be a little different than how some people are kicking it. I never feel a need to call anyone when I get back besides management. I always unplug the phone so there won't be any irritating messages waiting for me.

Why do I have this overwhelming urge to be deep into a Joseph Conrad novel right now? I'm in London tonight. I am in a city at night. Another city. I spoke to a few people today, mostly people at the counters of the stores I was in. To the people who recognized me on the street I just nodded and kept going. Sometimes I'm that guy and sometimes I'm not.

My load gets lighter with every passing month. If I have to deal with people, I just want to work with people who are doing something really interesting. The rest of it – spare me. Life is too short for bores. I'm so past it. I want to concentrate on my discipline and my work. Hit the weights with religious fervor and work a lot. Be alone as much as possible. What anyone thinks about this, I don't care. Life is short. Might as will cut the crap and get to it. The last couple of years have been a process of weeding out. Weeding out people and bullshit rituals that have come between me and doing the best I can. The things I put in my way to make myself think that I was giving it all I had. I was working hard but there was a lot of ego getting in the way. Ego and the need to establish myself. I had to rebound hard after Black Flag stopped. I had to rebuild the whole thing around me. That wasn't easy.

I would rather have experience than friends. Rather have money than love. Love didn't pay the hotel bill in Birmingham. When rich rockstars complain, I want to smack them. The big money they pull down allows them to do whatever they want. You can't be happy with a million bucks in your bank account? You're a fuckin' idiot. With a lot of dough, you can go places and expand your mind. You can buy time. You can go to an island for a year and do nothing but read. A year of no incoming calls. You could spend over a hundred hours a week, thinking without distraction. Imagine that. You could live like a king or the Unibomber.

A lot of people spend their lives never getting to know their potential. They show up for work, despise their boss and the way they have to live but lack the guts to walk out the door and never come back. In the end, they get what's coming to them.

12-18-97 Heathrow Airport UK: Will be on the flight soon. When I land I will go to the Roxy and be part of the Hollygrove Orphanage benefit put on by the Ringling Sisters every year. I hope I can pull it off seeing that I will be fairly ragged.

12-20-97 LA CA: 11.10 p.m. Went to the Roxy and did the benefit thing the other night. Twenty minutes stage time. I read a little of the journal I kept in Africa and that was about it. It was a bore for me. Some drunk woman gave me shit the whole time I was up there. Doesn't matter. I did my thing and didn't stick around for anything else even though I wanted to see Exene and Viggo Mortenson. He's such a great actor and poet and Exene is Exene. Amazing.

I walked back to my place. People called out to me as they drove by me. I ignored them. People said hello to me as I walked past them. I ignored them. I was in a bad mood from wasting my time and that being the last show of the year for me. People will ruin almost anything you give them a chance to get close to. There's a lot of kicks in the teeth in this business.

Now I am back in my room. My back pack and suitcase are on the floor. I have been back here for a couple of days now. I celebrated Joe's six years of death 12-19-97 by playing a lot of Sabbath. Started with Vol. 4 because I bought him that as a present many years ago.

The phone doesn't ring, a combination of the holidays coming up, my phone being unplugged for weeks at a time and the fact that not many people call me. I can't think of anyone I want to talk to anyway.

This is an alright place. I am surrounded by greatness. Recordings of the great ones are all around me. Stacks of books and art on the walls. These items are my shield against mediocrity. A refuge from all that noise out there. My own customized universe. Planet Zero.

I have been medicating myself for several hours now. Leadbelly, Lee Morgan, Coltrane, Hawkwind, the Field Recordings of Alan Lomax, Bill Evans, Joy Division, Link Wray, Scientist. Letting the toxins drain from my body. Not speaking for hours.

One of the greatest things I know is coming back to no one. There's nothing better than slipping back in under the wire and getting a little while to catch your breath before it all starts again. Not having to explain yourself to anyone. Not having to try and translate and talk about that which defies description.

My mind is working overtime trying to understand all the things I dealt with on this trip. Kenya was the most amazing place I have ever been to so far. Nowhere I have ever been to made me feel like that. How did I feel? That's the thing I am wrestling with right now. I feel as if I have been to the place where life started. I don't know anything about anthropology or the history of the planet but there was something in Africa that was huge and ancient and very dark. I sensed it when I landed on that air strip and the two Maasai were standing there just looking at me and my suitcase. Looking at them and the beautiful country they call home, that their ancestors from centuries ago called home, it occurred to me that the Listerine that I would spit out of my mouth into the bushes without thinking would do a huge amount of damage to a very small part of their world which they live in and treat like it's an equal living thing. It occurred to me that many of the things that I do daily, would destroy an environment like theirs. I deal with flight schedules, lawyers, all my bullshit ego trips, crime and these guys deal with cows, goats, lions and family. They can hang in the relentlessly brutal all natural jungle and I make my way as best I can through the one that they have to light artificially and pipe the water into. I know these are pretty generic revelations but when I was out there, they were hitting me pretty damn hard.

I lived in this beautiful dark place for a week or so and it's all I can think of now. When I landed at LAX a couple of days ago and looked around, all I could think of was how us city types are slaves to our luxury and convenience. That never occurred to me before. I saw how the Maasai were living. It's a rough life but the only thing that can screw it up is outsiders wrecking the ecosystem. If you leave them alone, things are alright. They might lose a few to treatable diseases but for the most part, they have all they need. I wonder what the suicide rate is in Maasai culture. I wonder if they even have a word for that in their language.

It's amazing to me that I covered so much ground this year and here I am back, sitting at my desk. What a year it was. A lot of hard breaks and a lot of good times too. I learned a few things. Some of those lessons felt like shots to the face but I reckon it's a good thing as long as I learned something.

Rest of the year was spent in relative solitude. Recharging, waiting for the holidays to be over.

1998

Part One

01-09-98 LA CA: Thom Panunzio is mixing the Black Sabbath concert in Studio D at A&M Studios. I'm going over there for dinner and to listen to him mix the show from December 4. This will be cool. I don't know if I was ever at a show that was taped for a live album besides one of my own. I hope the show is as good as I remember.

Later: What a cool time. Iommi was there. We ate and went into the studio to listen to what they had done before the break. They had been mixing 'Behind the Wall of Sleep' into 'NIB'. Sounded real good. They asked me what I thought. I told them that I thought it sounded good. They pressed me for more and I told them it wasn't my place to offer an opinion, especially when Thom is so on top of the whole thing. I asked if he was sure if he wanted my opinion. He said he did, so I told him. I told him what was bugging me about the kick sound and snare level. They fiddled with it and asked me what I thought then. I told them to tuck in the snare drum a little or something. I thought it made the mix more driving. They asked if I would come in the next night and listen to the mixes. How cool.

They worked on those two songs for the rest of the evening. It was great to hear this stuff. When I was there I thought it was a good show and listening back, it was still good. I know that sometimes the memory of the moment is better than it might have been in reality.

Thom had some good stories about working with Iggy on the *Soldier* and *Party* albums. He told one story about taking Iggy out to eat at Frankie and Johnnie's in NYC and Iggy ate his steak with his hands and freaked out the other customers. There's always a story with Iggy. A book about him would be the ultimate rock book. That thing would redefine the sport entirely. I have never heard so many stories about one guy in the music world. It seems like everyone who ever worked with him has an incredible Iggy story. Even a book of anecdotes about the man would be cool. He's a legend.

1-11-98 LA CA: Thom and Tony mixed 'Electric Funeral' tonight. Listening to the music while sitting next to Tony is something that I will remember for a long time. The jam in the up tempo part of the song is insane. Tony's guitar sound is brilliant, it sounds like it's melting.

Tony laid on some good stories tonight. I asked him about the *Born Again* record. He said that they recorded at the Manor in England. It's a nice place, you live on the premises. Nice piece of property. Ian Gillian pitched a tent and was living outside telling the rest of the guys that he needed the fresh air for his voice. They figured out later that it was so he had easier access to females. At one point the rest of the guys rigged the outside of Ian's tent with the pyro left over from the last Sabbath tour and waited until he was asleep and then set them off. Tony said it blew the tent off its pegs into the air and the concussion of the blast killed all the prize fish in the Manor's ponds. He said they were getting noise complaints from the nearby church hence the song 'Disturbing the Priest'. One of the nights Ian came back to the Manor after hitting the pub and decided to take his car around the go cart track on the property. He wrecked it and to make matters worse, it was Bill Ward's car. Apparently Bill got so mad that he took some rocks and sunk a small boat Ian had in a nearby canal. Gillian thought it was stolen. This is the story behind the song 'Trashed'.

I am a sucker for the stories. I love a good story. I will go a long way to hear it from the source. It's guys like these who have the great ones and you're not going to get them any other place. I live for moments, flashes. Every once in a while you're in a great spot and you catch something and you know that you're never going to forget it. I probably wear people out but fuck it. I want to know. You want to go nightly to a mixing session and hear the same song being played over and over? I do.

I got a free ticket to see Ratt the other night. I went to see what they would be putting across in 1998. It was not as hilarious as I thought it might have been. I don't know why I was thinking they were going to come out in those ridiculous outfits that they used to wear in the 80s. I guess it's the only way I had ever seen them. They were huge for a minute, like a lot of those hair bands, and then I don't know what happened to them. Kurt Cobain took them out I guess. I wanted to go because I figured people who would pay to see Ratt in 1998 would be at least interesting to watch. They sure were the first time around. Those bands had some pretty raw fans. I remember one time some of the Flag guys and I were handing out flyers to metal maniacs in line to see someone at the Troubadour, I think it was either W.A.S.P or Poseidon. One metal mamma had this large button on her chest that said 'Motley Crue' and I asked her if I could trade the button for one of these crass Pettibon inked flyers. She looked at me like I was insane and said, 'No way. You wouldn't *believe* what I had to go through to get this.' Oh don't worry, I would.

Ratt played at a place called Billboard Live. It's what used to be Gazzari's, a very famous hard rock club back in the day. It's where you could have seen a young Van Halen playing ZZ Top songs before they were signed. Ratt hit stage and everyone cheers. They are dressed very casually. They start playing and it's alright, I guess. The band can play, the singer sounds pretty much like he used to in his videos and the crowd knew the songs. A few minutes in, I am shoved in the back. I move to see a metal mamma holding her beer high to avoid collision, pushing her way to the front like it is her genetic imperative to be there to catch any stray seed that may inadvertently fly from the bass player's member. Of course, I am not one to stand in the way of evolution of any kind, dubious at it may be, so I graciously bowed and gave way. She looked at me like I was nuts.

At one point the singer, who hardly moved the entire time onstage during their 55-minute 41-second set, said hello to the crowd and told them to make some more noise which is a little silly because there's about four hundred people in this place. They did their best but it sounded the same every time. Then he said, 'Alright! Ratt back on the Sunset Strip. You like that Ratt shit? Ratt shit is better than cat shit, man. Cat shit stinks.' Everyone kind of looked at each other like 'Huh?' Everything stopped for a minute as everyone tried to figure that one out. I think the singer sensed that he had lost everyone in the place and quickly called in the next song. Easily one of the greatest bad stage raps of all time. I thought it was fantastic, right up there with the lyric he sang at one point, 'I'm gonna lick you til you're mine.' He kept asking for a joint between songs and no one seemed to be able to part with their stash or maybe it was because that the clubs are now smoke free. I noticed that before the show. I didn't know a law had been passed. I looked all around me and thought how considerate everyone was being by not smoking or maybe everyone had seen the light and they were no longer slaves to the tobacco industry and their murderous ways.

Near the end of the set, the singer said, 'This ain't no reunion, Ratt is back!' It sounded so sad. So completely empty. It was not that they played poorly. The drummer beat the hell out of the kit and played with a ton of energy and the guitar player did every note there was and the bass player had great hair and played well. The sound was perfect and the lights were fine but it was like a large well-wrapped empty box underneath the Christmas tree. The music was inessential when they were making it the first time, so what's the relevance now? It's like the Spice Girls reforming next year after it's all over for them a few hours from now, or *Spin* magazine doing an anthology of their best articles – there were any?

They seem like cool guys. It was their earnest playing that was unsettling. The singer talked about the new record that's coming out soon. Who does he think will be showing up for that one? Is anyone going to care? I mean, I hope they do alright because they seem like they want to play but I just can't see it happening. I've been wrong before.

They played 'Round and Round', the hit, as the last song in the eleven-minute encore. I was already outside talking to some people who were bummed out that they couldn't get in to see the band. It must be strange to go from selling millions of records and wearing all that eye shadow and headlining the big arenas to pulling up to a club and doing it in jeans and T-shirts in front of people who had one-hundred-year-old hair. I have never been all that far away from the clubs and, in retrospect, I feel lucky. One of our albums had a single and all of a sudden there was an extra throng of people at our shows for a month but that was about it. I never thought it was anything more than the temporary grace of MTV's almighty power. I like the people who come to see us play but they are fair weather friends and you see that they were perhaps only responding to a Pavlovian trigger such as airplay as much or maybe even more than what we are actually playing. I know at the end of the day, they would let me starve in the street and laugh as they walked by. It doesn't put me off them in the least. I don't expect anything else from them so how can I be let down? How can you be angry at a person for being a person? It's like getting mad at a rattlesnake for biting you – it's what they do. But I digress.

When Thom called it a night I walked up Sunset towards my place. A skinny man quickly walked past me. He stopped and said that he liked my videos. I said thanks and kept walking. He turned around and started walking with me. 'Have you seen a woman carrying a blue trench coat walk by?' he asked. I told him that I hadn't and kept going. He was right along beside me. His name is Scotty and he plays with Buddy Miles. Well, played with Buddy. Well, met him about twenty years ago. He went into the most insane high speed rap about his production studio he has out in Malibu and how he's taking Renny Harlan up there tomorrow. He said he is trying to exploit the power pyramid of youth, fashion and music. The guy was out of his mind. He told me that he wants me to be involved in every step of the huge project that he's trying to build and then he asked me what my name was, he had forgotten. There's no place like this town.

1-12-98 LA CA: In the studio last night. They mixed 'Fairies Wear Boots' and 'Electric Funeral'.

1-13-98 LA CA: It's a little past midnight. I went to the studio for a minute tonight and they were starting on 'Sweet Leaf'.

Next few months taken up by mundane LA activities temporarily relieved by short trips in America doing talking shows.

1-98
14. Pomona CA
15. Santa Barbara CA
28. Marquette MI

2-98
04. DeKalb IL
10. Queens NY
11. Toledo OH
12. Akron OH
13. Chicago IL
15. Ann Arbor MI
17. Lawrence KS
27. Atlanta GA

3-98
02. Athens GA
03. Orlando Fl
04. Knoxville TN
05. New Orleans LA
06. Baton Rouge LA
08. Missoula MT
09. Bozeman MT
10. Columbia MO
12. Winnipeg Canada
13. Minneapolis MN

4-98
02. Purchase NY
03. Burlington VT

04. Morristown NJ
05. New Haven CT
07. Portland ME
09. Nashville TN

5-4-98 LA CA: I was at A&M Studios two days ago on Saturday to finish the interviews for the Sabbath EPK. A few interesting developments in the Sabbath camp. Bob Marlett, the guy who was working on the tracks for Tony Iommi's solo album and the two new studio tracks for inclusion on the live album has been called in to remix the live tracks. I guess that they were not satisfied with the work that Thom Panunzio did.

Ozzy and Tony looked in good health and great spirits. As always, they have the great stories. What lives they have lived. Ozzy is really honest, he just puts it out there, if you can deal with it, cool, if not, then you have to make other plans. It's amazing that they all survived themselves and are still around. They have to be one of the only big bands of their time who has all the original members intact.

I did a long interview with Tony and Ozzy together. It was great sitting across from them, hearing the stories. I live for this stuff.

Bob was there and played me a version of one of the studio tracks that will be included on the live album. It's called 'Psycho Man'. I heard this before when I did vocals at his place for Tony's album. It's alright, I guess. The sounds are all there but it sounds like it's more of an Ozzy track than a Sabbath track. Bob gets some of the most intense guitar sounds I have ever heard. There's a certain clarity and separation he gets in the instruments that is phenomenal but at the same time it sounds very digital and a little sterile. It has plenty of power but no dirt. Maybe it's a little too clean. If I was Sabbath, I would be not exactly going for underproduction but I would be going after more analog warmth. One of the things that is great about the early Sabbath albums is that almost acoustic feel they have while being heavy as you can get. If you check the guitar sound on *Master of Reality*, you'll hear what I mean.

I asked Bob if I could hang out and check the mixes as they go down this week and he said that I could so I will hope that he calls me and I will get a chance to update this long story.

5-5-98 LA CA: Tony and Ozzy shipped off for Wales to start band practice. Looks like they will be working with Bill Ward for now, the real Sabbath tour is on. I think I remember hearing Sharon Osbourne saying that they'll be doing some European dates and see how it goes. I wonder what the year will be like for Sabbath. How many shows they'll do and if they'll go in and work on new tracks. It should be interesting. I'll be getting as much information as I can.

Next few months were spent in LA writing and recording what became the Get Some Go Again *album, working on film projects and waiting to get back out on the road.*

08-22-98 12.16 p.m. LA CA: Boris checks in from the Czech Republika with this burning missive:

Hallo Henry! I'm sorry for my English but I understand English very little. Thank you for your favour.

My name is Boris, have 24 years and write Czech Republic. You played in Czech 2X, both concerts they were splendid! On two concert I'm should collective photo, but such small, fat, baldheaded, technologist be insane.

I compilation all material for you and band.

I would like to read of your some book, but she don't publishing in Czech language. This book should be successful in Czech republic, sure.

I you very much for autograph, or publicity material, or answer in my letter. Thanks a lot for it. I wish for you, band much power, health and energy at further way music.

Good bye in future concert in Czech Republic. – Boris

The communiqué from Boris makes me think how great a feature length movie with this use of language would be. Could you imagine an intense courtroom drama with scowling, wildly gesticulating lawyers making a case for their clients, kicking it like Boris? Think of having the air flight attendant come on with English as a second language message. '*For making landing immediate time, incredibly. Broken moving not now stupid motor on flaming. I declaration emergency!*'

It's Saturday and there has been an abrupt change in plans. This being a travel story, it was going to start with a flight to England and then proceed to Scotland where I was going to do three shows at the Edinburgh Festival, return to London for press and then on to the shows that go until December.

All this changed the other night. Earlier that evening, I had done an instore at the Tower Records on Sunset Blvd in Hollywood. It was a good time. A lot of people showed up and some were quite memorable. I got asked out a couple of times, that was cute. Anyway, I got back to the office and found a script on the doorstep and many messages on the machine. Agent-manager-agent-manager. I called management and asked what was going on and was told that there was a good-sized part in this movie and it was being offered to me. I read the script and liked the part and now I'm leaving in a couple of days to go to Wilmington, NC, to work in this film called *Morgan's Ferry* for about a month. I will have a couple of days off before the speaking dates start in Austin, TX, in October. As much as I hated to cancel the shows and the press dates, I don't want to miss this opportunity. If I can pull this off, it will be three movies this year and the lead role in a television show. A non-actor getting work in Hollywood. An incredible scam.

The movie stars Billy Zane, Kelly McGillis and Johnny Galecki. Sam Pilsbury is the director. I talked with him today and he seems like a cool guy. It's an intense script about some men who break out of prison and wind up at a woman's house. She has no fear of them and it freaks them out. Kelly's character steals the show as far as I can tell.

It will be good work but hard. Going from this right into the shows will be a back breaker for sure but I have to go for it. I have a few days to get a lot of things done before I have to bail.

8-29-98 Wilmington NC: It's early on Saturday morning. Almost 0200. Got here in the evening from LA. Was supposed to get out here earlier but a hurricane was in the way. It was called Bonnie. I think it's stupid when they name them with a regular name. I have talked about that before, like calling El Nino 'The Motherfucker' instead. I think hurricanes should be given names like 'Hurricane Syphilis' 'Hurricane Richard Millhouse Nixon', stuff like that. These normal names are too lightweight, if you're going to do something, go all the way.

The way the papers handled the Monica Lewinski–Bill Clinton thing was boring. Since they were eyeball high in the gutter anyway, they should have at least had some fun.

The Secret Service agent diverted their eyes when he escorted her into the Oval Office. Monica knew this wasn't going to be just any ordinary visit to her President. Within minutes she was under numero uno's desk, using everything she knew to summon the executive potential. When the leader of the free world let loose, the warm splashing velocity of America's #1 executive's DNA paste nearly knocked her over. The urgency of the blast was not lost upon Monica. She now had an understanding of the weight of world leadership. The big guy was obviously under a lot of pressure, what with Iraq playing 'Anthrax, Anthrax, Whose Got the Anthrax?' The answer was obvious – bomb that sand blasted Bedouin Saddam Hussein and his towellheaded crew to the stone age and ask questions later. But in the interest of world peace, he had to use restraint. Monica was the perfect vessel into which our President could pour himself and with a rebel yell that shook the walls of the White House – he did.

After she regained consciousness and was walking unsteadily down the hall under the stern gaze of the Secret Service, she realized the importance of America's freedom and that she would do whatever it took to maintain that virtue on these shores, even if it meant losing a little of hers on the way.

I like that treatment better than the one that the press and smug Republicans like Orrin Hatch are giving the beleaguered Prez. I feel bad for his daughter Chelsea who must endure the next few years of school with her father's dalliance hanging over her head. While I am sure everyone around her is being cool to her and feels bad for her, they must talk about it after she leaves the room.

The whole rap about how he lied to the nation is a waste of breath. He was doing what many would do when busted in a similar situation. Deny. Priority one: cover your ass! To spend this much press time over it is pathetic and shows out the American media for the little bitches they truly are. I will never take another interview or press venture seriously again. I see now that any hurt I ever felt about mean things that any of them said was a waste of time. Their words are meaningless and they only influence the weak-minded.

I hung out with Billy Zane for a couple of hours tonight. We will be working together closely and it was good to meet the guy outside of the work scene. He is about as cool as they come. Smart, totally energized, a good guy. Earlier on I met the director, Sam Pilsbury, and a lot of the staff. All cool people. I spoke to Johnny Galecki briefly, he seems really cool. I guess I meet Kelly McGillis later on in the day.

I just came in from the street. It's late at night and still at least eighty degrees out there. It was like standing in a swimming pool of blood. Saw a fight break out tonight, two guys throwing punches. No one was connecting all that much.

A lot of people recognized us, it was pretty relentless. All were cool of course, but after awhile all you want to do is hang out and not have to do the thing. Before Billy got to the place I was sitting in, I was getting it full on. I would be able to space out for a minute and think my thoughts and then someone would break the spell. It's too bad. Sometimes, a lot of times actually, all I want to do is sit and stare off into space and think.

11.44 p.m.: Back from dinner with Johnny, Kelly and Billy. It was good to talk about the parts and hear everyone's thoughts on the characters. You can learn a lot. They all seem like good people. I am looking forward to this.

8-30-98 Wilmington NC: 7.48 p.m. 'Mood Indigo' on the restaurant system. I just came from the local used bookstore.

Asked the owner, an old man who spoke very slowly, 'Come on in, browse awhile.' I asked him if he had any books by Thomas Wolfe. He said that they go quickly and he puts them up front near 'that dude John Steinbeck'. I figure you have to buy a Wolfe book in North Carolina.

Even though the fan is blowing, it's still hot in here. This is where I should be. I am in my element. I am alone in a strange city. I am working, pulling my weight. I am away from people I know and doing something that I am not all that well-equipped to do. It will force me to use my brain and deliver. This is good. Too many times, I do what I know how to do. That's alright but I think that in order to take it to another level, one must go into some sort of unknown element and try to make do. This is one of the reasons I signed on for this movie. Also, I have to keep moving. Have to stay out here. I have a place to live but consider myself homeless. I live here and there. I bring it all with me. Less on my back, the better. The older I get, the less I need to feel I have a 'home'. I do my best to live minimally. I do that with all things. Property, people, everything. I save my money. I know that some day it will be hard to make a living and I will depend on the money I saved when I was able to work. I know that rainy day will come and the drops will fall as heavy as bricks and I want to be ready. Too many people in the entertainment business think that they will be there forever. Many of them don't think they have a limited time up there. I knew it by 1984. I saw others going out and I was not doing anywhere nearly as well as they were and knew I wasn't going to go out like that.

I was thinking today about the work, THE WORK! and how at the end of the day, it's all that really matters to me and how I should live more according to that. The work will always save you. The great ones always worked through thick and thin. When in doubt – work. Through the good and bad times, you gotta keep on working. You have to keep writing songs even when no one wants to know about you. You have to keep jamming no matter what.

8-31-98 Wilmington NC: 4.56 p.m. Was thinking about music critics and wondering if they feel frustrated because they know that the age of great music is over. I was thinking that every generation of music writers wants its heroes to laud so they can bullshit themselves into believing that they had something to do with the rise of these great talents. That's how lame some of these impotent, almost types are. Lester Bangs had Iggy, Lou, etc. Writers of years past had the Be-Bop greats, all the amazing sixties stars, the Beatles, Hendrix, etc. These days, there's nothing out there like that but that doesn't stop them from their need to surround the chosen few with accolades and precious studies of their dubious achievements. I read the articles and reviews and hear the records and know that nothing they write has any weight. I know they know. I guess they're pretty unhappy about it.

9-01-98 Wilmington NC: At the Cape Fear Coffee and Tea Co. watching two old men sitting in rocking chairs out front. They are homeless. A man just bought them bagels. I am looking at the man on the left: greying blond hair, black baseball cap, tan work pants, plaid short-sleeve shirt. Looks like he's worked all his life, hard and outdoors.

It's the first of September. Summer is over. It may be hot outside, but the summer is over. I keep seeing the back porch of a house I used to live at with my mother many years ago.

I like September. I like it that the summer is slowly dying and the cold is creeping in. When summer starts to wane, I always feel like I have lost a friend. Something about heat gives the summer a life of its own. You battle the heat, it keeps you from sleeping, drives your thoughts insane and makes your blood run hot. It's a constant daily consideration, staying cool and getting some sleep in the hot nights. In the spring I ready myself for the bestial months of summer. I know that I will think of women of the past, listen to music I don't think of during cold months and reread works of writers I associate with summer, like Miller, Wolfe and Fitzgerald.

Don't compare yourself to others. Compare yourself to yourself. How about that for a bold idea? Throw out the notion of referencing yourself against others. It would be so easy to compare and put yourself down. You can all too easily waste time and obscure your own potential by trying to match someone else's. I figure that the great ones thought differently and let their truths guide them no matter the cost. At the end of the day, you can't fuck with it. When you compare, you immediately ensnare yourself with a ton of variables and assumptions that can pull you off the trail. Anyone who thinks for themselves and acts upon these thoughts stands a chance. One can be met with resistance and scorn. 'I really can't stand your music.' That may be, but can you stop me? Will your words break me? The answer tells you everything. To do the thing all the way, you have to be pretty damn unsinkable. If you really want to get it done, you have to prepare yourself for what becomes of a real moving and breathing individual. You can always go the way of most of them, mill around and wonder what happened when you end up at the end of the line feeling like you didn't get what you deserved. The road is always wide open for those who want to cruise the middle lane. If you want to do something else, it's going to hurt, all things connected with excellence do to some extent. It's always worth it.

All work and no play makes Jack a dull boy. All work and no pay makes Jack a mean motherfucker.

9-03-98 Wilmington NC: It's 10.14 p.m. on Thursday night. I think that the great age of music has passed and now it's time for the meek to inherit. Who am I to stand in the way? For a while there I thought I had been betrayed. How can I have been betrayed by strangers and the corny music they make? I say go on with it and I'll go on with mine. There's room for all I reckon.

From them I expect nothing. Nothing. From media people I expect distortion, ignorance and musical illiteracy. If I can keep the work in front of all of that nonsense and do the right thing, I'll be fine. Otherwise you get swallowed but the peripheral. Focus and self-belief is all. Movie people like you when you are making them look good and making them money. When you aren't doing that, you're history to them. I can deal with that.

9-04-98 Wilmington NC:
Travel the world alone
Walk through magic nights
Let the dead speak to you
Hear the ancient call
Discard the present and its plastic values
Turn a deaf ear to the tin music makers

I saw some things on television that made me think. I saw a thing about Andre Agassi. He said when he had domestic bliss, his game slipped. Made me think of an interview I saw of Donald Trump where he said that when he started taking vacations and enjoying his marriage, his game slipped. I think you have to chose what you want to do. I don't think you can have it both ways. Either you choose the work or you choose the other life. My life gets harder and harder it seems. It's cool. I just say 'this is hard' and keep jamming.

9-05-98 Wilmington NC: Due to rain, we have lost a day and a half on the schedule. It is Saturday. We work tomorrow. An 0630 call. So far, when we are working, it's been great. Everyone is cool. It's the down time that's a drag. There's not a great deal to do here but I have been getting in good workouts and that is good for me.

I have been watching the news which is depressing as hell. You can't watch any news program for more than a few minutes without hearing about Bill Clinton's moment with Monica. I know I can't be the only one so bored and sick of it. It's a ball that won't hit the ground because the media won't let it. If they talk about it, then it's news. I am disgusted. It's strange for me to feel that way about something like this. I must be getting old.

Nostalgic insert: It is the Labor Day Weekend. I remember this holiday well. It was the last few days before school started. I remember this weekend hanging like a death sentence over my head. The summer holiday that I suffered all those months of school to get to was over and another nine months of incarceration was about to start. The last day before taking that walk to the bus stop to get back on the school bus with the other inmates was a slow and dreary day. There was momentary elation at seeing all the others before first period, a feeling of camaraderie that soon vanished as the bell rung and the full horror of the classroom closed in. It only took a moment or two to see that these were people that I would never have anything in common with and I was stuck in an unendurable hell with them for the rest of the year and that all communication with them would be fake and forced. It was acting class all day, every day. I'll never forget that school uniform. It seemed like I had just gotten it off when I was putting it back on again.

9-08-98 Wilmington NC: 10.32 p.m. Long day today. I can handle it. I gotta think like a champion. Gotta be a champion. It's so easy to quit. Quitting is the easiest thing there is. Gotta be like Mohammed Ali, like Sinatra. Never quit. Have to get up too early in the morning? Work too hard? You can always quit. You can always do less and in America, you can always get by with less. You can always get by with being mediocre and normal. You can let it beat you down and join the droves. It's all there for you. You can retire at any age. Or you can do something else. I know that I am not much and that certainty makes me hit like a hammer and never quit.

Doing this movie has given me a lot of confidence. I feel good that I have stepped up to the plate and took the brave swing. It doesn't matter if I hit it out of the park as long as I go down swinging.

Cut like a scalpel. With less hanging off you, you speed along. Human baggage, addictions, they all distract you from the work. They become your downfall. I think it's lame when people have the talent and all they can do is sell it out and dissolve themselves into the lamest possible parodies of what they once were.

Been reading Hemingway and Fitzgerald at the same time. Both are amazing but Hem makes Fitz seem neurotic. Hem makes me think of a lone man walking on a trail, close cropped hair and gnarled features. He has shattered the glass walls of solitary nights with the weight of his existence. He has traversed the world many times. He knows that he is alone. So many years, so many miles have passed that he is friendless, motherless, free. Look at the scars on his hands and face, it's the consequence of freedom, of experience.

Hard not to get soft. I try not to drag myself down with what some would consider success.

I don't answer to you, that's the important thing. If I let outside voices discourage me, then I have allowed my resolve to slip. I'll take resolve over conviction any day. The flesh will wither no matter what you do, but the rest can grow stronger as time goes on.

Been watching Clinton. He answers questions hypothetically, just like Ted Bundy did. Satan chose to follow his own will and got thrown out of Heaven. Now he collects the weak and kicks ass all over the world.

9-29-98 Wilmington NC: Just been doing the movie and the lifts and that's about it. Been too out of breath to write anything. It's going well and everyone is cool to me. Having a great time hanging out with Roscoe Lee Brown, one of the actors in the movie. He was friends with Miles, Parker and Billy Eckstine. He told me the reason that he rarely curses is because those words hardly ever express what he wants to say and besides that, Eckstine was the best curser he has ever heard and could never hold a candle to him. I'll never hear Mr B's music the same again. Roscoe does a great imitation of Miles. His stories were so cool, he knows he has me in the palm of his hand when he gets going on the jazz stories. I'm all ears for that.

Been thinking about Hemingway after seeing the documentary about him on A&E. What a life he had. What is there to learn: Alcohol and fame helped destroy him and his genius. His huge ego was also a factor. When he got popular, he seemed to lose his power and got swept away with being 'Papa Hemingway'. I love this quote: 'Write the truest sentence you can.' That's all you need right there.

Hemingway lived hard, he went for it. He went through three wars. The documentary had interviews with two of his sons. They were respectful but you could see that he hurt them. I remember one saying that he was a great dad when he wasn't busy being Ernest Hemingway. I can dig that, but he had to write *For Whom the Bell Tolls*, didn't he? What a book.

What is there to learn from that: You can't do the real thing and have too many attachments without something suffering. In Hem's case, he had to take care of the awesome talent that he knew he possessed and play catch up dad to three kids. He shouldn't have had the kids. He should not have had children and then left them to their mother. I think that guys like him leave a path of destruction because they need a woman to wait hand and foot upon them, to worship them and take care of them but at the same time, they need to be alone to deal with as he termed it, 'Eternity or the lack of it'. You can't have it both ways. One person's genius is another's cross to bear. Hemingway gave the world something huge. He gave the world some of the most beautiful writing ever. I live for great writing and great music. For as long as I can remember, I have been preoccupied with both.

I am enduring the chatter of two women at a table in front of me. They are supposed to be studying but all they're doing is talking. Every once in awhile, one of them talks about the book that is in front of her as a jumping off point for bullshit. What a waste of daddy's money. All that info being pumped into the mind of a twit. Chattering birdbrains who will probably just settle down and breed and not use any of the knowledge that may have accidentally seeped in over the years. No doubt about it, on the whole, the population is getting dumber, fatter too. You can thank technological advancements for helping obliterate the need for common sense and aptitude.

My questions are: When is someone going to stand up and split the sky? When is someone going to conspire against the odds and mediocrity and make some music that burns holes in the night? When will the useless chatter cease?

There will come a time when resources run so low that the real is going to get so real it will be on everyone's doorstep, rich or poor. There will be no protection. What then? The music I hear these days tells me that we are almost at the end of the line. Corny, weak and apologetic, or by turns, smirking and infantile.

I want to be hurled into rooms. Shot to destinations that shatters forever the notion of destiny and fate. There's no such thing as either. You choose it all. The test is whether you have the strength to live up to your potential. There is victory and defeat. The rest is what you tell yourself on the way.

09-30-98 Wilmington NC: At 9.30 tonight I go in for the last night of shooting. I'll get out of the deal around noon. I have a flight a little while after that. Three flights to get to Austin, Texas, for the first show. I have to do press on show day and then the shows are pretty nonstop. At one point I felt a little tense. How was I going to be able to go into these shows having just come off this movie, which was a lot of work? I felt like calling someone and hearing a voice. I snapped back to the reality that I am on my own and no one wants to deal with anyone else's stress. I know I don't.

You have two choices as far as I can see: do it or don't do it. As soon as you want to say it's all too much, you can go back home. There's lots of knockout drugs for you to take. Alcohol, tobacco, television, a mediocre job. You can go to that and go into a deep freeze, or you can be like the few and rise to the occasion. It's all yours to choose. That's all there is. Who can help me to deal with stress? You? My mommy? Lift it or don't.

I passed on a chance to be on the *Rosie O'Donnell Show* today. Press woman set it up without asking me beforehand. There's no way I could do that show. Rosie's the worst. I wouldn't be able to restrain myself. I would get thrown off that show. She is so offensive to me. Press woman was really bummed out that I didn't want to do it. I imagine it was no small feat to get me on that show. Management bummed as well, I can't blame them.

7.35 p.m.: In the Cafe Phoenix for the last time. Taking stock: the shoot was cool. By the time I get to Austin, I would have been up for about 24 hours. So what else is new? It'll be a lot of running, bleeding and dying tonight. You know, the usual stuff.

I am looking forward to getting this done and getting on to the shows. Those talking shows are hard to do and there's a lot of them, over fifty. We'll see how I am at the end of this run.

10-07-98 Washington DC: 1.17 p.m. In the coffee place, sitting in the same seat as I was last time I was here in May for Alec MacKaye's wedding.

The sky is grey and the weather is mild. I have taken some photos of this area, my old neighborhood. It's funny to walk down the same streets as I did when I was fourteen and have the context change so much. Now people call out to me from cars and come out of bars because they saw me through the window, it's cool but it makes it hard to have a moment to try and remember the days.

I am looking at the window where the Shit Lady used to live. Grey house with black shutters. We gave her that name because she used to throw her German shepherd's shit out of that window in paper bags. The front of the building was littered with them. We used to call out to her using her new name and she used to shake her fist at us.

I love this neighborhood even though some of it has changed over the years. Being here also makes me feel lonely for those times. It makes me lonely for a happiness that I can only imagine. I don't know why I think it's going to be found here. I guess this is the last place I used to live before all the music and touring started. It seems like a different life ago. It was. From 1981 to now has been a furious blur. A lot of stuff. I come back here and see the old places and it trips me out. Sometimes I'll sit on the stairway I used to sit on after I had done the night shift at the job I had before I joined Black Flag. Still looks the same. It's strange to sit there and think that I was in the same spot twenty years before. Sometimes it makes me sad that those days are gone. I wonder if other people think about stuff like that. I don't know, I don't ask. I figure there's things you don't talk about to others. I like my thoughts, no one can take them from me.

It is October, my favorite month of the year. It was Thomas Wolfe's favorite month as well. I'll always think of Wolfe during the month of October. I'll always read him in this month as well. He said that October was always about returning, returning.

10-08-98 Washington DC:
I must be humble
I don't want to get my hands caught in the machine
I am stupid and move slow
I must shut up, shut down, look out
The machine is the master material waster
The thud you just heard was my heart
Hitting the bottom of the dud bucket
I know, I know
You're still out there swingin'
I'm trying to write a brighter song
But the words keep coming out wrong

You're too busy destroying yourself
To fix the hole you tore in me
You're too busy smelling your own blood
To finish me off

No matter who's in front of you, all you see is yourself. A junkie without junk is a warrior without a war. When you're shut off from your own pain, you can't see it register in anyone else. And when you leave, I feel so useless and alone that I think the world has been surgically removed from my life and all I have left is this hole and the memory of you.

10-09-98 Washington DC: Same coffee place, same seat. I went with Ian to the record store yesterday. Same store we've been going to since we were young. Yesterday and Today Records, 1327 J Rockville Pike. It was good to check out Skip and the store. I have known that guy about twenty years. It's amazing to me to still be able to walk in there and see him. I go all over the world and come back again and there's the store and there's Skip.

There's a beautiful sadness here. It's in the trees and how the air smells at night. It's in the way the smoke from chimneys fills the air, in the street light's glow. I wish you were here with me. I wish you were my friend and wanted me. That's what I wish. To see the grey sky and these streets. To smell the air at night and walk with me underneath these trees. Maybe you could teach me something. Maybe you could help me. You know how I am – impossible.

10-13-98 NYC NY: I'm in the dressing room at Irving Plaza. I have some good memories of this place. I saw a lot of bands play here. Bad Brains, UXA, Cramps, Dead Kennedys, Fugazi. I played here with Black Flag and my band as well. The last NYC Black Flag show was here.

I don't have any nostalgic feelings for this town. I walked down the streets and they're just streets. I lived here for a little while and it wasn't all that great. It was pretty interesting to be a New Yorker for a minute though.

October is breathless and people of the city are relieved to be spared the heat.

10-15-98 La Guardia Airport: Waiting to go to Rochester. Spent the morning doing MTV. Boring and alienating. Met the singer in Cake and he was cool and funny.

I am lonely. I like it and I hate it. It's kind of cool to be lonely, you know you're alive. The women look so beautiful. I like the way the cold air brings out the life in their faces. I think if you're alone inside yourself, it's hard to get out to anyone else. I am working to get out of myself a little more as time goes on. It's hard for me when I spend so much time thinking about getting to the next place. It's always the next place. I don't want to know, I just want to move, just keep jammin'. 'If you're ready, I'm ready,' that's all you need.

It's cold here. The flight has been delayed thirty minutes. It's Thursday, have been up for hours. I have a show tonight and then an early van call, a three-hour drive, border crossing and all day press tomorrow. That's the deal. It keeps us apart.

1998

Part Two

10-20-98 Columbus OH: Much different than other shows I have done here. More people than usual and a much better venue.

Ohio is flat and the people are trapped on the flat plains. The endless small towns, full of American flags and bad food. All that time and television. You want the real America? It is here that you will find it. Ohio, Michigan, these are the places where the American slow death plays itself out over seasons. Football and raking leaves. All that heritage. Depressed towns that are now shells of the boomtowns they once tried to be. No one told them it was a joke and the joke was on them; that the American Dream is only for a few, that the rest just serve their time in this tortured land of beautiful fugitives. Small towns are the suppliers to the American Machine. Soldier boys, food, patriotic air, good sturdy racism and separatist spirit.

The American is a nomad. A bastard son. A criminal wherever he goes. Cut loose in his own country to wander and wage battle. The parents are merely stand-ins and those who raise the child for its life of brutality along the highways and streets of the city where it scrapes along, in search of home. The American, always lost, always homeless. Momentary relief when living abroad. Away from the cold mother America who does not embrace or welcome its own when they come back, never waves goodbye when they leave. Come, go, America never notices. Business class, body bag, it doesn't matter. The American travels the world looking for home in other countries. Always alone, always American, he'll never get it off of him no matter what distance he puts between himself and his crime of birth. The stain can never be removed. The blood never cleansed.

America will always kill its own for better ratings.

10-21-98 Cleveland OH: 1020 hrs. Check-in lady had some attitude. Today is a fake day off. No show but an in-store and press and whatever else.

10.01 p.m. Chicago IL: I did this in-store thing today. I met a long line of people. Near the end of the ordeal, a woman came in with a group of retarded adults. She asked if they could meet me. I told her to keep them all to the side and let me get finished with the line and then I could hang out with all of them with no interruptions. So, when the line had gone away, I hung out with these people. They were so cool. I did photos with this one guy, I think his name was Igor, he was very intense. One of the women and I walked around the store and checked out things and she gave me her take on all the different items, it was so cool.

The woman who takes care of them told me that she has taken them to meet people in bands and other notable types and they're usually mean to them and don't want to meet them. That's strange. That doesn't sound like anyone in bands that I know.

October is slipping away faster than I thought. I always find myself on the road in this month. I try to take it in as best I can. It's stupid, but I always think something's going to happen. I will figure something out, some great mystery will make itself known to me. I don't know what it is that I am looking for, what it's supposed to feel like or anything. It's always been this month for me. The magic month of the year. It's an alone month. Not like summer months where the heat makes people seem closer, streets seem more crowded, voices louder. October is a month of longing for the undefinable. Walks in the evening that make one happy to be alone and on the move. It is not yet the time of winter's death and silence.

Tonight, I walked by a club that Black Flag played with Husker Du in December of '81. The 730 club was it? No feelings of nostalgia hit me. I don't have much of that connected with Black Flag. It was cool but there was a lot of flat stretches that we just had to occupy and endure and it was alright but nothing I remember with that much happiness. It was a damn good band though. It's funny to read what these corny music critics write about Flag. It's funny because you can tell they were never there. When I read a music writer's take on Black Flag, it's easy to tell a lot about the writer. I have found most of them to be full of shit. The real story is only known by a few. I am fine with the rest of them getting it wrong. Thank goodness there's great writers like Peter Guralnick to write books like *Feel Like Going Home*.

10-29-98 Portland OR: In America, running like a fugitive. No sense of community. Freedom freezes me out and turns me hard. I see a factory. I see men and ruined shelters. I see men in steel caves with hot sparks flying around their heads like a furious meteor shower. I see the open road and all the opportunities to lose everything in this land. Go and erase your past in a few hundred miles. I'm stopping here to talk to a room full of people, other drifters like myself and then going back out on the dark road. Over, ever, on. My American song. A moon over my windshield, silence behind the wheel. Stopping by a box of beds to rent space to lie amongst the other strange convicts. The land is painted and blasted beyond recognition. It roars in song and tradition. A history of fists. Jail, Army, marriage, divorce, death.

I meet them every day. On streets and in stores, restaurants, hotels, airports, the show, everywhere. I can't help but like them. I love their energy and the excitement that they instill in me. Their eyes make me hate the cheap, sniping land they scrape to put food in their mouths. I curse the land that might murder them and turn their dreams into bitter memories of a life denied, a place that will take their good intentions and turn them mean and twisted. In their eyes I see the limitless potential of a single life, and in that, all life. Glorious and full of blood-filled dreams and real life horror. Restlessness and anticipation of the things that will some day be theirs.

I want to go. Another town. Now. Portland is like a lot of places in the Pacific Northwest. A community slammed down in the middle of dense forest. Not like what I see in the South.

Alligators and dead cars on the front lawn. The faces of the great Pacific Northwest have the hardness of the pioneer. Solid, grim, warily hopeful. Sometimes I wonder if my eyes will wear out from all the things I have seen.

I'll take this backstage room, the pre-show compression. One floor below me, they are sitting and talking. They came to see me. What they might not know is that I came to see them too. Without them, there would be nothing tying me to the Earth. I might just disappear into the night, like so many do in America, to towns and cities, into rooms with shades drawn and walls that murmur and floors that creak. I'll take this room and the stage that waits. Minutes from now I will be with them in this American night.

11-04-98 LA CA: Nights from now, winter will be here. I see your face lit by a candle.

'It's hard to be around you.'

'That bad?'

'That good. I loved you the first time I saw you.'

She looks down for several seconds. Then lifts her head slightly and looks off to her right.

'Well.'

'I'm sorry. I should never have said anything.'

'No, it's alright. I don't know what to say.'

'It's alright, you don't have to say anything. I am sorry if I upset you.'

'It's alright, it's just that I . . .'

'Of course, you'll miss your train.'

'Yes. Right. Well, it was nice to see you again.'

'Yes. Well, goodbye.'

'Goodbye.'

And then the world swirls down a night drain and the road opens wide. Winter will seal off this moment from the dull grey environs of the city. A place that makes a man want to escape it and someday return to rule it, to make it bow before him in a mechanical gnashing of automated teeth and melting miles of electric wire.

11-05-98 LA CA: 2.41 p.m. Waiting to go to Phoenix AZ for the last show in America for the year. I did a TV show called *Loveline* earlier today. It's the televised version of the radio show that I have done so many times. It was cool I guess. I think that the audience was hand-picked. They all looked like models, their hair and faces were picture perfect. It's another racket but it's cool, at least young people can get their questions answered about sex and maybe a few lives will get saved. Glad to be done with that and getting down the road to the next show No matter how good a place is, I always look forward to leaving it.

11-07-98 En route to London UK: It's about one in the morning. The plane is pitching pretty good. Makes writing difficult. Must keep writing. Must keep punching through the days that stand before me.

Last few days have been a blur. Finished the US dates on 11-05-98 in Phx. AZ, then flew to LA for a few hours and now I'm heading to London. It was good to get out of there. The phone was ringing more than usual. Most of the time I only get calls when someone needs something. The calls are to the point because people have gone the 'Hi how are you?' route before and they know that just makes me want to hang up. How am I? I'm doing the thing. I don't want to hear about who's fucking who over. I talked to someone the other day. I had less than an hour to be alone in my place before I had to take off and it took a good-sized portion of that hour to get off the phone. I lost my temper and smashed the phone with my fist. We both survived. I can be such an idiot. Why do people talk so much shit? Why do so many people have such mediocre lives and feel the need to drag others through it? So much that passes for normal conversation is excruciating to me. It's like talking about cardboard. Fucking load up and go, damn it. Life is too short for the rest. I am operating on not much sleep. I have only slept a few hours here and there over the last few days. I look like shit but I feel alright. I want to hit a gym when I get to London and break it up. I will have a hard time making the jump to UK time. Traveling east is always hard for me.

I feel the depression setting in. A combination of exhaustion, loneliness and other factors. This will be a hard tour. A lot of depressing venues to blast through. Gigs in England will drop you. The thing that bails it out is the fact that the audiences are very cool. The cold, damp, poorly lit backstages in these places are hard to take. It seems like they were built to pound you down like a nail. You just have to power through it. Loneliness is fucked but it's part of the deal when you travel a lot. Whatever. Get the work done or don't. No one besides you will notice. You deal with it and get the damn task done. One of the great things about doing these shows is that I do them on my own. I have no help up there. I do my thing and I don't rely on anyone to help me. Sometimes people put me down but it doesn't matter because I know they couldn't pull off what I pull off nightly year after year. Either you do it or you don't. It's that easy.

Last few days have been busy. Got to LA from San Francisco for shows and press. I don't remember much of the events leading up to the show at the House of Blues. I think I unpacked and dodged phone calls. Hilarious. My guest list for the show was about five people. A couple of them were favors. Shows you how many people I know in that town. Of all people, the wife of Black Flag's Chuck Dukowski called, asking if Chuck could be put on the guest list. Dukowski got married? He has to get his wife to call me? I don't get that. Does it matter? Played some wild shows with that guy many years ago. That was some shit.

I did the LA show and thought it was pretty good for an LA crowd, they seemed more lively than usual. For some reason I was signed up for an 'in-store appearance' at the House of Blues gift shop. I was on stage for nearly three hours and now I have to stand at the front of a line of people and sign stuff when I could be in my own room? The people in the line were great so I didn't mind meeting them at all, just wish I could have gone back to my place and listened to some music instead.

I met with Oliver Stone about his next film called *On Any Sunday*. He was interested in me playing a part on the football team. I would like to be in an Oliver Stone film before I die. Some people don't like the guy. I think he's awesome. I like the way he carries himself. He delivers the goods and doesn't give a fuck what people think about him. That's the way you have to be. He came into the meeting room, hair a mess, looking rough. 'Working late last five nights.' Yeah he was. One thing he said in an interview years ago is still very inspiring to me. 'I'm exhausted so I'm not going to make any mistakes.' He makes some damn good films. I thought *Nixon* was great.

I don't have the size for a football player but it's cool that he was interested in me for a part. It's energizing to be around that guy. He said, 'You and I are too intense not to make a film together in this life.'

After that I had to go and be on *Politically Incorrect.* That was pretty cool. I hung out with Lynn Redgrave who was also on the show. I thought she was cool. Met David Brenner. I have always liked that guy. He was funny as hell. Bill Mahr let loose on this woman, a Republican, his favorite target. He always has one of those on the show so he can blast them. The woman, Charmaine Yoest, was a good sport about it but kind of opened herself up to attack. He laid into her. Glad it wasn't me.

'What color is this coffee mug?'

'Blue.'

'Right. What color is the sky in the world you live in?!!'

Brutal. Crowd goes nuts. She smiles through it but you could see that he got to her. Republicans on TV shows are always hilarious to me. You can talk about anything and they will turn any topic into a platform to talk about the good deeds that the Republicans are doing for all Americans, even those silly-not-smelling-the-coffee Democrats. They always seem to be able to bash Democrats as they discuss policy. Amazing ability, that.

I finished there and then had to jam to get to a show I had at Occidental College. What a non-event that turned out to be. Inept staff, glumly standing around. Uninspired students putting on a show. The people whose idea it was to bring me there were barely into it. About a hundred in attendance. People walking in and out all through the show. Felt like I was on display. I did my thing and it felt like a chore. I would have rather had a night to myself in my room. Won't be seeing that place again. So glad to be out of LA and on the way to the next thing.

11-08-98 London UK: In the hotel's breakfast room. I have the music cranking in my headphones so I can hear myself think over the caterwaul of my fellow masticators.

I got to the hotel yesterday . . . 'Come and stay at the beautiful Hotel Yesterday. Accommodations feature unmade beds, damp towels in heaps on the floor, old newspapers and half filled cups of cold coffee. A feeling similar to *déjà vu* pervades these halls. You get the feeling that *someone else* has been here before. Visa, American Express and Mastercard welcome.'

Anyway, I got here yesterday. Saturday I walked around. It was unbelievable. I have not seen so many people waiting to cross the street at intersections since I was at the Shibuya Main Station in Tokyo. I stood surrounded by who knows how many deep waiting to cross. The two sides step into the street and collide in the middle. Christmas presents slam into each other as shoppers push and heave themselves through the opposing human wall. An endless mass of pinched faces, bad skin and stunted growth. London is a hard city. England is a hard place. I like it though. I used to hate it.

I have to do some press today. English journalists are weak and too hilarious to take seriously. I can't bring myself to anger when they rip my spine out with their polysyllabic diatribes, taking out their bad skinned, stunted growth, rotten toothed frustrations on my new release or performance. I look forward to their quivering voices and limp, clammy handshakes. I am giddy with delight as I anticipate their questions concocted in their cramped, gaseous, garlic and tobacco smelling flats. What a wonderful way to spend a cold Sunday before a major gig the next night. It begs the question – could it get any better than this?

On the other hand, some of the hardest-working crew people I have ever met on the road are from here. Intelligent and hard. They get it done.

It is a tough, rainy rock they live on. It's canned and trucked in for breakfast. The air in the rooms is over-breathed. The sleep is churning with perspiration and grey dreams. Still, there's something aching and eternal about London streets at night. The tired people on the subway and the hard resolve on the faces of the elderly as they clutch their packages and stare fixedly at some obscure point on the floor beyond their swollen feet.

I have been here so many times I can't even estimate. At least 35 separate trips. The place is familiar. Makes me think of October of 1986 when I came out here to record songs for what became the *Hot Animal Machine* album. Lived in Leeds for a couple of weeks. An exciting time. I was 25 and just out of Black Flag. Chris Haskett and I worked on those songs hard.

That was twelve years ago. I have not taken my hands off the wheel since. That's what fucks so many people up. They take their hands off the wheel and detour for a little drug addiction, a little marriage–divorce or some other shot at oblivion. I think to do it, you have to sacrifice a lot of normal domestic tasks. I include bad marriages and various addictions as generic, domestic concerns that sidetrack one from the work. Oh, but that's so extreme. Whatever. All I know is that a lot of people I know from bands and people I was in bands with are fucked up and scraping. The one thing they have in common is that they detoured into addictions and destruction and tried to haul their human wreckage out into the world and sell it as entertainment. They get out there with their plot loss and damage and it keels over and dies in front of them. The funny thing is they wonder why. So many times they find something else to blame it on. Anything but the three-year battle with cocaine; it was the woman, the job, whatever, never them. They can't deal with the fact that you have to work your ass off all the time. What the fuck were they thinking?

Coming to London makes me remember the sleepless tours through Europe with Black Flag and the Rollins Band. Grinding it out until the parts fell off. Coming back to my shitty room with nothing to show for it but my journal and enough money to pay rent and phone and the fact that I survived it and delivered the goods under strained circumstances. Remembering how fucked I felt getting here yesterday made me remember the time we got here in 1988 and had a show the night of our arrival. We were totally fried and still pulled it off. That's it, that's what it's all about. It's about going another mile when you are sure you cannot go another step. You had it in you the entire time and the greatness inside was just waiting to raise its raging dragon's head. Once you realize your potential, it's hard to say that you failed at something, you just realize that you didn't try hard enough or more likely, you didn't want it that bad. Once I saw its face, I was unable to turn away. I was only able to be at odds with it, confront it and see the truth that a lot of times, I didn't want it bad enough to pay the price. Those who talk shit about me have no idea what they're messing with at this point and would have no idea how to deal with it if they had to. It's like getting called down by a side-liner. Makes me think of Hemingway when he wrote about how a crowd turned against the bullfighters, throwing trash into the ring and jeering. One of the spectators should have been thrown into the ring with the cape and left to deal. Point is, you'll always get called down by someone who can't pull it off. They will put you down if you're in a ditch below them or on a tightrope above them but never on a level playing field. They are false stones in your path. Don't listen, just proceed forward with the force of your life. Don't ever blame your shortcomings on others. It was only you who got you where you are right now. Deal with it.

In 45 minutes I go to the dismal Geffen office to do about seven hours of press. A company about to get field-stripped into corporate wasteland. *Corporate wasteland. It's only corporate wasteland.* The vibe at the Geffen press office in LA when I was there recently was brutal. No music, no birds singing. Vultures circled the boxes of Hole records. The great days of Geffen are over. Bye bye Axl. Bye bye smug marketing guy, time for you to fall up the corporate ladder to a bigger office and an extra zero on your yearly salary.

Hey, I can always go home and quit. I've been waiting for this time since the mid-80s. Saw it coming before it knew I heard its footsteps. This is the lean time. I am 37. No longer afforded the luxury of youth. I have to stand on my words and actions. I've been preparing myself with every breath, with every moment, with every sleepless night and grueling scheduled detail. Now it's all about lean tissue and guts. I can see the age on my face. No one is calling me good-looking. My tattoos are fading and the ink is running. My hair is going grey. I'm running on guts. Got any? You gotta grow them. Smash them until they grow tough like caged dogs. No beauty is lost. You get to see the real face of it after the blossoms have fallen off the tree. That's why I would rather see the face of a beautiful woman than a pretty girl.

Girls aren't beautiful, they're pretty. Beautiful is too heavy a word to assign to a girl. Women are beautiful because their faces show that they know they have lost something and picked up something else.

Now is the time I get to see what's inside. From here on, it's all about guts. Think the first half was rough? The second half is a killer. I can't think of any other place I'd rather be. I don't want to be in my twenties again. I want to be here right now staring into its face. Every step has been a blast, no matter how bad any of it was. It's all a blessing. Still here. Always a lesson to learn. I just wish all the parties concerned were here to see it.

11.05 p.m.: In room number 859, trying to stay awake to get on schedule. I seem to be doing alright. Will be glad to get the shows going. The day of press was alright, boring but what do you expect from these fucks? One guy was hilarious, 'Don't you think that weightlifting is another addiction? Don't you think that a lot of muscles denotes a bit of misogyny?' Hello? Real world come in please. What miserable pieces of shit these people are. I spent a whole day in the very depressing Geffen press offices. Glass partitions, no air. Glossy magazines all over, musicians portrayed as glamorous fashion mavens, pictures of Beck everywhere. It was more than a man can take. So not my world. At one point I looked at Tony the press guy, gestured at all the magazines and said, 'What a shitty world you live in!' Tony is very cool but the world he navigates through daily is so lame to me. The world has been taken away in the night and a fake one has taken its place if one is to take these magazines seriously.

I can see that he doesn't know what to do with me and when you are on Dreamworks and you have to have Geffen people do your press stuff, you always can be sure that they are a bit put out doing work for another label. I can totally understand. I am always polite to the Geffen people even when some of them have at times, given me that elitist attitude. Their hands are smooth and they work in offices. I know, I know.

I asked for a copy of Hole's *Celebrity Skin* CD and for my sins they gave me one. I played it all the way through and listened very carefully. Now that is one bad record. Just horrible. The voice, the tunes, the production, what a waste of money. It's like a Courtney photo session, you can dress it up in nice clothes and find a flattering angle, if one exists, and even with all the plastic surgery and airbrushing, it is what it is. Not even the mighty Michael Beinhorn and Billy Corgan rewriting tracks from *Adore* could save this dog of a record. You can hear all the work done to make the drums sound alright. I wonder if the band's drummer even played on it. Courtney Love, only in America. Well, maybe in England too. You know what I mean. An insult to real bands everywhere. Hole should tour with the Offspring. It could be called The Almighty Crap Tour.

11-09-98 London UK: I watched a show last night about the phenomenon of shell shock. I sat on the edge of the bed staring at the screen, trying not to cry. It was so hard to watch. The narrator said that all sides of the war reported that their men were breaking down and experiencing all kinds of intense physical abnormalities. The footage of these guys twitching uncontrollably, unable to walk correctly, hearing, sight and the ability to talk disappearing. One man's trigger finger became paralyzed. Watching these men's limbs flailing and twitching, the expression on their faces, one of humiliation, helplessness and fear as they tried to sit in front of the camera and retain some essence of dignity was excruciating to watch. One man was court-martialed for high cowardice for showing these symptoms after being warned to stop faking it and get back out there and fight. In those days, one served up to four years on the front lines. He had already been on the front lines for two years. Anyway, he was executed via firing squad. He refused to be blindfolded. He stared down his assassins and took the bullets. His wife was sent a certificate in the mail informing her of his death. His daughter still had the certificate. How great would it have been if one of the shooters had the guts to throw down his rifle and walk out in front of the condemned man and said shoot him and kill me too. They shot one of their own guys. I think it would have been great if they had all turned their rifles on the commanding officer and told him that the only one who was going to get shot was him if he didn't call the whole thing off.

Makes me see that we have been existing in a war culture since then. Now people are desensitized. After decades of John Wayne, Rambo and all the wars that there were no reasons for, like Vietnam where people are still wondering what the hell that was all about, after all that, we feel nothing. It's something on CNN. The guys in WWI were real people, not sickened and numb like we are. Is that a little overreaching? Like I care. It's what occurs to me. It's hard to care at this point. You see stuff on the news about these countries that kill the shit out of each other year after year and sometimes I just want to pull the shade down and forget about it. Sometimes I figure, alright that's how you are, I can't do anything about that. It's like trying to talk to an adult, some people you just can't reason with.

I get sick of some of the aspects of this business when I'm in England. The press here is so completely corny. All the shit you have to do just to get people to come to your show. At least I love the shows and the audience.

I am listening to Johnny and the Hurricanes. First got into them from an instrumental 50s compilation record I had when I was young. I lost it and it took me years of combing through used bins before I found it again. I used to play that one a lot in my room. I spent a lot of time in my room when I was living with my mother. We moved from place to place and I always set up the room like a small camp. Had some food and water in there so I could go long periods of time without coming out. Listened to music and read. When I would leave the apartment I would walk alone and stay out as long as I could. I see now that I have not changed much. I still prefer my own company. Things make more sense when I am alone. The nights are better when I am alone. Travel is tops when alone. It's all more interesting when I am alone. It's when you find out what it's all about. When I'm with someone else, it's cool sometimes but not as cool as going solo. Discovering things alone is the most amazing thing I have ever experienced. Like when I was on the beach at three in the morning in Madagascar under that bright moon, no one in sight, that's not going to come again and if there was anyone there, it wouldn't have been the same. When I am alone I don't have to get my ideas pulled apart by the sheer proximity of another. That all sounds good until you are so lonely you think you're going to blow away in the wind. I feel that way all the time. I'm not made of stone. I just feel worse after trying and failing at a relationship than I did when I was on my own with my loneliness not having a woman to attach itself to. I guess I don't have that particular strength needed to bounce back from that kind of shit. I'd rather go without than take that kind of pain.

Can you be yourself all the way when you're with someone else? Isn't it true that you cover up at least a little to keep up appearances? To be something you're not? That happens with me. It's a compromise. I guess if you find the right person, it would be cool. Also, fuck all this shit, do what you're going to do. You want to fall in love? Go ahead on. I am on your side. Wish it would happen to me.

11-11-98 Glasgow Scotland: I don't have a show tonight. I have a day of press in London and then I will try to get to Amsterdam to get the travel over with as I start the first of five shows straight there tomorrow night.

Last night's show was good. I love this country. It's savage and beautiful. Flying over the green, raw hills is amazing. The people reflect the land they grew up in. They are tough and vibrant. I imagine Americans used to be like that a century ago when they had to do more things by hand. The Scots are a good audience as well. Really into it and very energized. Last night was no exception. I was in a theater called the Pavilion. The weather outside was fairly cold and raining on and off.

Not much to comment on as far as yesterday. Getting over jet lag pretty quickly. Nothing like a bunch of shows to get you wired and in line. It's good to have two under my belt over here. I have this strange fear that if I take a couple of nights off I will lose my ability to perform. I have to stay out there or I get very pent up. It makes the time between tours strange and tense. I figure I will walk out there and nothing will come out of me. I also have a fear that I will walk out onstage and not be able to stay awake and will fall asleep. I don't know where that comes from. I guess all the years of trying to get sleep on a consistent basis and failing.

11-12-98 London Heathrow Airport: I did an interview with UK comic Eddie Izzard yesterday. We did photos as well. Apparently this will show up on the cover of *Time Out* magazine which seems to be a big deal here. I got some video of Eddie before I came over here and it's fantastic. He's funny as hell. He tells no jokes, he just kind of goes and it's brilliant. The more I watched, the more into it I became. I've never heard anything like that guy. We hung out for quite awhile and he gave me his new record called *Dress to Kill.* Can't wait to listen to it. When I get back to London, I am going to get all his stuff. He's a really great guy. I admire that kind of talent.

Off to Amsterdam again. I can't count how many times I have been there over the years. Not a place I find all that interesting but it's a good gig. I'll always take a good gig. I'll take the bad ones too. I'm an easy date.

11-13-98 Amsterdam Holland: At the American Hotel in the breakfast room. Good show last night. Lots of people and the mood was good. Last time I was there for a talking show, my throat was wiped out and it was hard to get through, so it was good to get back in there and kick ass.

Got to the hotel very behind on sleep with soundcheck only an hour away. Managed to pass out for twenty minutes and walked over the Paradiso like I always do. Been playing that place since 2-12-83. Turned 22 there. Sitting in that basement backstage room brings back so many memories. Black Flag and Rollins Band stuff. Shit man, Joy Division played there, everyone passed through that place is seems. It's cool to keep coming back to the same venue.

This is a city I keep coming back to but have no great affection for. Now London, I have been knocked around in that town many times but I love it and like to walk the streets I know. I have been walking the same streets here for as long but it doesn't mean anything to me. That is one of the cooler things about traveling, I like to return to cities I have been to before and walk the streets. Especially outside of America. I like being a citizen of many cities all over the world. How could anyone want to stay home when the entire world stretches out before them? How can they be satisfied with so little? Don't they hear the voices of all the rivers, seas and mountains call out to them? Or have their ears been dulled by the roar of the work place? Have they been bludgeoned into a stupor by television and the failure of dreams that didn't have to die? Some get out and some don't. Many don't want to go anywhere though. They're happy with what they have. Maybe it's better that way, imagine the lines at the airports. Perhaps I have it all wrong. Maybe I'm nuts running around all over the world trying to see things. Maybe I am not being responsible not getting a real life. Maybe I am avoiding myself by all these stunts. Maybe it's time to buckle down and get that job at the copy place and shoulder that American load and get that ache in my back that tells me that I am pulling my weight, or at least the boss's weight. I see these people who aren't 'running away' from life. I see them in traffic.

I see them getting divorced, fighting to see their kids. I see them overweight and bitter. I hear them telling me bullshit like 'It must be nice man, you're lucky.' Oh fuck you, you make me tired.

Amsterdam always makes me think of Jeffrey Lee Pierce of the Gun Club. We were together here years ago doing a festival in 1985. He left me a note to meet him at a bar. I still have the note, the bar is still there, he's gone. I miss that guy.

I sometimes wonder what keeps bringing me to these corners. I can find pieces of my life strewn all over the world. Some people grow up in a town or city and walk those streets for the rest of their lives. I see nothing wrong with that. I do the same thing I guess only it would take you a lot of miles to get to all those streets. I feel like I have scattershot my existence all over with all the years of travel. I have never had a reason to come off the road. I sit in my place and there's nothing for me. Nothing for me out here either but at least the scenery is always changing.

Will be good to get out of Amsterdam. I don't dislike the place, it's got nothing for me but the show. Probably the tourist factor wears me out. I don't know many people here. I don't know many people anywhere, that's just the way it played out. Must be the way I wanted it. I see them when I see them and that's good enough for me.

I do think of Ian MacKaye though. He is one of those amazing people who gets better as he goes. I don't think it's anything he works at, it's just the way he is.

At the airport: The sky is grey. Several planes are lined up outside. I'm in Holland, en route to Copenhagen, Denmark. I am alone and everyone around me are strangers, other travelers. All with different reasons to go somewhere, different worlds they live in. A universe sits around me talking and drinking coffee. To my left is my back pack that I have carried with me since 1985. Denmark to Sweden to Germany to Brussels, and onwards. Lit points on the map. Stops along the way. Cities to explore with my loneliness. I could always go home. I could always get that safe little job and take shit from some frustrated insult merchant. On the other hand, I could go out here until it breaks. What's there to keep me in one place? If this isn't living I don't know what is. My extended camping trip. How could anyone stay at home knowing that the world shakes and glitters outside their door? My place in LA is a reference point. I go there now and then, look around and plot the next way to get back out here.

And then on the other hand, sometimes there's days I don't want to be alive. Days of suffocating depression blot out my thoughts and I don't want to exist. I get on planes and hope they crash so it will be over. I have lived with these spells of intense misery for as long as I can remember. I walk through these corridors of black rout for what seems like years and then the rage inside builds and I'm burning and I want to break the record for breakin' the fuckin' record. Know what I mean?

I live to destroy time. I don't want to live in harmony with it. I hate that word. Since time is going to kill me off eventually I want to fuck it up on the way down the drain. I want to leave it with scars and a limp. I am the monkey on time's back. This is not a heartbreak, this is not a skirmish. This is one long march at the speed of a blitzkrieg.

If you're going to write, then write. If there's plans you have made, then execute them or be damned. Time is your wings, the key. If you let it slip by, it is acid that drips upon your soul. The only thing that makes life interesting to me is that you can go. I am on my way. To where? To the place I will leave and be on my way. Every step is one on my way. I'm on my way to the way to the way. Life is all points in between. For now I will be totally selfish. Totally self. No thoughts of kids. Someone has a family of five as I write this. That's plenty. They had my kids for me. The world will not miss any people I don't create. The world is full of people as it is. In traffic you wish for less of them.

11-14-98 Copenhagen Denmark: At the airport. Morning. Cold, grey, raining. Show last night was good. Audience was great, who would have thought?

I was so burnt before I went on. I was trying to doze off in the backstage area but had to do interviews before I went on and couldn't get unwound from them. I hit stage and woke up immediately. Sometimes it's hard for me to leave the stage. I look at my watch and see that I have been on nearly three hours and there's so much more I want to say but I don't want to wear them out. It feels like I have only been on a little while. All of a sudden I am walking back to the dressing room with the ache returning to my bones and eyes.

Fuck it. I don't care when this string of shows ends. Might as well stay out here for the rest of my life.

5.42 p.m.: In my room in Stockholm. Coltrane live at the Village Vanguard playing. I love it when Coltrane plays soprano sax. I have traveled with his music all over the world. He fills lonely rooms with strength. His music, like Phil Lynott's, goes everywhere with me. There's nothing like it when Coltrane has laid out of the mix for awhile and then he comes back in. The world changes, the air in the room reconfigures. In the time he has been away, he has evolved somehow. I have never heard anything like that guy. His relentless search for new music on just one live album is breathtaking. It's like he's lived several lives in the space of a few nights onstage. That's what it's all about isn't it? To keep smashing through your own limitations and go until it breaks apart. Coltrane found the truth in music like no one else. He gets me inspired to get out there night after night and do these talking shows. I feel like I'm him up there, blowing it out every night until I am exhausted. Giving all and then walking off spent. When I am hanging out in some cold backstage area I think of Coltrane sitting in the same kind of place waiting to go on, waiting to give it everything he's got.

I am alone in this room. Can't get the ache from my eyes and I'm too keyed up to sleep. Loneliness hammers me sometimes. I don't know what to do about it. If I stopped traveling I don't think I would be living life to the fullest. I have to suffer this lash to see the things that I want to see. The truth I seek is out here. It's the stage that awaits me every night that doesn't allow me to be at ease. Every night I have to prove myself. Every morning I wake up, stripped of credibility. I have to go out and prove it all over again. Sometimes every waking moment is just waiting for the show that night.

What is this all about? How come I don't write fiction? All I know is my life and my perspective. This is all about the airports, the stages and the lonely boxes I live in. Rentals, temporary alliances, border to border. Life pounds me, I pound life. The critics don't know because they don't venture out. To quote Alan Vega, 'What do the poets know?'

11-15-98 Stockholm Sweden: At the airport waiting to go to Berlin. Last night's show was cool. The audience was really good. I don't know how they end up being so on top of a language they probably don't speak all that often. The night didn't start out all that well. I got to the venue at 8 p.m. for a 10 p.m. stage time. The record company people weaseled in a photo session as well as the interviews. It's hard to say no because they're working on your behalf and you have to respect that. I did all their bidding and, as usual, it took longer than they said it would because they never plan things well and since they don't have a show that night and know nothing of the pressure coupled with exhaustion and jetlag, they have no concept of pre-performance time. Add this to the soundman who didn't have his shit together and had to be walked through a soundcheck involving one microphone. I ended up with about twenty minutes to get it together before I was out there hitting it. The Universal rep promptly split. Seeing that they have little or no regard for my time, I'll just figure that they merit the same treatment. That's the way it is around these parts.

Glad to be leaving Sweden. Never a big fan of the place. Too many hassles at the border. Too many uniformed men telling me how it is here. You can have it, sorry to have intruded on your glacial privacy. I like the audiences though. I always see women here that are so much more beautiful than the ones in fashion magazines and movie posters. Some of them don't even look real. Hooray! – or something.

Thomas Wolfe was right, the American is never home. Never at home. Always restless. Always getting it where he can as he moves along, rootless and alien.

5.49 p.m.: Berlin Germany. At the venue. I remember this place from February 1993. I did a talking show here and it was a drag. I was so glad when it was over. It was the classic too hip German thing. Sometimes these people are fuckers and you have to straighten them out. I can't have that vibe in here tonight. Disc two of Coltrane at the Village Vanguard is on. Everything goes better with Coltrane. I remember the first time I came here with Black Flag. It was February 1983. We played the SO36 club. Brutal show. All the shows on that tour were fuckers.

I love the streets here. The small colored lights in the windows, the iron, the grey. The history of the place can still be seen, even in the new buildings. At night, parts of Berlin are like a dream playing out in front of my eyes.

I always associate Germany with cold, beauty and loneliness. Nico albums. I have spent so much time here in the fall months. German cities are landscapes of mechanical promise. I always think of the record that Die Haut made with Nick Cave back in the eighties called *Burning the Ice*. The song 'Dumb Europe' with the frozen drone of the guitars and how the song begins with the line, 'Fucking cold in Europe', makes me remember being in those cold clubs waiting to go on in front of a hostile or indifferent audience. So many nights it was one or the other. Sometimes they would be both, we liked the variety. It took me a long time to be cool to audiences here. The tours with Black Flag here made me hostile. I remember the first time back in Vienna, Austria, after I was there with Black Flag in 1983. It was 1987. A guy said some shit to me and I hammered him right there. I bounced some guy's head on the floor a few years later, someone got it on video and I watched it after the show. Interesting.

Listened to a lot of Lou Reed on that tour. *Street Hassle* and *Take No Prisoners*. Critics ripped *Prisoners*. Shows what little you know, dick boy. What a great record. I still play that one. I could use either one of those right about now. I talked to Lou Reed on the phone a couple of years ago. I was in my NYC hovel and the phone rings, 'Hello, this is Lou Reed.' The voice, whoa. We talked briefly about a project I had going that he was interested in contributing to. He didn't end up working on it but he was cool and it was awesome to talk to the legend. It was one of those cool moments that I will never forget. I hate it when people think they're so cool that they let things like that slip by because their ego obscures a great moment. I would hate to think that I could end up being too cool to dig the less than huge things in life. I think it's lame that some people con themselves into such a contrived state of aloofness. Is there any other way to be aloof? I don't think anyone who is doesn't work at it. That kind of cool takes work! Not enough respect for their own mortality! Throw them in a cage with a damn polar bear, that'll fix 'em! Time to take it to the stage.

11-16-98 Berlin Germany: At the old airport. I like this one better than the larger Tegel Airport. This one has the vibe I used to get in Berlin before the Wall came down. There's something different about the city now. It's still cool but it feels just like another city in Germany when there used to be something here that I had not found anywhere else. Berlin had this amazing tension, things about to go any minute. Fleeting love, long nights of deep discussion, hushed voices in smokey rooms. The Wall that went and kept going. The crude, corny reminder that men can't get their shit together. We'll build a wall, that'll fix it! Come on. Even thousands of miles away, I used to listen to music that I associated with Berlin and the Wall to get that feeling. Like the stuff Bowie recorded here at Hansa Studios, the song 'Heroes'. The German bands Malaria, Die Haut, Einsturzende. Auslanders like Nick Cave and the Birthday Party remind me of Berlin. Nick was a bit taken with the city for awhile and wrote some amazing stuff in Berlin. When I think of my first time here I remember the cold and the hard travel. I like hard travel in cold conditions. It makes my brain work harder. My loneliness makes things beautiful in the cold. I remember traveling for weeks through the hostile tour grind, breathing tobacco filled air in dimly lit, cold clubs. Sometimes thinking of a woman who didn't want me or didn't know I existed. Even at it's worst it was amazing. I was lucky enough to know it, too. Emotion in the lead, passion above all. People feel this way for a time and then something happens. Life creeps in and shines a search light into previously darkened sanctuaries of thought. Moonlit fields of a shared breath, the memory of placing a hand over a woman's breast and feeling her racing heart. The hand being covered by hers to make sure it doesn't leave. Oh, to be wanted. But then it's time to go. The train pulls away from the station and you're gone again and she is a memory. The mundane rigors of maintaining a human life set back in. The magic leaves with the rising sun. The beautiful loneliness evaporates with the steadily increasing light and clamor. The path back becomes obscured into non-recognition by passing seasons, stacks of paper in brightly lit rooms where people move like ants on speed to ringing phones and rush to meals untasted and kill their time senselessly without knowing it. On and on into stern, packed oblivion. The city inhales and exhales, roars and swings. I'm going, but not like them. I have trapped life's searing pain in my bones and it kicks the walls of its prison nonstop. Go. Go hard. Go more. Go again.

11-19-98 Hamburg Germany: At the airport. Flight delayed. Who knows when it will come. We wait indefinitely. Have not checked in here for a couple of days. The 17th was a press day and that was alright, just a lot of talking and trying to stay awake. Yesterday was the show in Hamburg. Great audience. German crowds have always been pretty good for this kind of thing but now they're just smokin'. It was great to see all the people who work at Universal in Hamburg there. They are so hard working and supportive it's not to be believed. I wish all the people I worked with in the music business were like them. Most of the time I merely feel tolerated, nothing more.

The shows have been good but the travel's been a day to day tedium that's been wearing me out. Looking forward to Ireland tomorrow. It's an interesting place. So sad and beautiful. Some people go out so hard there. You see a lot of pain on some of the faces in the galleries of the street. I will hopefully see Phil Lynott's mother Philomena. She's so great.

I have been thinking about the Amazon River lately. I want to go next year if I can get the chance. I don't know why, but images of what I think it will look like have been flashing in my brain for days now.

I must maintain this urgency. It is in the rhythm of life. Life is furious. It explodes in foliage and rots in damp heat. Follow *that*. Jump into the river that takes you to it. Otherwise life is a pause before death. I don't comprehend how people have been able to suppress their lives enough to work in the same place year after year while the hate they had for the place that might have saved them by giving them the push they needed to get out, dissipates into complacency and they just toughen up and resolve themselves to a life they don't want. They justify it with things that their fathers told them about responsibility. It's a strength of character I don't possess. That life reeks of death. An unhurried, languid death that doesn't walk, but ambles down the hall. Old footsteps dumbly decaying out of hearing range. The blood thickens and the world slows down. The blues fade and the reds become muddy.

I have noticed that in all the hot places I have been to, like Brazil or Italy, that the culture is hot as well. The music is more passionate than in cold places. Tango music could have never come from Germany. Some of the most harrowing, violent and passionate music in the world comes form these hot zones. Civilizations that come from the soil and never leave it. The music is intense and it's made to move you, wreck you a little. The way they live is never far from the cruel and beautiful madness of pure life. Can you deal with that? Or is that too much all the time? So many have been removed from the front lines of life by technology, bundled away from the world by digitally rendered clarity.

11-23-98 London UK: In the hotel, waiting to leave for Bristol. Yesterday was a day off. Took hours to get from Dublin to London. Not that the flight was all that long. It was the hassle of the airport and getting through London. Had a good day off with the remaining hours.

6.41 p.m. Bristol UK: Backstage room not so bad. It's a UK environment though. Cold, damp room, florescent lights overhead, gross sandwiches with buttered bread. Basically a room specially designed to drain you of your will to live. I knew these were going to be here to meet me. Easily one of the most depressing and recurring themes in my life. The UK backstage area. Makes me think of skinny men sitting in sweaters, smoking and drinking pints of beer, their faces an explosion of acne, their hair, oily and matted. I'm wrong about this? No I'm not. Seen it. I like England because the people here have a lot of backbone. You would have to, to be able to stick it out in a place like this year after year. Narrow streets, damp rooms, bad food, it's all yours. But the people, the people are tremendous. I like them better the more I come here.

Topic change. This room makes me think of the fact that I am alone all the time. With the way the last few forays into the world of relationships with females have gone, it makes sense to cut out the middlewoman and live alone. Spit on desert floor and walk crunching, frozen trails where no footprints exist ahead of mine. Why not travel through seasons of cold and heat in rugged conditions and give life a fucking shove? Why not stay out and go long? Why not live like I said in the song 'Starve?' I don't see any reason not to. I see them loading themselves onto busses to go to a job they don't like and I think to myself that it might be good enough for them. It's obviously good enough for them, they're doing it. I see them walking through a slow, screaming nightmare. Not me. I'll do whatever it takes to escape that mortal hell.

11-27-98 Manchester UK: Yes, this is the England I know so well. Backstage at Manchester. Yellow walls, florescent lights. Cold and damp. Hang me. The venue is vibeless and cold. I knew this was waiting for me. Robert Pete Williams is playing on the box. Been getting some good listening done in these grimy backstage areas. Good rockabilly stuff and music from central Java. I have to raise the amount of new music I listen to every day. There's so much good stuff out there, I want to try to at least put a dent in it before I die. And in rooms like this, I might just go out sooner than I want to.

Got here from London a few hours ago. Two and a half hours on the train. Not bad. I stood in the station for an hour before the train came and looked at the strained and pinched faces of the people waiting. They were carrying their bags, looking tired and overworked. So much movement. It puts lines in your face, creases in your heart and miles between you and the rest of the world.

Right now in this dressing room, I am thinking thoughts of power to get myself roaring for tonight. I will have a damn good time up there. Have been away from the stage for a night and I miss it already. It is what I am good at. In shitty rooms like this is where I belong. This room is my heritage! It's not for everybody.

11-28-98 Manchester UK: Almost 1.30 in the morning. Show was good tonight. The kind of audience I hope for. They were sharp and had a lot of energy. I'm doing different stuff up there all the time now. The slog has been a little grueling but the shows have been good and that's what I came here for.

Have been thinking about the press days I have been doing while here. Hanging out with the press people here makes me see that I don't really know anyone. I do most things alone. Most of the people I know are industry types. Managers, press people, etc. I don't think the Geffen UK press people like working on Dreamworks acts. Maybe they don't like working the acts or maybe they don't like working me. I always get the feeling I am tolerated but that's it. Perhaps I lack the essential element of hip. They are pretty cool to me though so I can't complain. Even in the interviews, I don't answer the questions as much as say things that I want to see in print for whatever reason. I learned that from David Lee Roth. I don't mind meeting people after shows. Actually, I like those people a lot. I have a great crowd all over. A sharp bunch like what I do. I figure I am lucky. There were times when I didn't like the crowd that came to see me.

Like the last year of Black Flag. All the Nazi guys that were into us, that was a turn off. Things are better now. There's a woman I know, who I would go a great distance to know better. Definitely a lot of things I'd like to tell her. Don't know if she would want to hear any of it but still. If I was a woman, I wouldn't want to know me, I'm just a walking itinerary. I don't know what to do about that though so fuck it.

I hate it when I hear myself say that I 'know' someone because I have met them a couple of times. I think I know a few people and that's it. I've met a whole lot of people my life. It's the nature of the business I'm in. My hand is a hello-how-do-you-do whore. It has touched many.

I think to be close to someone, you have to do the time and the miles. Time is one thing, but there's nothing like the miles. Like the guys in the band. I know those motherfuckers. We have done the time and the miles. Have we ever. That's why I will always love them. They are the best. I have seen them go through it. I know what they're made of. That's what I'm all about. Let's see you go out there with many continents as your neighborhood. Can you go long? Can you hit the trail? I'm not talking about some little fucking camping trip. What kind of mileage are you made of? Are you a three-day pass or are you A.W.O.L.? The truth is found right before you collapse. Not until then. The entire lesson is taught over years and learned in an instant. Don't say you know when you don't. Don't wear stripes you have not earned.

11-29-98 Birmingham UK: It's almost 0330 hrs. Been sitting uselessly in front of the TV set watching a movie about the Beach Boys. It's pretty cool, it's about the Beach Boys, how bad can it be?

The show was alright, not great. Audience was dull and there wasn't many of them. It'll be better next time right?! I get out there every night and give it my all but sometimes it's hard. Some of these crowds are the great energy drain. I come off stage feeling so spent and I realize that I got nothing from them at all. That's the breaks. It's not an easy job.

The same girl shows up every night and sits in the front row It's a little distracting. I feel like I am being stalked. I'm just grinding it out, small shows in small towns. It's cool. I am used to the long haul. Being alone on planes, backstage, hotel rooms, you name it. I go for hours, sometimes days without speaking to anyone but myself. It's what I know but not always what I want.

How does anyone connect with anyone? The woman I was with recently is great but I see that I upset her balance. I have only good intentions but I feel intrusive and strange. I want to be with her but I think my presence stresses her out. It hurts to know I have this effect. This is why I just book tours, go and keep going. What is there to stop for? I try to connect with someone and find I'm too strange, too inherently fucked up, too something. You're better off as that thing on a stage. I see people together all the time. I can't understand how it works. When I go out with women I feel like Travis Bickle. Like I'll do something really horrible and have no idea why I sent her running away. I think it's one of the reasons I have sometimes ended up with psycho women. At least I don't freak them out. This one's different. She is real and she is rare. I don't know if I am all that easy to be around. I am working hard to figure myself out before I die.

7.03 p.m.: Norwich UK: Played here a couple of times. At least once with the band and once doing a talking show.

Exhaustion is getting its teeth into me. Been feeling it the last couple of days. Overall lack of energy and depression are give away signs.

Today's drive was about four hours of countryside and small towns. Council housing painted yellow, churches that are centuries old. Cold and wet the entire way. The road beat my eyes back into my head as we drove east out of Birmingham. These last shows are going to be hard. I have weeks of travel before I'm done. This is the tough part of the year but it's also the best. I hit this point around November. I am out of gas and keep going. This is it right here. This is where you find out what you've got. I like to see if I can get through it. I learn something every time.

The dressing room is typically dingy. A long counter under florescent lights. Narrow strip in which to sit. Toilet stall right behind me. One electrical outlet. White tile walls. Two sinks and a mirror. These rooms pound the words out of my mind. They turn me cold. I imagine I am a lizard. Not much on my mind. Show to do. Have to think of what to say to the three hundred odd people who may wander into this place on a raining Sunday night.

This kind of thing is easy. Either you break it or it breaks you. It's one or the other so you deal with it. Either the audience owns you or you own them. I trust the road because it will never be my good friend. It's always there but it will kill your ass if you stay out on it long enough and it will not care. It never says it likes you and will be there for you. It always will be there but it doesn't exactly take out ads proclaiming its sincere intentions on your behalf. It just waits for you to take your shot and expire en route. Now how cool is that?

12-01-98 Coventry UK: Another grand day off. Of course it was a day of press in London. I will be loose by 6 p.m. Other than that, it's a day of tedium spent with weary press people who would rather be doing something else, myself included.

Let's take a moment to contemplate the sheer horror of this town called Coventry. We arrived yesterday to the mangled snarl of confusing roads that strangle the city center. With the hotel a mere one hundred yards away, your journey to it has just begun. Just begun you say? Why that hotel is right over there, why don't you simply drive over to it and be done? Oh no, no, no! That example of efficiency would require streets that would allow such a minor feat to be accomplished. You've been on streets all over the place but perhaps not in the confines of Coventry. Following the letter of the law would have the harried and exhausted traveler taking a seemingly endless, serpentine route of one-way streets that take him right back to the very place he started. Why not drive a straight line down the street in front of you to the hotel. No, it's a bus lane. Only busses get to go to the hotel. Potential residents of the hotel must pitch a tent in the park and play 'pretend it's a hotel'.

Finally, Rick the road manager had endured just about enough of these silly streets. He had definitely had his fill of me and my commentary, 'You limey faggots really know how to put a city together. Fuck America, I'm moving here for I too want to drive around all afternoon past downtrodden people milling around, contemplating their future on the soggy streets of Coventry. Boy this is one well concepted city, yes sir. Oh wait a minute, is this an example of some post WWI construction? An example of how the city fathers, given a second chance to build the place really took some time and no short amount of consideration and this is the shining example of efficiency they drew up? Hell, I'm honored to be driving in circles here in Coventry. No really, honored. Honored and moved almost to tears.' Rick, unmoved by my impassioned speech, punched the roof of the vehicle and broke about every traffic law Coventry had to offer at that time.

We finally got into the hotel several minutes later. There were no casualties. Well, a few, but I don't think they noticed.

12-03-98 Newcastle UK: A little before 0200 hrs. The show here was very good. I like the club atmosphere better than the sterile lecture hall. The crowd was live. I wish they were like this every night.

The press day in London was slightly interesting because I had to do some MTV stuff. My favorite little group of bitches. They have a channel called M2, it's all the same bullshit. The music they play is weak. MTV has crippled music and they are the enemy. I don't give a fuck what they say, do or think. So with that premise, I went in. They asked me to pick out some videos and talk about some of them. My video selection as follows:

The Cure – Love Cats: Just to see that silly man run around doing his 'Love Cats Dance' if nothing else. Isn't he something?

U2 – Discotheque: O, Christ! No, I'm not taking homeboy's name in vain. Yes, I'm calling on Christ. Why, my brother? Year after year. I think of this song and the turgid record that spawned it and I am filled with Joy. Joy? Yes, joy. Rays of buttery golden sunlight showers down upon me as I rejoice in the fact that the record didn't sell and the tour lost money and the promoters took a bath on the whole thing.

The Smiths – The Boy with the . . .: Didn't write down the rest of the title, what the fuck is it? Do I care?! The Boy with the Broken Dick? I like Morrisey, he's no dummy. He took the press pricks for a ride and they ended up kissing his ass. Of course they had to dismantle him in the end when it was time to bring in the new crop of morose, pasty-faced look-at-the-ground-while-you-play lads and turn them into the next apathetic icons to take their lap around the sun like a moth circling a streetlight. I know, call me a poet, go on say it! He inspires me. Calling your band The Smiths, that's putting it all in perspective isn't it? No one will ever be able to accuse you of wanting to stand out. You British fucks always try to hide your ambition lest you fail. You can't bear to have all the other mediocre wheel treaders catch up to you in the pub and tell you that you aren't very good. Hilarious that The Spice Girls are the most relevant band that the UK has coughed up in years.

Morrisey – November Spawned a Monster: Again the man with the mind and the song titles that can't be beat. It makes me want to put on my little sister's clothes and run through the house singing the words 'November spawned a monster!' over and over again until my breasts grow heavy and melon like and my lips swell and I become 100 per cent voluptuous, unlike the song's creator, a study in pale tea and tobacco addled insomnia.

Jesus Jones – Right Here Right Now: How did anyone go for this one? Great hair. The now classic 'JJ' look. Sounds like JJ-Man wrote it while watching television. After the uprising when the Space Brothers have taken over the land, many British people will be sent to Mars. Or Belgium. And it will be his fault.

Blur/Petshop Boys – Girls and Boys: I like this song because it puts two groups of pale near deads in one video. Could anyone ask for more? You could ask for a Black Sabbath album to be played instead.

Edie Brickell & the New Bohemians – What I Am: She set thousands of college boy's hearts alight. Now she breeds with Paul Simon. Figure that out. She made a third record awhile ago. I think it was called 'number 200 on the Billboard chart and Sinking Like an Anchor'. No wait a minute, that's my record. Anyway, this song asks a lot of questions and it lead me to ask a few myself. Here's but a few:

01. Why wasn't this band put in a bucket of warm water at birth?

02. If there was a god, wouldn't he or she have stepped in to stop this woman?

03. What kind of guy would buy her records who wasn't trying to lure a co-ed into his dorm room?

04. Where are all those New Bohemians these days? I can see them now, beansprouts stuck to their beards, living in boxes outside the Greyhound station. Get VH-1 on the line, I think there's a documentary to be made!

05. Edie, Edie? It's the lonely college boys from the Midwest, we're calling to ask if you want to do some bong hits through red zinger tea and 'talk about spirituality' like Alanis says in her song.

The Cult – She Sells Sanctuary: Because they changed their image as they 'evolved' from The Southern Death Cult to The Death Cult, to The Cult. It occurs to me that if you changed a letter in their name you could get in a lot of trouble so you journos, watch those typos. One T-shirt designer did and lost his job over it (even though the shirt sold rather well in the UK). Besides sanctuary, she also sells seashells by the 'C' section of the used CD place down the street.

Sisters of Mercy – Lucretia, My Reflection: Never heard the song, never saw the video but you gotta love the Sisters guy. I respect him for getting through his set while opening for Black Flag in 1984 and having the audience try to disembowel him. Oh, the hatred! Oh, Lucretia!

SS Sputnik – F1-11: It was an eighties thing. Most of us have recovered. The man from Haircut 100 is still in Intensive Care from the beatings but he's showing strong vital signs.

Offspring – Pretty Fly for a White Guy: They're like Raffi for white suburban teens. They could be Rosie O'Donnell's house band. Perfect music for virgins. The racism in this song is a prime example of America's obscene day-to-day operating standard.

Holy Barbarians – Space Junkie: It's the Cult guy. What a name for a band! Plot? It was here a minute ago! You better reform The Cunt before the heating bill comes in.

Why these? I picked out videos I knew were going to be lame or videos that had hilarious titles and just went off on them. My concept was that if I was to put together a show that was so totally diabolical that it might get some of these kids to stop watching MTV for an hour and read a book or something. I couldn't hold back. Seeing the look of bummed out-ness on the face of the interviewer was worth the whole trip to London.

A lot of modern bands just plain suck and someone has to say something because most people who derive an income from these dolts can't. You go to a place like MTV and they're kissing ass as a vocation. As a fucking career. I'm not in the MTV Club, they're not doing me any favors so I have nothing to lose. Even when I did have something to gain from those fucks, I fucked with them.

Got in a good workout today. There is a great gym here. I've been to it a couple of times. Usually burly guys in there lifting heavy. Everything is old and beat. There's this old guy who has been there both times. He's like something out of a movie. Tough old bulldog of a man, really friendly but into lifting weights and that's it. It was good to talk to him. The Iron is so good to me. Pick it up or don't. It's so simple. So many things in my life are that simple.

12-06-98 Heathrow Airport: A little before 0900. Waiting on the flight to Moscow. Moscow? What was I thinking?!

The agent called several weeks ago and asked if I wanted to do two shows in Moscow. I told him that it would be very difficult because of the language barrier and he agreed. I then said I would of course do the shows. How can I not take the opportunity to go to a country that was frustrating beyond belief to deal with two times for two? Bad food, no food, long lines, slow long lines, traffic jams, corruption! To do two shows, not one, two! In a place where English is rarely spoken. It will be a nightmare. So let's go!

Either go or don't. Go home or go out there into the world and see what happens. At the very least it will be an adventure in linguistics and logistics. At the very worst, well, let's look on the bright side. The bright side of Moscow? To quote Lee Harvey from *Stripes*, one of the great films of our time, 'There was one?'

The last two shows at the London Astoria were cool. It was great to see TV Smith and Gaye Advert there. On the second night, Scott Gorham from Thin Lizzy was there. Such a cool guy and a smokin' guitar player. How many hours have I spent listening to that guy?

The Astoria, what a cold pit of gloom that place is. I love it. I always have a great time there. Crowd around the heater in the dressing room and watch the steam come out of your mouth.

So, OK. Moscow, round three. This will be one for the books. I will be using a translator, how the hell is this going to work?

In a few days, I bet I'll know some things I don't know right now.

I slept about two hours. My eyes ache and my thoughts are scattered. The temperature in Moscow is well below freezing. I am armed with two sweatshirts, no hat. I'll be fine. I like the cold.

Later: In seat 24-J for today's claustrophobic flight to frozen, bereft Moscow. City of the dodgy water. Everyone seems to be bringing two to three large bags on board. No one can fit all the packages, cases and winter coats in the overhead compartment. The place is packed with humans and baggage. Mere galley slaves are all we are. Waiting meekly and hopefully for the gruel that is rumored to be slung at us if we don't get beaten down for some unseen insubordination. The overburdened passengers close and reopen the overhead compartments to see if articles have shifted during our stay on the ground, looking over and over again to see if by some act of tourist class magic, there's now room for their overpacked suitcases and about-to-burst packages. Alas, there is no more room. Now the travelers seem to converge around my seat. There is a great deal of interest in a small pocket of space directly above me. A large man complete with big furry hat repeatedly bumps his pelvic region into my right shoulder as he tries to pack a suitcase the size of a duffel bag into this space but fails. Undeterred, he tries again and again with slow mechanical resolve as the line of passengers waiting to sit down lengthens all the way into first class. They wait patiently, their eyes are dreamy and docile like a cow's. *Lines? We know lines. Ah, me.* And they do. The people are waiting to get into their pack 'em in, sit 'em down and strap 'em up economy seats, complete with fetal position contours. If this baby goes down, no need to bend over to hug your knees – you're already there. The man standing over me opens the compartment one up from mine. No, not that one! Any one but that one! Too late to warn him. Too bad I couldn't tell him that the inmates in the seats ahead of me had taken up every available square inch of that space by vigorously slugging their coats into said space and together, with much effort, managed to close the hatch. Like I said, too late. The man opens the hatch and like angry lions let loose from a cage, the coats fairly lunge out of the compartment and land on top of their owners. After a few more minutes of coat smashing and other assorted struggling, we were all battened down and ready to go.

The flight is nearly four hours. After I land, I have to do some press I stupidly agreed to. I have done press conferences here before and they were really lame. I sat in a room with a bunch of journalists who while looking very intense, had either nothing to ask me or were too taken aback. So for the most part we sat staring at each other until one of them would ask something like, 'What do you find of Moscow?' All the other journos leaned in and knit their brows awaiting my answer. Imagine an hour of this. Imagine an evening of it with a bad meal to follow Yes, it was one of those uneasy instances that this business is all about!

So why did I sign on for this? Oh come on! You got to go. What else are you going to do, go home? This is where you see what you're made of. Most never get the chance. I know I am fortunate. I would be betraying that by not going for it. This is some awesome stuff. Russia. Russia! I can't wait to be back there. The place fascinates me. By the time I am due to leave I wonder if the planes will still be running or if I'll get stranded there.

The plane is now descending into grey clouds and lonely setting sun. I wonder what Thomas Wolfe would have thought of this place.

12-08-98 Moscow Russia: About 0300, Tuesday. Got in on Sunday afternoon. Customs was a mass of people standing in a lineless herd, waiting in the airless room to get into Russia. After maneuvering through the crowd I managed to get into the place after about an hour. I remembered then that there was a lot of waiting in Russia.

I got picked up by Nick Hobbs, the man who brought the band here two times before. He lives in London, manages Pere Ubu, does experimental theater and I'm sure a ton of other stuff.

He is one of the more extraordinary people I have met in the last few years. He picked up Russian by coming here often enough. He's innovative, hard working and honest. I like working with this guy.

We went to the hotel and checked in. Nothing like the Russian hotel experience. Hookers and the armed men who protect them. An hour later I went to the new offices of MTV Russia to do interviews. Can you believe they have that disease in Russia now? That's it for that place. It's all downhill now. The people there were cool though. Young and energetic. It was good because their set up wasn't slick like MTV UK or the NYC version which is a big put off, where I find myself so totally repulsed that I am barely able to be cool. MTV are the harvesters of musical death. In their hands, music has become a sterile, cute, horror show of mediocrity and weakness. The Russian version is wonderfully underfunded, amateur and refreshingly fun.

The interview took a little while to start because they couldn't get the camera to work and there were all these people kind of standing around uselessly holding video cassettes and rolls of duct tape. It was how I figured it would be. Finally it got up and running and they couldn't get the shots lined up so I helped them out with that. It's probably the closest I'll get to getting some control of MTV.

They have all these different shows but no guest so I did all of them. I don't know how that will look. An all day Hankathon.

I did an interview with their fashion girl. I think that was my favorite one. By then I had been there for three hours after they had promised I would only have to be there for two. Well, you know, they had to figure out how to use the microphone and the cameras kept malfunctioning. Hey, we're pioneering it here and I'm in on the ground floor. By the time it was time to talk about fashion, a topic I know so much about as it is so central to my life, I was in rare form. I told the shaking young thing that I actually knew some of the world's top models. This gal bought it hook line and sinker. I told her that I had Claudia Schiffer over every other week – to mow my lawn. I had Kate

Moss over to do the windows and vomit her lunch on the lawn to fertilize it. I had Naomi Campbell doing something, I forget now. That's about all the fashion model names I know. At one point, the girl figured out that the world of fashion was lost upon me. After a boring, endless, suffocating three hours spent doing 55 minutes of interviews, I was finally let loose from the environs of MTVsky.

After that, Nick, some of the MTV people and members of the Russian promoter's office all went and ate at a really cool restaurant. Got back to room number 526 around 0200.

On Monday, show day, I slept late, read a lot of Thomas Wolfe's *Of Time and the River*. Soon enough it was show time.

I went to the venue to soundcheck and see what I was going to be dealing with. No monitors, a bad wireless mic. OK. Eventually monitors were brought in and they sounded bad too. No sound, no sound problems is the maxim I live by when in the east. All the seats had headphones installed and they would be listening to the translator. I knew I was going to have to speak at a slower rate of words per minute because of the language barrier. I knew that the translator, Peter, would have to listen, articulate the information and then shoot it back at the audience, so everything was going to be on a ten-second time delay. Oh brother.

I sat down with Peter to talk about his translating skills and found out that he isn't a translator but merely a guy who knows a little English.

'So, you're a translator.'

'No.'

'OK, that's cool. But your English is great, right?'

'Pretty good.'

'So, tonight's show will be a disaster.'

'What is disaster?'

Soundcheck was over quickly because there were really no sounds to check on. I went back to my room and worked on ideas to jam on that night.

I hit about ten minutes after eight in front of a few hundred people. The monitors started feeding back immediately. This was perfect for me. I turned the monitors away from me and explained the no sound, no sound problem theory. The audience sat silent and still. Only the gig to go. I plowed bravely on. I talked about the first time I came to Russia in 1994. I talked about Thailand, Buddha, Africa, racism, men and women. I didn't go on too long. I didn't want to wear them out seeing as they had to deal with me and Peter the translator.

Everywhere I went, I had the bodyguard action. It was intense. They silently waited for me outside the door of the dressing room and then walked me from there to the stage and then back. They hung out as I talked to some people after the show. They walked me out of the place as well. I have been surrounded by security guys before but there's something about the way these guys do it that makes you think that something might happen to you.

After the show was over I went to the same place and ate. The people who Nick are working with are cool and very friendly but don't seem to have all the pieces together and it's a little frustrating. Good thing it's only for a few days. A week of this and I would be up the wall. I can't stand it when the people who are running things are late or have to constantly be reminded of things. It makes me think that I am on my own and should just put the show on myself. Yeah, like I could pull that off. When we're at the restaurant, they just kind of sit around and smoke and talk and nothing seems to happen and then I ask if we're going to eat and they seem to awaken from their stupor and ask for the waiter. Just makes me wonder what's on their minds.

So, there's another show tonight, for I bet about eighty people and then I'm out of here. Didn't see much so far. The streets remind me of being in Hungary but with lots of prostitutes. I counted thirteen in a line outside the restaurant tonight. The hotel I am in this time is a nice one. I prefer the not as nice ones really. There's nothing like a drafty room with no hot water and a prostitute calling your room to see if you want to be serviced to let you know you're somewhere other than your own place. A hooker calling your room! What a time we're having!

12-09-98 Moscow Russia: Nearly 0400 hrs. Trying to sleep. I leave for Israel in a few hours. Three days off and then the last show of the year in Tel Aviv.

The second show was better than the first one. At least I had a better time of it. The audience seemed a little looser than the previous night.

I had to do four interviews afterwards. They tried to sneak them in before the show but I told them no. I am hitting stage in thirty minutes and one of the promoters comes in staring at the ground, all sulking like he just broke a neighbor's window with a baseball and announces that I will be doing four interviews, uh, now. Uh . . . no I won't. He looks at me slightly incredulous. It's on the schedule! Well your schedule is ridiculous. We'll see the press weasels later. The word 'no' means 'yes . . . eventually' to these guys. So, I do these wacky interviews with press types with intensely bad breath. Always my favorite.

The best part of yesterday was walking around Moscow with Nick and riding on the subway system. The train stations are amazing. We went down some really steep escalators to the platforms which are these amazing high ceiling affairs with statues, stained glass, it was like being in a subterranean castle. Nick told me that the unwritten law is that you don't litter here. I looked around and could find no trash on the ground. It's funny that these people who have nothing treat this place so well and then you go the New York City subway and the platforms and trains have been trashed completely.

It was a trip to walk around the streets. Some of the apartment buildings are so beautiful. Massive stone buildings. They look like they'll be around forever. We went to a friend of Nick's to hang out for awhile. Cool guy, married. We sat in his kid's room and his wife put out some food and stuff to drink. Some cheese and crackers, fruit, juice, water. It was so cool to be kicking it with this guy in his abode knowing that I don't come from here, if I wasn't with Nick, this would have been nothing more than a lit window I would have walked past. Instead, it's this whole world. This is what it's all about. It's why

I can't stay home. It's why I wonder how people get by with so little when all these worlds, all these possible universes exist if you go past what you know. What good is what you know unless it gets you to the parts that you don't know? I got more from hanging out at this guy's place for an hour than I do in a lot of places. For me, the big deal is in the seemingly obscure. Big magic in small places. The old folks selling whatever they have in front of the train station to get by. Nick said that most of them, Ukrainians he speculated, will be renting space in the train station that night to get out of the cold. Americans have it pretty good in comparison. Makes me wonder why some Americans have to trash their country. They don't know what the real world is like. They don't know how good they have it.

Oh yeah, this is wild. We were walking to Nick's friend's house and he says we can save time if we take a cab. He sticks his hand out and this small, fucked up car pulls over immediately. I get into the back which is piled up with all kinds of stuff. Nick talked to the guy and the guy takes us about half a mile and we get out. I ask him how he knew that car was a cab. He says that it wasn't a cab. People are up against it here and if they can make a little money somewhere, they go for it. Nick said that ride cost us about fifty cents.

After the show I came back here instead of going out to eat with the others. I got tired of talking and listening to people. Depression makes me withdraw and I wanted nothing more than to be alone. So, with three security guys around me, I went back to my room. I said goodbye to Nick, as I won't see him in the morning, and kept walking. He said, 'I'll see you when I see you,' which perhaps is a take on something he heard me say to one of those interview people when one of them asked me if it's true that I don't have many close friends. I told the guy that with most of the people I know, I see them here and there, now and again. I see them when I see them. It's true, right? How many people do I really know? You go and do your thing and go somewhere else and do something else. You see people when you come through their town or when you are on the road with them and that's that. I don't know when I'll see Nick again.

Does it matter? He's an amazing guy and there's a lot of things to do and see out there and I'll see you when I see you. I have always, always been compromised when I have put too much into any one person. I have always done better when I keep to myself. I figured that out when I was very young. My parents were cool but I was done with them around age fourteen. I listened and went through the motions but I wasn't there.

I guess that's not all entirely true. I think about some people fairly regularly. People like Ian, Vega, Selby, Bajema and some others. But then again, I see them about two times a year. It's good when I do but then it's always on to the next thing.

I am now thinking of the woman I spent time with recently. I like her a lot. She makes me think differently. I am so used to being alone. So used to loneliness. I am used to a loneliness that has no face. I am used to that formless loneliness that comes in the night when I am awake, staring at some ceiling somewhere. I think of women I saw that day and invent conversations over the murmur of city traffic. I am used to the shifting, gaunt loneliness that runs alongside the vehicle. The coyote you hear howling from miles away. A loneliness that sometimes looks you square in the face with eyes like Hank Williams before it runs out of the range of the headlights in the middle of nowhere. This is the beautiful loneliness that has followed me, haunted me, spoken to me for years. It is a force that allows me to work relentlessly, to travel and go beyond exhaustion. To live in alien landscapes for hundreds of days a year and miss no one and no thing. A loneliness that finds me when I have returned to my place after a few days to push me wordlessly out the door, back to the world. Onto continents, through time zones, across borders, into confusion and sleep deprivation. A loneliness that makes music burn in my brain. A loneliness that elevates life to an altitude only traveled by a few With her kiss, this magic world vanishes. With her hands on my face and my name on her lips, all of a sudden the loneliness has a face, a name, a memory. Something is lost and something is gained.

10.51 a.m.: At the airport in Moscow. Waiting on the flight to Tel Aviv. Today was filled with typical, wacky Russian hijinks. The ride was about twenty minutes or more late. This is expected, no, it's demanded damn it! I don't want to be on time, I want to panic and wonder if I'll get out of this place on the day that the plane ticket says. I want this extra stress in my life. If the ride came on time, I would have hidden myself for twenty minutes. I'm in the back of a van with the promoter woman. I don't say anything. There's nothing to say. We did the shows. They were 'interesting' and now I'm trying to escape like the other two times I have been here. After a few days, I am done with this place for quite awhile. Of course, no drive to the airport would be complete without getting pulled over by the police. We were lucky though and were on our way quickly enough.

I got to the airport a little while ago. I gave customs women my passport and customs form. She asks me how much cash I have and I show her the few dollars and pounds I have. She starts searching my wallet. Finally I just took the wallet away from her like *OK, game's over.* She just grunted and waved me on. What a place.

11.02 a.m.: Now sitting on a freezing bus, hopefully going to the airplane. It's cold in this motherfucker. People around me are weighed down with packages of all sizes. I guess no one cares what you check in. The bus is filling and I hope we will be moving soon.

I have a four-hour flight and a day of press when I get to Tel Aviv if I get there in one piece. I never think I'm going to get out of Russia. Something about the airport says, 'We are closed for no reason all of a sudden. Try again . . . someday.' I am always happy to leave Moscow. It has been a good trip though and I will come back again if possible. The people were cool. The food was good, I saw some cool stuff and I pulled off the two shows. If I can get out of here, I'll count this as a good part of the trip. Actually, it's all the good part. It's always better being out here, wherever that is, rather than 'home' where everything is known and I don't have to use my brain as much. I'd rather have the adventure than the comfort anytime.

Been on this bus for ten minutes now, oh we're off all of a sudden. A minute later and we're near the plane but not allowed to get off the bus. It's cold but we've got Rock and Roll to keep us warm or some damn thing. Some men are out there, standing next to the plane. They are laughing and rubbing their hands together. They stare in at us like the shivering experiment in human storage that we have become and laugh more.

My esteemed colleagues are being escorted into first class from a different bus, hence the hold up. Today's carrier is the wonderful Transaero.

Minutes later: I am now seated, the smell of airplane food is filling my nose.

12-10-98 Tel Aviv Israel: It's 0213 hrs. I am on the balcony of the hotel, looking out on the Mediterranean. I can see ships lined up at a dock. The steady roar of the ocean mixes with the sound of traffic. The air is cool and moist. For some reason, sitting here is making me recall a night in May of this year when I was in Washington DC, sitting on the steps of St. Luke's, looking up at the intersection of Wisconsin and Calvert. An intersection I grew up walking through almost daily for years. I have crossed that intersection with varying degrees of frequency for over 25 years. And now I am sitting with the memory of that night on this night. Memories of a single night always lead to memories of other nights. Night time is the best. For me, night time is the only time that matters. I am alone, looking out on this amazing sea from a great height. The night is starless. A solitary green light flashes in the distance. All around me are strange and fascinating lands. Egypt, Lebanon. I am alone and silently alive. I am a living secret making invisible history that cannot be proven. A small moment of perfection.

To think that several hours ago I was riding on crowded underground trains and walking the frozen streets of Moscow and now I am in Israel. This is living. This is beating the grind. This is ultimate experience. A solitary victory. Last year at this time I was in Africa sitting outside my tent, looking up at the night sky.

I got here hours ago. Met up with the promoter, Zev, and came to the hotel. Did some press and photos and then had some time in my room. Later, Zev and his wife took me out to a good Middle Eastern place in a somewhat rundown part of the city. So far, people have been extremely warm and friendly. Many people have told me how great Tel Aviv is. So far, so good.

Another couple of weeks before I have to go back to LA. Sometimes I think I am living life to the fullest and sometimes I think I am avoiding it by doing all this travel, the shows and living out of suitcases in rented rooms all over the world. But then I think to myself, what am I missing out on? Walking into the same room every day? A 'real' job? Of course I have been thinking about that woman and what she means or could mean in my life. I think it's great for two people to be together. That is a good number. I think, that to keep it alive though, you can't spend every day together. It wears out the magic. Love means nothing to me if it's not fortified with fierce, painful longing, brief explosive instances of furious passion and intimacy and then a sad parting for a time. In that way, you can give your life to it and still have a life of your own. I think some couples spend too much time together. They flatten out the potential for experience by constant closeness. Passion builds over time like steam. Let it rage until it's exhausted and then leave it alone to let it build up again. Why can't love be insane and distorted? How can it be vital if it has the same threshold as normal day-to-day experience?

Why can't you write burning letters and let your nocturnal self smolder with desire for one who is not there? Why not let the days before you see her be excruciating and ferment in your mind so on the day you go to the airport to pick her up, you're nearly sick with anticipation? And then when desire shows the first sign of contentment, throw it back in its cage and let it slowly build itself back into a state of starved fury. Then when you are together, it all matters. So that when you look into her eyes, you lose your balance, so that when she touches you, it feels like you have never been touched before. When she says your name, you think it was she who named you. When she has gone, you bury your face in the pillow to smell her hair and you lie awake at night remembering your face in her neck, her breathing and the amazing smell of her skin. Your eyes go wet because you want her so bad and miss her so much. Now that is worth the miles and the time. That matches the inferno of life. Otherwise you poison each other with your presence day after day as you drag each other through the inevitable mundane aspects of your lives. That is the slow death that I see slapped on faces everywhere I go. It's part of the world's sadness that's more empty than cold, poorly lit rooms in cities of the American night.

12-11-98 Kibbutz Ayelet Hashahla Israel: 0300 hrs. What a day. Jerusalem. Whoa. The Fourteen Stations of the Cross. Jerusalem Slim drags his cross up the Via Dolorosa. It's looking bad for our man at station number 4. He says goodbye to his mother, I think I read that he said, 'If I don't see you no more in this world, I'll see you in the next one, and don't be late.' Pretty cool under pressure I'll say. After dragging the cross that he will be nailed to another four stations, all the weeping women start carrying on and he cools them out, playing it bad ass like Cool Hand Luke. I think he said, 'Don't cry for me baby. I am a man of danger. I have soul and my rap is strong.' By the time this pre-Lenny Bruce superstar hits the top of the hill he's surrounded by a bunch of cowards armed with hammers and closed minds. Judging by what I read of the incident, he knew he was a charismatic motherfucker and was determined to make this his finest moment. He must have been playing to his fan base who surrounded the crucifix. 'I know nobody came here to get mellow tonight now did ya? I know that no one out there came here to get even a little bit mellow. ANYONE WHO WANTS TO GET MELLOW CAN TURN AROUND AND GET THE FUCK OUT OF HERE, ALRIGHT!! DO YA HEAR ME?!!' Do you believe the balls of this guy? I can see why people all over the world dig J. After he moved the stone and made his last rounds and was ascending, that parting shot was so great. 'Rock over London, Rock on Chicago! Next time you see me coming you better run.' And then there's something about a highway that I couldn't make out because there was a lot of wind hitting the mic. You know how those field recordings sometimes leave a little left to be desired sonically.

I think that a lot of people misinterpret the man. Like these idiots with their signs 'God Hates Fags'. I bet JC would have found that to be so lame. So many people doing so much bad shit in the name of Christ. He would have bummed out to see how many people read him wrong. What the fuck do I know? I know dick about Jesus Christ but he seemed like a straight shooter with a lot of guts. He was definitely rock and roll.

12-12-98 Tel Aviv Israel: At the hotel. About half past four in the afternoon. Got in last night. Burned out in my room for the rest of the night. Body is operating in typical December fashion. I am depressed, exhausted and underweight. This is usually how December is for me. It's the last stretch before the finish line which is when I crosswalk into my place in LA. Last year it was a let down. I busted my ass to get back to town in time for the benefit I do every year for this orphanage. It's the one night I redeem myself for being such a jerk the other 364 days of the year. I go from Madagascar to Johannesburg to Germany to London to LA to get back in time. I land at LAX a few hours before the show. I get to the venue and have twenty minutes onstage. I am jet lagged but holding alright. I get up there and read this journal thing from Africa and a drunk woman heckles me relentlessly. I don't know what I did to this lady but she had it in for me. What am I supposed to do, punch her out? I do my thing and leave. I walked home determined that I wasn't going to do that benefit anymore. I don't need the hassle. It's all your fault to put yourself in the position to let others fuck with you. Instead of complain I just change up my strategy. I'll just mail in some money next time. They can stick the benefit up their ass.

Tonight is the last show for the year and I am looking forward to it. I watched the CNN news loop a few times last night. Depressing about Bill Clinton. I watched his face as he spoke to the camera. He looks tired, haunted, almost flat. I've never seen him so gaunt. It looks good on him. Makes him look concerned, like Lincoln. I think it's lame what he did, well, lame that he got caught – but the media and the Republicans are making too much out of this. Is that all you fuckers can come up with? Republicans are weak. The whole thing stinks. Meanwhile, an entire nation's progress gets put on hold because of all this. It's old news. I went through the international issues of *Time* and *Newsweek* about an hour ago. Families of Ford, Clarke, Kazel and Donovan, the four nuns murdered in El Salvador still look for justice. Now there's an issue. Rape, murder and horror. A little bit of sex in the White House has more importance than that? That's where we're at. I see clowns like Orrin Hatch and the rest of them speaking so eloquently about morality and the idea of right and wrong. About as meaningful as anything coming out of Sting's wife's mouth. Where did the Sting and his idiot mate's reference come from? Two drivers I have been with lately who have driven them and told me what miserable shitheads they are. Made me remember when Versace died and I heard Sting's wife make some hilarious speech at the memorial. So dramatic. I imagine they are surrounded by people who tell them how incredibly right on they are. Will be time to go to the venue soon. A show, finally.

12-13-98 Tel Aviv Israel: It's about 0300 hrs. What a great crowd. A-1 supremo. I wish they all could be that great. What a great way to end the tour. Eighty-one shows this year. Not too shabby. That's the most talking shows I've ever done in one year.

I really like Israel. I wish I had more gigs here.

Now I am in my room waiting for sleep. There was easily one of the worst films ever made on the TV awhile ago. *The Invaders*, starring Sean Young, universally known as Psycho Sister number 1. An alien comes down to earth to knock up Sean. Gestation is a mere three days for this ET tyke. A chase scene ensues through the woods and mountains as the ET male who gave her the otherworldly wood tells her about his people, etc. Finally, the ET babe is born. The Space Brothers come down with the big ship to take ET man and child to a different galaxy or wherever. They looked like tired, substitute schoolteachers in robes if you ask me. This diabolical waste of film comes to a end and they roll credits and you want to thank them for letting you off. You figure this must be an old flick as you would hope that our Sean could get better work at this point. The film is copyrighted 1997! Brutal. Never bet all your money on one horse. Best to have a few jobs to go to lest you find yourself having to make a film like *The Invaders*. One of those Baldwin brothers is in the movie. They all act you know! Didn't you know? Well, they do. I guess they all can't be Alec, but they'll get in the show just the same, even if it's *The Invaders*. *The Invaders, Johnny Mnemonic*, it's all good work if you can get it, right? What awesome film does this line come from, 'Bullshit, Mr Hand Man!' That's right, son, *The Sound of Music*. Nothing gets by you. Alright, moving on.

8.43 p.m.: On an airplane about halfway to Cairo. This is so cool. I am going to Egypt. I remember being on tour in 1985 thinking that one day I was going to go to Egypt. Somehow, thirteen years later I am finally getting there. I want to see the sights and all but the one thing that's worth the price of admission is the chance to sail on the Nile at night., I have wanted to do that for years. I have thought about it before. Falling asleep so many nights I used to make believe that the bed or piece of floor I was on was a boat sailing silently through the mysterious Egyptian night. I had the time and the frequent flyer miles so I booked five days on the Nile to see the sights.

I hope I get back to Israel soon. I spent a couple of hours in Jaffa earlier this evening. It's a few miles away from where I was staying but it felt like another country. Small streets, Arab-owned stores, women with the full head wrap, beautiful little kids running around. Felt like I had entered into a time warp. Tonight I ate lamb and humus and watched the sun go down over the Mediterranean. The streets, the age of the buildings, it was a small, fascinating world.

11.42 p.m. Cairo Egypt: I was met at baggage claim by a guy named Samir. Samir warned me that the drivers in Cairo are like no others anywhere in the world. I hear that everywhere I go though. Italian drivers are crazy, Russian drivers are crazy. Basically, everyone who gets behind the wheel thinks that everyone else is crazy. But after what I just saw, Samir was right. Most of the traffic lights just flash yellow. No one seems to pay attention to the lane markings. People drive between lanes and drift all over the road. People use their horns nonstop. Rarely was there more than a few inches between us and another car. It was like a stock car race. It's all up for grabs. I thought it was cool, all the chaos and everything.

We passed through a neighborhood that was really rundown. Samir said they were poor folks who made most of their income making pottery and other things for tourists and export. The neighborhood looked like the streets I saw in Jaffa if Jaffa had been shelled. I thought the place was beautiful. Clotheslines and narrow hallways. Poorly lit rooms could be seen through the windows. After that we crossed the Nile and I got my first look at it. Looks like any other large river I have ever seen, I only got to see it for a moment.

I am sitting outside my room in a plastic chair. In front of me is a courtyard with bungalows. I can hear nonstop traffic, car horns and what sounds like gunshots in succession every once in a while. The smell of car exhaust is ever present. I noticed that all the way here. Cairo is one polluted city.

Had to come inside, mosquitoes were getting to me. The room has the overwhelming, pleasing smell of insecticide, always good.

The bellman was very disappointed with me when I took my room key and found the room myself. I am in room number 213. Samir said that a lot of people are looking for that one dollar tip. Samir is very informative. So informative at times I was getting an info-OD. 'This is our form of public transportation,' he said, pointing to a bus. 'Is that a . . .?' I wondered out loud. 'A bus!' Samir exclaimed proudly and the mystery was revealed to me.

On the other side of the highway as we were driving here to Giza, a presidential motorcade flew by at top speed. A long line of Mercedes with vans and motorcycles in the front and rear. Reminded me that two nights ago I stood right in the spot where Yitzhak Rabin was shot a few years ago. Zev took me there. It was next door to the venue. There were flowers next to the spot. A few years ago I went to the second floor of the Lorraine Motel and stood where Martin Luther King's body fell after he had been shot. I thought it was the entrance. The security guard was mad as hell. One night, after finishing a show in Dallas, I went and sat on the grassy knoll and looked at the spot where JFK was killed. It was intense to be there with all that history. And now I'm in Cairo. This is great, ultimate. Tomorrow should be epic. The Giza Pyramids are down the street from where I am sitting. I can't believe I'm finally here.

12-15-98 Cairo Egypt: 0259 hrs. I have a 0515 lobby call to go to the airport. Flying to Luxor to meet the boat and see the sights.

Spent a good part of the day at the pyramids. I didn't know there were so many of them. The Giza pyramids were stunning but it was the Sphinx that was most amazing to me. Like the pyramids, the Sphinx looks surreal. The tour lady told me that it was Napoleon's men who broke the front off it. I want to find out more about that. It was incredible to stand in front of it and know that Napoleon had been there. What kind of scene that must have been to come upon these monuments at that time.

What got me was the general tonnage of everything. Each block and beam I saw in Giza and Memphis were several tons each. How the hell do you go to work every day knowing that your job is to push a sixteen ton block up a hill to make the first part of a building so the king's entrails can be prepared for the afterlife? And what can you, the stone dragging hump, look forward to in your afterlife? You get to resume serving the king. What a drag. In service even after you're gone. Well, at least you have that to look forward to.

I went down a shaft in one pyramid with a 'guide'. Big fella in his garb. His handshake was a vice grip. 'Hello American. Merry Christmas. Boy oh boy, here we go.' He took me and two

British guys down to the bottom of this pyramid. We're all the way down there and one of the Brits turns to me and says, 'You're Henry Rollins.' We're in the bowels of the earth and he recognizes me. The world had gotten too small. Guide man barks out a couple of lines about the pyramid and then it's time to go back to the surface. He turns and flashes a wad of folded one dollar bills. 'American. My friend. Merry Christmas. Happy New Year.' I had no money and told him and started up the steep plank back up and he kept calling after me. 'American. Please, something. Merry Christmas American.'

The drives to the other sites were fascinating. The street life in Egypt is intense. The men's faces are sometimes so hard and fierce looking. Their eyes come burning out of their faces like Miles Davis.

Men pulling water buffalo near a canal. Two men kiss on the cheek. Old men sitting alone on rocks. A man arranging his prayer rug. Laundry hanging from an ancient house. Piercing blue sky, crops, brown water, chickens and dogs in front yards. Men sitting in dirt, staring at nothing. Women in clothes that only allow their eyes to show. The men look eternal, from a dream. The fierceness of their gaze is unsettling. Men sit at a table drinking tea. Men and women carrying things on their heads. The little boy with the memorized rap, 'Hello, how are you?'

0626 hrs.: At the airport. Waiting on the flight to Aswan. Tired of the nickel and dime. People try to hustle you left and right and after awhile, you're ready for something else.

0943 hrs.: Now on the boat. The Nile is outside. Magnificent. I am still cooling off from the drive here. Fuckin' guy meets me at the airport and tells me that before we go to the boat, we're going to the 'Alabaster Museum'. So what the fuck is that? It's his friend's fucking store. 'Meet my friend. He is friend to all Americans.' I think to myself that must be such a shitty job. I could never be friends to all Americans. The guy goes into some tired spiel about alabaster and on cue, two workmen start doing their little number. I am taken into the store and the guy tries to sell me stuff. I ask him if this is a store and he says no, it's a factory. Oh. I just stare at the guy. His shoulders drop. 'Do you want to buy something?' I leave. We proceed to the boat and now I'm lining this guy up. I go to check in and he tries to take over the process. I smell another scam so I take the paperwork and deal with it myself.

I go up here to the lounge area and wait for the room and he comes up and tells me that his work is done and now he's going and do I have something for the driver? That was it. I look into his eyes and start talking to him real slow. You take me to a fuckin' store and now you want money for something I already paid for? The guy bums and starts talking real fast. Enough. Goodbye. It's not like I've slept any or will get much sleep today. Sometimes I'm not in the mood for the bullshit. I hate not knowing the territory and having to take it from a prick like that. But it's part of the deal sometimes. I just remember that I am not home. That's all I need to remember and everything snaps back into perspective.

One thing that was cool about the drive here was seeing the sky and the people. Black-skinned women dressed head to toe in black. So beautiful and intense. Nubians. Back on the African continent again. The clothes people wear here are amazing. The men in the one piece thing and the skull cap. The women in various states of cover, always great. I sound like an MTV host. Hello, need brains please. Don't delay my order. Thanking you much, very. Please to happy.

Where do I belong? American. I get brief flashes of the idea of home when I am with Ian. He'll say something or we'll be somewhere in the old neighborhood and for a second, all things are in alignment. It's a moment. Then I go back to my regular routine. Counting the minutes, checking the schedule to see where I'm supposed to be. I get the feeling of home mostly when I'm alone. The location doesn't matter. I'm in Egypt. Suits me fine. I got a small bag and a backpack. The weather is fair. I'd just as soon sleep outside.

I'm looking out the window at the handsome men in their cool clothes. The trees shade them. Boats are sailing past our boat against red sand dunes and blue sky. The Nile water is churning. Small white boats are parked on its shore. The Nile! Tonight is going to be something. The night I have been thinking about for years.

Ten years on and loneliness is my traveling companion and friend. I think loneliness makes things matter more. There's a lot of loneliness in America. It's the loneliest place I have ever been. Americans are the loneliest bunch ever. So many looked like they just walked off the stage from a play and they don't know what to do next. Americans get played by their own. Sold out by their government. Made to watch as the President goes to great lengths to fix problems all over the world but nothing seems to happen in America. Poor folks are still poor. So many people illiterate, or semi-literate. The ghettos howl and moan and nothing seems to change. No matter who's elected, it's always the same. That might lead one to believe that some problems cannot be solved, but think that way and nothing will ever happen. It is discouraging. Look at that word. It means to have the courage knocked out of you. One needs courage to deal in America. You need to have guts to be able to make it there. It's one of the great things about the place. But it can be hard to get a hold of that when it seems to be relentlessly obscured by corny music, flimsy news media and politicians who don't move boldly and get it happening. Every year, same hatred, same fear and ignorance and so many cool people go down in it. The American is born dysfunctional and must fight his way out just to be normal. He's shot out of the cannon to make it or not. Pass, fail, doesn't matter to the coroner. I have never been any place like it. I sometimes think about family, mine. I think about them around this time of the year. People ask me what I'm doing for the holidays and I just look at them. When they mention the family members they're going to be with and the time they have to spend, they make it out to be something they don't want to do. So if you don't want to do it, then why the hell do you? I wonder how many people would rather just sit on their ass over the holiday and cool out. It's like that scene in *Cool Hand Luke* when Luke gets the others to lay down all the tar on the road real fast and then when they all sit down, one of them asks Luke what they're going to do now and he laughs and says, 'Nothing'. The ritualization of human kindness is so lame. You have to pick a day to call a truce and be civil to people you don't care about? That's weak.

5.52 p.m.: Went out today with some people from the ship. We did a lap in a sailboat. We sailed by some rock islands called cataracts. Palm trees on the side of the shore, ancient, crumbling structures high up on the bank with the setting sun as a backdrop. I thought it would be beautiful but not as much as what I saw. My fellow tourists are, for the most part, in pairs. Like in Kenya, I am the silent loner in the back with the sunglasses. Never used to use them before. People stare at me too much these days. The shades give me some relief.

The year is starting to hit me. This time last year, I was in Madagascar burning out alone in a bungalow on the Indian Ocean. I was feeling depleted, defeated and deserted. This year, not so bad. I'm getting gasoline in my blood thinking about 1999. Another thing that happens to me around this time of the year. I have already discarded all the achievements of the year and look ahead to the next year to make it all over again. I always start at the bottom of the mountain so I stay pissed off and motivated. I look to vanquish. Beat that ass and stand the fuckers down again and again. Go until depletion, rep out until failure if you have the guts. Go until the mind and body keel over and there the lesson is learned. Like I said years ago, there will come a time when the energy I took for granted is gone. After that, it's all about guts and defiance and not freaking out in decisive moments. It becomes a measure of your character. What the samurai called Makoto.

12-17-98 Edfu Egypt: 0258 hrs. Ship parked. We pulled in hours ago. Don't know exactly when. It's like looking out the window of the tour bus. Night time. Florescent light, a soda machine. Darkness

Spent the day seeing the sights. Huge temples. No block of stone less than several tons. If you were standing in the middle of all those pillars at sundown, looking out at the Nile in some year 'BC' you would know you were living in a magic age. At sundown we were at some temple. I bailed on the group to be alone amongst these immense ruins and look at the profiled face of Horus and get pulled into the terrifying magnificence of this age.

This trip has been good but frustrating. I can't understand how anyone can talk while they walk through these places. I am always silent. Awestruck. If you shut your mouth for once, stopped talking all that useless, time killing bullshit, you might be able to tap into the eternity that stands before you. Instead what I get every day is groups of people with their guides, stomping around, all the chatter, the idiotic, ceaseless chatter.

You, tour guide, what do you do? Try to be funny as you vomit out dimensions and facts that you have memorized. You repeat things you read in a book and then at night you shove a fork in your mouth. You are not much. The people who built these places believed in something much bigger than a paycheck. Did they know they were building something that would stand for thousands of years? Oh, yes. They probably dreamed of quantities of time unfathomable to you. So instead of your unsharpened humor that barely conceals your boredom, tread lightly with awe-inspired steps.

I didn't notice anyone else pick up on it, but what I couldn't stop staring at was the engravings left by people who had been there before. We were at some temple and in several places, about eye level, were fading signatures, mostly Italians and Germans, 1850's. I saw one from February 11, 1861. Damn close to one hundred years before I was born.

What was heavy about these engravings was that they put the structures into some kind of context. It's hard to get my head around the dates and figures that keep coming up. So many years, so many tons. When I see something that's man-made that's four thousand years old, part of me just shuts down. What was it like for these travelers to come upon these places without all the tourists around? When it was all silence and mystery? Couldn't have been the same as when I was there hours ago, amidst gortex-clad and Nike-booted swarms, point and shoot cameras whining and winding all around. Perhaps the travelers hired a boat that was paddled by men. Not the motorized one that was followed by the second boat with the armed security that I came up in. Their grandchildren would know of WWI. Perhaps the ancient voices spoke to them. Whenever I walked around these places, I tried to imagine what it would have been like to have come upon these mute monuments. To stare at huge hieroglyphs frozen in profile while you stood in shocked silence.

So now I stand back from the group or go ahead to be alone for a few minutes with the pillars and the walls and time.

I live in an American time frame. That's why I needed to see 'Karl Bielmann, Berlin 02-11-1867' carved into a wall that is thousands of years old. I'm on a four hundred year clock. Saw a relief of Antonio and Cleopatra. Whoa. But it's also heavy to stand in the dressing room of the Paradiso in Amsterdam and know that Ian Curtis and D. Boon had also been there too.

The only thing tying me to time now is that soon I will be with her for a week. She will come to stay with me in LA. She does not know that to me the place is only some rooms in which articles I've accumulated reside in darkness and in the off position for most of the year. That I walk into the place as much a visitor as she will. She does not know that I have no home. No matter where I go, I feel the need to move. When I live in a hotel, the agreement is good for 24 hours and then it's pay again or get the hell out. She does not know that I walk the floors of my place as I do a hotel lobby or airport gate. That when lying next to her in a dark hotel room I have felt the brother horror retreat into the shadows briefly. She does not know that I have not one shred of faith in the concept of home and that while I know that she would never try to hurt me, I expect her to leave me or find something about me that will be intolerable, some unchangeable aspect of my nature will repel her and she will be gone. She does not know and will never know that I will always seek the blasted, frozen trails over the welcoming hearth. Pain and the need to prove myself obscure much of my potential, dubious as it may be. The road is the only master I acknowledge and the only thing I take my orders from.

Other than that event, I am on a ship in Egypt. I stood at the front of the ship last night and stared into the wind, looked down at the silent Nile, looked up at the star-packed sky. For a couple of hours I stared into the darkness and wind. That instance of time was perfect. The ghosts came out. The banks of the Nile spoke. The palms whispered, the small boats on the side uttered countless centuries of this river. The river flows, always forgetting. The river is more powerful than time.

An American in Egypt. An American in Ohio. Both the same. Both homeless. Both driving nails into time's hands and feet as another life is strewn like ashes over the side in high wind. No particle ever touches the water, they're just left to swirl in the winds of the world. For the American, America is lost inside him as he is lost inside it. He treats the world like America because the world treats him like an American. I wonder if the reason that so many Viet vets talk about the time they spent in the jungle as the most defining time of their life is because when they found themselves crouched deep in the jungles of a country they knew nothing about, to kill people they didn't know for a cause that wasn't made clear to them – maybe in the middle of all that alienation, and the government's obvious unconcern for their lives, they found their home. The blood of their annihilating ancestors spoke to them and for a time, they actually belonged somewhere. Maybe this became more evident when the survivors came back to their homeland to find that no one could speak their newly acquired language of horror, that many hated and feared them, that many barely noticed their absence. Maybe that's why some went back.

12-18-98 Luxor Egypt: 0047 hrs. We're docked here in Luxor. We are out early in the morning. A few things on my mind. On 12-19-98, it will be seven years since Joe Cole was killed. It's hitting me hard this time. Maybe harder than last year. Every 12-19 that goes by is hard. I miss you, man. I wonder about the two guys who held us up that night every time 12-19 rolls around. I wonder if they think about Joe at all. And if they do, what they think. I will be checking my watch to make sure I don't miss LA time.

The day of sightseeing was good. I can't get my head around the size of these temples and how well built they are. I watched a man doing repairs on a pillar. He was whacking away at it with a hammer and the pillar just kept taking the shot, no problem. It's only a couple of thousand years old, maybe a few centuries more. I was talking with two of the others in the group about how people marvel over Mt Rushmore; the 19th Dynasty posse could have done that over spring break. Americans get all bent out of shape over Rushmore, I wonder what they would do if they all saw the things I just saw. Oh fuck it. Doesn't matter does it? Go. Don't go. Lift it. Don't lift it. It's easy.

Everything in my life is easy. Do it or don't. That's all it boils down to.

At 0800 hrs we go to see the Valley of the Kings and Queens. Hours later I'll be on a plane to Cairo. I get a few hours of sleep and then I have three long flights back to Los Angeles. I think I have over 25 hours of flights and layovers altogether. Good thing I brought a book.

I like this small room with the window that looks at the Nile and the river's bank. I did my thing. Hung out under the stars and sailed down the Nile like I had always wanted. Was it great? You bet. Life is a blast no matter what happens.

7.44 p.m.: At the airport in Luxor waiting on the flight to Cairo. The next day and a half will be quite the pull. Four long flights. I don't care. I am Egypted out for now. I am looking forward to something else.

The boat was showing the movie *Heat* and I was recognized by the staff and some of the people on board. Great time to be out of here.

The British couple next to me are trying to keep time with the piped in music by banging their hands and glasses on the table hard. Their time is lousy and I want to see them bleed

12-19-98 Cairo Egypt: At the airport, waiting to go. 0730 hrs. It is appropriate that on this day it will take such a long time to get back to LA. If my calculations are correct, I'll be flying or burning out at an airport for the next 26+ hours. This is a Joe Cole day in Hell. Brought to you by the folks at Waste Management Industries. This will be a long and brutal one. Thank you Joe Cole for giving me this day of travel hell.

'Some days are longer than days – they're eternities.' – Davo One of Joe's favorite lines.

I am tired of this relentless siege of nickel and diming that happens here. You get out of the cab at the airport and guys come running up to you, telling you that you will need your passport and ticket to get on the plane and then they try to take your luggage inside. Even if you take your own luggage and tell them to fuck off like I do, they persist all the way up to the security gate until a cop tells them to take off. In every toilet, the man is there, standing by uselessly, waiting to be tipped. I half expected to see him in my hotel room last night. How hot would that be to have the men's room man everywhere? Have a guy in your home that you would have to tip all the time whenever you did anything. I like this place a lot but it will be cool to get away from all the guys trying to sell you something. They left me alone for the most part. I must have a low rent vibe coming off me. In the market places we would go to, the vendors would call me 'Rambo', cute right? Those guys are like flys around here. The rest of it is amazing and I hope I can get back here some day.

The woman across from me has the worst painting bubble-wrapped and leaning against her leg. If that's going on the wall, the rest of the house must be a fucking disaster.

Tourists trip me out. I haven't felt like one since I was a little kid, traveling with my mother. For the most part, the people I encountered were seasoned travelers but there was one family from New Zealand that was classic. There was the bounder of adventure father with a lot of questions for the tour guide. He's going to get his money's worth, every Kiwi dollar. Don't try to fool him either because he's an authority on the place and will tell you a thing or two. Then there's the sulking, ultra-bored daughter, the son with the Pink Floyd shirt that never came off and the wife. So many times, intrepid dad cut people off to be the first one through the gate at a temple. He was intense. He always held the tour guide in some contempt, knowing perhaps a little more than he did, not much, but just enough. Wifey did the whole treat the locals like the brutish, swindling, mongrel tribe she knew them to be but she had no fear, no one was going to pull one over on her. Oh man, I gave this family a lot of room to work. Wherever they were, I moved well out of their way. To be within earshot of dad would be too close to boredom for anyone with my new and improved, patent pending, low boredom threshold.

I thank my lucky stars that I was spared the rare and multi-level hell that is the family vacation. The son and daughter, trapped in a day to day tedium with mater and pater, unable to get drunk and reckless, unable to smoke hashish and break windows. To pillage, to riot, to burn! To go screaming through ancient temples and desecrate hieroglyphs thousands of years old, destroy and deface pillars and reliefs, only to be cut to pieces by the uzi toting plain clothes security who roam the sites with darting eyes and ninja stealth. This is your chance, your one fleeting moment, your rendezvous with danger and destiny!

On the other hand, New Zealand! Hail New Zealand. You New Zealanders know how the rest of the world sees you. You're that little island next to Australia. In fact when you go abroad, no one asks you, 'Hey, with that accent, you must be from New Zealand.' I'm sure you get tired of people asking if you're from Australia and that confused and uninterested look they give you when you tell them where you're from. Most have no idea. Maybe that's why you have been witnessed on several occasions introducing yourself to people, accosting them actually, grabbing them by their lapel or arm and shouting, 'I am from New Zealand and my name is Ben! New Zealand is not a suburb of Australia. We are a separate country! We are not 'almost Australian', that's not funny. Come and visit us sometime, we have hot and cold running water and photographs of our trip to Egypt!'

Later: A few hours into the flight. Some movies really suffer when they are cleaned up for airline use. Today's on board piece-of-shit-critic looks at and comments upon the diabolic, strained and thoroughly unreal non-epic *Lethal Weapon IV*. Like most blathering critics, I'm an ass getting paid by the word. Also, I came into the film part way through, does it matter? I came in at the part where Danny Glover's house has been torched by Asian bad guys. I think it would have been a cool idea to put in Deep Purple's Roger Glover instead, that guy rocks. If you have a bad script and talented actors, as you do here, trapped in a plotless excuse to endure obligatory car chases and explosions, massive amounts of destruction that no one seems all that bothered about, you better make your money back by slapping the name of a successful movie as the title and add a number to it. Get it out to as many movie houses as you can and see if you can recoup your costs on the first weekend and get it to video as soon as possible. It's the way they work every Stallone film. I once asked a high-ranking Hollywood agent if anyone in those high towers who puts up the money for the Stallone films ever thinks that the guy is any good. He said no but studios know that they will make their money back in video sales and rentals and that's why this guy keeps getting work. I figured it had to be something like that. I have seen some of his later films like the one he did with Sharon Stone and they're brutal.

It was hard to watch Mel Gibson wince while in character. The pain on his face as he burns hundreds of calories and massive amounts of lean tissue trying to breathe life into this threadbare story line was hard to watch. Even the mighty Mel can't save this one. At the end, Glover's daughter gives birth to the child she had with Chris Rock. Chris Rock is capable of having sex? At the same time, Rene pops one out from her coupling with Mel. Our boy goes to his wife's grave to ask permission to get on with his life. He hits an emotional impasse and is pulled out of the murk by Joe Pesci, who tells him of the best friend he ever had, a frog named Froggy. I was touched. No I wasn't. In the words of the only two film critics who matter, the guys on the 'Breakin' Into the Movies' show in the movie *Hollywood Shuffle*, 'We gave this shit the finger.' See you at the movies.

Wow, that was fun. If I had a sudden loss of integrity I could write for *Entertainment Weekly* or *Spin*.

Later: On the plane headed towards Dulles Airport. I hit my stopwatch when I walked out of the hotel in Cairo to start on the journey back. So far, fifteen hours, fifteen minutes in. A little over halfway. I have not slept much as the above review bears out. When I was on the ship the other day, I watched about ten minutes of the horrendous *Ace Ventura: Call of the Wild*. This is funny? Jim Carey is funny? That guy puts me off my fuckin' food. I watched about half an hour of *Dumb and Dumber*, *The Cable Guy*, suffered through *Liar, Liar* and *The Truman Show* multiple times due to bad luck on airplanes and thought they sucked. Shitty movies, pussy music, fuck all y'all. Watched the 'Fugee All-stars' on TV in Tel Aviv, face the truth – they sucked. Fuck you.

The movie version of *The Avengers* is on now. I have Sabbath in the headphones. Computer-generated insects are attacking Uma Thurman and what's his name. The two thugs chasing them are the idiot from Black Grape and Eddie Izzard. A man with more talent than most. I guess he needed the work. The Black Grape guy is a walking billboard for why you shouldn't do drugs.

I read a review of a movie I was in called *Frost* in *USA Today*. They gave that shit the finger. Hooray! I'm in another stiff.

Several hours from now I will be in my room. Always interesting to be back there. Strange to walk in there after a long time out here. I get back there around this time every year. It marks the finish line to the year of work. So was it a good year? I think so. I came a long way. When I think of the fact that Joe died for nothing, it takes away the feeling of accomplishment for me. I know he would not want me to think that way but I do sometimes. He was the one with the talent. He had the talent but he hadn't grown into it yet. He was on his way there though. Another couple of years and I think he would have had it happening in a big way. He could write music, was a great photographer, a great writer, interviewer, etc. He would have been a real all around Man Ray. And the guy who killed him? What do we get from that guy? All he can ever claim credit to is that he cut down one of the great ones and past that, his life doesn't mean anything.

I get along alright because I am a maniac who works too much. I work out so my body can take what I put it through. I keep a hectic schedule so I don't slip. I know myself. I am human, fragile and prone to all the mortal shit. With an iron work ethic, one can pull oneself up a few degrees. It's like going out for a run, if you can get out the door, you'll be fine. It's the couch that'll kill you. If I didn't get out on the road all the time, I'd withdraw to the point of living in one room of a house. As it is now, I can be in a hotel room for twelve to sixteen hours at a time, never say a word, never wonder what's going on out there at all.

As cool as it will be to be back amongst my books and records, I will be relieved to be back on the road in a couple of weeks. I miss the audience when I am away from them for too long. I hated getting off-stage in Tel Aviv the other night. It's been 12-19-98 for over seventeen hours now. Looks like it will be 12-19 for about thirty-three hours by the end.

12-20-98 LA CA: 11.13 p.m. got to my place around 0100 this morning. The place always looks so small when I come back. Fucked around for awhile, unpacked. Hit the sack around 0200. Couldn't sleep and have not slept yet. I am not all that tired but my brain is gone. Ran errands today. Body was cramping bad. Now I'm just here, waiting for the next thing. Whenever I get back here, my life seems to go on pause. LA, what am I thinking?

Appendix

02-01-97 LA CA: Past two in the morning. Spent the night working doing work on other people's books. A French company is putting out a book of Alan Vega's photographs. The company asked me to do the captions for the photos. The man said that I was one of the only people that Alan trusts. That's cool. I have spent no small amount of time on Alan's behalf and believe in the guy 100 per cent. I get this package of photos and I am told that they need it all done right now. No warning. Deadline yesterday or something. So there I was on my last night home, trying to get everything done and deal with this art project too. Now I leave in a few hours and I feel a little burned by the French guy. But Alan is the man so it's alright.

02-03-97 Tokyo Japan: 9.23 p.m. Got in OK. A woman named Miwa met me at the gate and we went into Tokyo.

I got some good records at the local Wave record store. I ate some good sushi. It's good to be back here. I should get to sleep soon, there are a lot of interviews to do and I have to get used to the gym I will be going to all week.

Nothing to report yet, nothing has happened. It is good to get out of LA and on the road. I feel better out here.

v02-07-97 En route to Hong Kong: 5.52 p.m. The time in Tokyo went fast. Didn't do much except interviews. There was a lot of them. Checked out a bunch of record stores and found some cool stuff.

Nothing much to say about the whole ordeal. Just did a ton of press and boring photo sessions. The interview thing in Japan is a drag because everything goes through a translator. The guy says something to you in Japanese and of course you can't understand but you look at him anyway to let him know that you are respecting him by listening. The translator tells you what he said. As you listen you look at him and nod. You answer the question while looking at him, even though you're talking to the translator. The translator tells the interviewer what you said and he nods at you to show you he understands what you're saying. It's a somewhat strained affair that leaves me drained at the end of the day.

The people who work at the label are pretty cool. I don't always know where they're coming from. They are polite but they never loosen up. They seem to tolerate me more than relate. The translator, Kazuyo Tategami was great. She would rip on me all the time and that made it fun.

Chris and I are now going to Australia by way of Hong Kong, where we will have a short stop over. It will be good to get to Australia.

Tokyo is a city that turns its inhabitants into robots. The culture seems to be derived from the construction of the city itself. The way people are is determined by how they deal with their lifestyle. People close their eyes on the subway so they will not have to deal with other people. I have never seen anything like that anywhere. All these people sitting there pretending that no one else is around. The politeness thing there I will never get used to or understand. It never seems real to me. I see people walking with surgeon's masks on all over the place. So many people smoking.

At the Roppongi Crossing, you see black guys handing out fliers for sex clubs. Rarely did I see anyone of any other color handing them out.

The non-Japanese that I have met there are always strange, with little exception. I met a trainer at the gym who is Canadian. He has been living there for nine years. Why? These people seem like exiles. Definitely a different type. What would inspire you to go to such an alien place and set up camp? Oh yeah, the gym, what a trip. It's men only. I got a three-day membership there. When you walk in, all the other men put their fist in the air and say something like 'Heyyy!' It was cute. The last day I was there, the trainer had on these really short pants, they looked like hot pants. We were down in the weight room and from the level above I heard this very queeny man call out the trainer's name and say, 'I'm ready for my lesson now!' It was very obvious what was going down. I just looked at the guy and he looked at me, shrugged and said something like 'It's a living,' and went up the steps.

02-11-97 Sydney Australia: 3.18 p.m. Been in Australia a few days. Been going OK. A lot of press but it's cool. Saw the Beasts of Bourbon play the other night in Melbourne. Hung out with Mick Geyer and as always it was too short a time. He was brilliant. We sat and had a distended discourse on the genius of Nick Cave, always a good topic. He is one of the only people I can think of that I look forward to seeing. It was so cool that he happened to get back to Melbourne right around the time I got there. That guy has turned me on to so many good writers, musicians and films. I don't know where he stores it all.

11.10 p.m. Back from a long day of talking to people. It was OK except for a couple of things. One radio station guy I had to talk to on the phone was a drag with all of his bullshit, but I dealt with it. I hate having to be put through other people's corny shit but that is part of it right now. Why do these people feel the need to act like such jerks? I guess they think they have you where they want you and they can work out their little power trips on you.

Now listening to the new Kim Salmon record. Kim is amazing and this record is one of the best things he has ever done. It would be so great to be able to put out Kim's records in America. No one would buy them though. It's frustrating but it's true. There's so many records I would like to put out. They wouldn't sell and the artists would get all bent out of shape and then all of a sudden I am seen as Satan. I think I'll pass.

02-12-97 Sydney Australia: At the airport waiting to head out for Bangkok. The Australian press was OK, there was a lot of it.

I have a day off tomorrow. It was either go to France a day early or hang out in Bangkok for a day. I don't have anything against Paris, but I have been there many times. I have never been to Bangkok so this will be interesting. I like the fact that I will be there on my birthday and I will be there on my own.

02-13-97 Bangkok Thailand: A little after midnight. Went for a walk around the neighborhood. Men offering me taxi rides to Pat Pong, where the women are. Strange smells mixed in with rotting garbage. Old men sitting outside in the hot night. I am 36.

The cab driver who got me to the hotel asked me if I was single and when I told him I was, he lit right up. 'You get Thai massage in bathhouse. Girls beautiful here. Everywhere else no same-same.'

Australia was alright, not that I remember much of it besides the press stuff. I guess there wasn't much besides that. It has not occurred to me to see how many days I have been gone. I used to count them. Now I don't. Days away from what? From where? It doesn't matter. It's great not to miss anyone or anything. It's the only time I feel free. That's what fucks a lot of people up. They get attached to someone and then they can no longer perform the tasks they have to without the other person around. I remember all the times I was with a woman and missed her, it was a drag. I would like to see the years go by and have less and less people know me personally. I think that would be great.

I walked around Bangkok for hours today until the heat beat me down. I walked down this one street and I was the only round eye I saw for a long time. People were coming out their places to look at me. They probably thought I was lost. It was fascinating. I saw a woman selling an elephant tusk, she was just sitting there with this tusk next to her, women walking up the street with sticks across their backs with baskets on either end.

The heat and the pollution were intense but still the whole thing was cool. I was on my own, walking through Bangkok on my birthday. I live for stuff like this. I like to travel by myself. These moments are the best. I think it was Mark Twain who said that the great moments are nothing without someone else to share it with. I feel the exact opposite. I think there's nothing like a trip like this on my own. I look forward to the years ahead when I can be on my own for weeks at a time. There's so many instances where company would just blow it.

Sometimes, when something really cool happens, I wish that Joe was around. Like when I was on Ozzy's jet, sitting across from him, listening to him talk about how Black Sabbath recorded the *Paranoid* album. It was so cool. It was about 65 per cent cool. It would have been ultimate if Joe was sitting next to me, which he would have been if he had not been killed. It's times like that where I would like to get the shooter, cuff him to a light pole and smash the brains out of his skull with a bat. I remember looking to my left and knowing that Joe would have been sitting right there. Now when anything cool like that happens, it's alright but not what it should be. It never will and that will always bug me. I can't think about it too much or I'll do something really stupid.

I leave for France in a few hours. It was a cool stay here. I thought it would be a good idea to come here and I'm glad I did it. Easily one of the more interesting places I've been to in awhile. I feel good about getting out of here though. A day off is good but it's good to be back at work.

I have been depressed a lot lately. I don't know what it is. Maybe it's a result of all the bullshit I've endured over the last several months. I am adrift. I am on my own. No one knows me all that well. I feel good about this and will do my best to distance myself even more from people. I don't know why this occurs to me as the thing to do, but it does. When you mix with people too much, that's when all your troubles begin. I guess I am tired of the way people make me feel when I get too involved with them. I always seem to lose something. I don't know if it's bad luck, bad choices or what, but I know that I am always alright on my own. People make me hurt when I get too close to them. I don't think it's anything they try to do, it must be something in me. I think it's lame to blame others for pain you're feeling. If you can't handle it, move to some place you can. Well, here I am. Nowhere suits me fine. Nowhere feels just right a lot of the time.

02-18-97 Köln Germany: 0720 hrs. Doing the European dawn breakfast ritual. I have been here so many times before. In 45 minutes I go to do a voice over for Saturn, a car company. Yes, even in the middle of a press tour, I am able to do even more! I am doing the voice over because they are paying me ten thousand dollars. I need money to pay the lawyers who are defending me from the mean record company millionaire who thinks he owns me. The lawyers need more money to eat more lunches and buy more suits. I must pay them or they will leave me to get torn to shreds by the other lawyers. Ten thousand dollars is a handful of sand thrown into the Grand Canyon as far as what they are owed.

Fact is, Terry Ellis of Imago Records is trying to destroy me. It's hard to walk around with all this in my head and deal with all the things I have to. Oh, it's just business, you know. No big deal. Just a drama involving people who want to own other people and don't care about the music and the hapless musicians caught up in the bind.

Ellis lost his deal with BMG and now runs his office with no staff. He has been selling off all the bands on Imago like they were cattle. He's not even in business and he wants to put out our records. I went to Dreamworks and he is suing me for breach of contract. It's going to be expensive and as always, the musician gets screwed and the lawyers and the bosses clean up. I don't hate the guy, he's just a business man and all I am to him is a piece of property. I don't put any emotion into it, it's just business. Still, it doesn't make for smooth sailing.

All the years of hardening myself has paid off. This is the time I need to utilize all my inner resources to deal with the work and stress that the coming months will bring. This case has nothing to do with anyone in the band. It's just me, lawyers and management. It has been hard on my managers, Gail and Richard, who have been generating the paperwork and working with the litigating lawyers and the labels. They're the ones who deal with it on a more day to day basis, especially Gail. I don't see where she gets all the energy to deal with these fuckers. This, along with other factors, makes my days very hard to get through. It is hard. In my mind, they can't break me. As long as I keep to myself and don't confide in anyone, I will be alright. When you start spilling your guts to people, you weaken the rivets in your frame. There are ways to get the stress out. I have shows to do and weights to lift. When things get tough, I have always found that the best thing to do is deal with it on your own as much as possible. No one will ever understand what you're going through. They have their own thing they're dealing with. Everyone has tough things to deal with in their life and don't want you adding to their burden unless they're getting paid to carry it. As much as I hate the lawyers in this whole thing, I kind of get off on them as well. They are the truth. They are there to make money off your misfortune and nothing more. When the case is over, they're on to the next case and sometimes when they see each other in the hall, they shake hands and laugh about that last case. They both made a ton of money so what's the problem? They are crass and they know it. At least they don't hide it. Right on. I love it when it gets brutal. This is what it's all about.

Sometimes it's hard to rally myself to stand up to this every day but I find the way to do it. As bad as things get, I have been through worse. Terry Ellis will never break me. He's playing for money, I am playing for my life. 'I am alone' is my mantra.

02-19-97 Hamburg Germany: 0810 hrs. In the breakfast room of the hotel. I was in this hotel a few months ago.

Doing all these interviews puts a funny slant on artistic integrity for me. What's there to talk about with these people? The integrity of the work will never be fully understood by those who didn't create it in the first place so what's the use of critics? I guess the weak need to be fed so they give them fake jobs.

Thinking about it this way makes all these interviews hard to do. It feels more redundant than ever. Yesterday a journalist tried to assign all the values, rules and regulations of punk rock to me. That pissed me off. A bunch of fucking weak links in the food chain and I have to adhere to their values? What tragic, fucked up, make-believe world was this idiot living in? I saw a picture of the Sex Pistols playing some outdoor festival yesterday. Johnny Rotten – what a pathetic heap of crap that guy turned out to be. That's punk rock. There's your leader, you dumb pieces of shit. Fetch.

02-20-97 Stockholm Sweden: 0740 hrs. Another day, another breakfast room, another cup of throat-ripping Euro hotel coffee. This stuff puts the 'G' in grind, I'll say.

I saw a picture of the Oasis guy hanging out with Mick Jagger. The old-school and the dropped-out-of-school meeting. What Oasis don't know is that they will be out of the picture so fast it will make their heads spin. I just hope the lads invest their money because it's not lasting for long. I wonder what their conversation was like? 'You're brilliant mate!' 'No, you're brilliant mate!' It's funny to see the Stones and then look at footage of the Beatles. I love both bands but I get the idea that the Stones are major posers. Mick and Keith's detachment is a little too well-studied for me. The Stones are awesome but Mick Jagger does not possess a drop of soul in his body. That's why I like them. The Stones are evil, like Exxon. How about that song they were playing on the Steel Wheels tour? 'Between a Rock and a Hard Place'. There's Mick out there singing about how the poor are having a hard time of it. It was like seeing Satan cry for the homeless. A great acting job. You think with all the lines in Jagger's face, he could find some soul in there. I guess after you spend your entire life mimicking, you get lost. I see this image in my head of Keith Richards tipping his cigarette ash into the outstretched hand of a beggar.

And how about that London music scene? That's a music scene? No music, just a scene. Weekly music newspapers move faster than the sickly little bands can cough and stare at their feet while they limply crank out records. The records they make are not made to be bought or listened to. They're only made to be reviewed by frustrated people who, after failing at all else, now make a living slinging endless pseudo-intellectual drivel onto paper that rings so cheap it disgraces the poor tree that was sacrificed to make it.

The interviews have been going well enough but I don't know where I'm getting the energy to do them all. Maybe it's because I'm so fucking mad all the time about the level of bullshit that this business runs on that I'm drawing energy from it. Nothing like a little fury in the gas tank to get you down the road.

02-21-97 Oslo Norway: 0825 hrs. Lots of snow outside. Today will be interesting, Scandinavia is a strange place. I have always found the people to be friendly enough but enigmatic. I don't know if I have ever done any press in Norway.

11.50 p.m. Copenhagen Denmark: The interview thing was really strange today. I was interviewed by this one kid and one of his opening shots was that he played our record to one of his friends and he said that it was not hardcore. I don't know why I cared what this guy said. For some reason it got to me and I decided to work him a little. I told him to call his friend down here and I would beat the hell out of both of them and there would be their hardcore experience for the day. I waited for him to make the call. He didn't of course. He said that he was so nervous that now he couldn't ask any more questions. I bet there won't be a favorably slanted interview in that magazine. I don't care. You give it and you get it back. The other guy who interviewed me was introduced as the leading interviewer in all of Norway. Whatever the hell that means. He just sat in front of me, smoked, drank beer and was boring. Knut Hamsun, the great writer, was Norwegian, anything else? OK. Norway, it was great.

02-26-97 Milano Italy: 0918 hrs. I keep imagining that this is the Italy that Hemingway saw. The hotel is old and very grand. Last night I looked out at the fountain and the rooftops and tried to imagine Hemingway standing in the same place. What words would he use to describe what I saw?

Italy is one of the most beautiful places I have ever seen. It's great to be here and not have to do a show. I like the people but I don't like doing shows here at all. Bad PA's, criminal promoters, the worst. But for mood and food, architecture and weather, Italy is amazing. I think Pisa is one of the most incredible cities. The canals at sunset, the streets at night.

Too burnt to write much now. The interviews and travel have taken it out of me. Tomorrow I will be in Spain. How great is Spain? I have had many good times there. The first time I went there I was seventeen. I saw a bullfight and the matador got gored pretty bad. He didn't get killed but he got carried out of there. The bull was thrashing him pretty bad. The bull had him pinned against the wall and was driving into him with his horns. I took pictures.

'Were you there for the end of the world, man?'

'Yeah, man! I took pictures!'

03-02-97 NYC NY: Back from the press trip. I got in last night. Took a second to get used to NYC belligerence factor. Customs guy didn't look at my passport and almost missed the customs form with his stamp he was so bored. Nothing like this place.

Drank a cup of coffee in the usual place, sat in the regular seat. I got bored after half an hour. Other than that, seems like not much has changed over the last three months in the Village. I went to the record store last night and checked that out. No one bothered me.

I have depositions on Tuesday and Wednesday. Not looking forward to it but on the other hand I don't think they can do anything to me anymore. I have grown pretty numb to the whole thing. Not like I am not paying attention or anything, just I don't freak out at the bullshit that surrounds all of this like I used to. There's nothing like sitting in a suit across from a corny lawyer that I could kill with my hands, having to take his shit. This guy is hilarious. No balls. He gets all bent out of shape and goes in and out of character. He telegraphs all his moves. I can almost ask myself his next question because you always know the direction he's going in. The fact that he has nothing really to ask me makes it all the more ridiculous. 'Mr Rollins, have you ever heard of a magazine called *Details*?'

'Yes.'

'Would this be you on the cover?'
'Yes.'
' "Imago is a cool label to be on." Did you say that?'
'I guess I did if it's printed there on the page.'
'So the label was as you say, "cool"?'
'Sure.'
'Define "cool." '
Do eight hours of this for a few days and get back to me.

I have been doing a lot of thinking. I see the errors of my ways a little more clearly now. I learned a lot from a book I just read. There are some things I will never do again. I will leave people alone more often than ever. I see now that the things I did as an attempt at friendliness were oppressive and a drag. No wonder people acted as they did, I gave them no choice.

So, I am sorry. I am sorry and I never meant any harm. I will be a better person.

To myself, these reminders: Don't think that you can do any good. Don't tell people things. Don't try to get them to be you. For instance, don't make them tapes of songs that they have never heard. All you are doing is trying to impress them and make them more like you by getting them to like the same things you do. You want the company of others as long as they are like you. If they are different, you try to make them into you. That might be the reason you lost the nice girl.

03-03-97 NYC NY: Good workout tonight. Trooped there through shitty weather. For a minute I didn't want to go. Figured it was too fucked up outside. It makes me mad how lame I can be sometimes. Soon as I walked in and saw all the lame motherfuckers in there, I knew I had done the right thing by going. I like working out with people around. It makes me go harder. I just want to kill.

No depositions tomorrow. Their lawyer is sick. Maybe he couldn't stand himself any longer. Depos will now be re-scheduled to the beginning of April. This bullshit is such a pain in the ass. Terry Ellis should leave me alone. It's only now that I see the extent to which this man wastes my time.

It's a pretty rough deal. You get signed to a label and basically they loan you the money to make a record. They get the money back and ownership of your record. That's a great deal if you own the label. The bands are out picking cotton.

03-04-97 NYC NY: I have hours to kill before I have to do press. I have to talk to someone over at *Spin* radio. They have a radio station now, isn't that just so cute? I am so lucky. I get to go and talk to a woman who works for a magazine who rips me every chance they get. Well, the magazine is so poorly written, it's more their problem than anyone else's. I feel bad for their readership. No I don't. I wonder what this will be like.

So what am I feeling now? Some boredom and a craving to go to the gym. That will have to wait until tonight. I don't want to talk to anyone outside of business. I have some calls to make today and I don't look forward to them. They are a reminder of a stupid person that I once was. I am looking forward to getting over the last year. I am looking forward to not being everyone's boy. Things are getting better as the weeks go by. Maybe by this time next year, things will be alright.

Later: I got through a little of the interview with the *Spin* lady and then I couldn't take the hypocrisy anymore. I told her something like I have no respect for her or her publication. She was cool and said that she was sincere and trying to make a difference. I can't remember now, I am wondering if I used my now standard 'Hitler was sincere, who cares about sincere?' line with her. At one point she gave up and that was it. She seemed like a nice enough lady but you know, you are no better than the people you work for so flick it. The press lady who has been taking me around really bummed on that one. I think I bum her out all the time though. The company she works for works with Sting so when I am in there, I can't help but rip on the guy. I saw that his last record only went gold here and said something like, 'Good. It's about time he fell off' and they bummed. I also bummed them out when I said that when I heard his crap song, 'Let Your Soul Be Your Pilot' I was trapped in a crowded car in Grenada, Spain and couldn't beat the driver to death with a baseball bat. With a trembling voice, the press lady said, 'He wrote that song for his friend who had AIDS.' Like this is supposed to shut me up, right? I think I said something like, 'If I was dying of AIDS and someone wrote a cloying, moronic song like that to me, I'd rally my remaining strength and beat that person to death with my bare hands.' Of course, I'm winding the lady up a little but she took it hard. At least she's dedicated to him. I think ol' Sting is very talented actually. I think his wife is hilarious. I wonder if anyone ever just tells her to shut the fuck up. I would in a hot minute but then again I'm negative, bitter and on my way down.

03-05-97 NYC NY: Had to do an interview about Black Flag today. I wasn't going to do it but I was the only one who he had not interviewed so I had to make sure I got my two cents in. He said that Ginn had nothing good to say about me but he also had nothing good to say anyone in the band. You would figure that he would have liked at least one of us.

It was depressing to go back to that bullshit. Greg will always hate me and the rest of the people in the band. I ask people who know him why he doesn't like me and they basically say the same thing, that I am successful and he's mad about that. I don't get that at all. He's the one with all the talent. It was always evident that you were dealing with a higher power when dealing with Ginn. He was one of those guys. One of the great ones. I don't care all that much that he doesn't like me. Of course, I wish things were different but it's been this way for so long, I have gotten used to it. It's Tuesday, Greg Ginn hates me and I have to get on the R train. It's like that.

I have tonight on my hands but I don't feel like doing anything. I wish I could just fall asleep. I feel like getting some coffee but where I am is far from everything.

Today was a drag. Too many people get in my face in this place. Today was no exception. The coffee place was fucked up. No longer a place to hang out. I will get used to being locked away from people from now on. When they need the idiot to talk to they will have to find another one.

03-06-97 En route to LA: Today was another depressing one. American press is such a vicious little game of bullshit. Some of these people are so crass. Talked to a man from *Alternative Press* today. He says he is sorry about the fucked up article his shitty magazine did on me a long time ago and wants to do another one. I told him that I was thankful that he took the time to talk to me and all and I would think about doing something in the future. It was good to hang up the phone. I am sure he means well. I know that management will not be happy about that but I just don't think one should come back to the place where one got torn up. It's basically saying that it's OK to fuck me up. That you can do it and at the end of the day, I really didn't mind all that much. At this point I don't care. I think we can live without doing all the stupid magazines. I know *Spin* won't want to talk to me. Thank goodness. A bigger load of crap between covers would be hard to find.

03-10-97 Orlando FL: Tonight was one for the books. I came here to be at the NARM thing. The North American Recording Something. Universal had a soiree and I was there to meet people and do photos with the reps for accounts, Target, Block Buster, etc. I didn't mind. I always like to meet the people who actually move the records into the stores. They're the ones who make it happen. I am asked to do photos with some Universal artists and I said sure. All of a sudden I'm in this half circle with all these people and we're standing around some Universal big wig, an ancient man who winced when I shook his hand. Chris ck is to my right. I tell him that I really like what he does. He just stares at me and says nothing. OK. I am introduced to Erykah Badu and I smile and say hello and she just looks at me. OK. Those two, Mary Blige and I were doing all these photos and it's all so fake. Really friendly! I look off to my right, all the way at the end of the half-circle of people. Oh god. Sammy Hagar. What a strangely eclectic evening this is turning into.

The photos are over with and now it's time for me to stand in one place and meet a bunch of people and have my photo taken with them. I don't mind. They're all cool and it's not so bad. I look over at a table and see Mary and Eryka, am I allowed to be on a first name basis? *Hello Eryka? It's Henry, Henry Rollins, I met you briefly at the NARM soiree in the Universal tent in Orlando last week? I thought I would call to say hi! Hello? Hello? Eryka? Are you there?* Anyway, they're sitting at this table with some other people and there's two serious bodyguards, impeccably dressed, standing by, glaring at people who walk too near the table. No one got to meet them. Great way to get the people who order your records to remember you. I'll try that next time. I'll carry Sting's head around on a stick and see where it gets me.

The only celeb type I got to meet was Sammy Hagar. He was the only one of the Universal artists who would talk to me. He was cool. I have been working on a book with David Lee Roth and it's not the most pro-Hagar camp on that side and I was thinking what DLR would say if he saw me shaking hands with ol' Sammy but what the hell, he was cool and it was an interesting night. It was intense as hell seeing him that close. I might not have any of the Van Halen records he's on but I still listen to Montrose. Isn't it funny that you can rip on a guy and then you meet him and he's cool, you think he's alright now? Makes me think that I was full of shit the whole time. Now will I have to be nice to one of the guys in U2 if he's cool to me? What if everyone in the world was cool to me, then what? I would have to like everybody. I feel like my entire body has been licked by a dog. No! We must keep hating! At least a little every day. Keeps the blood thin. Humor without malice is like a Pat Boone record on eleven. Malice without humor is like the LAPD. So now do I get to tell everyone about my new friends. Eryka, Mary, Chris and SAMMY HAGAR, MAAAN?!!

03-11-97 Somewhere FL: Did an interview this morning with a DJ named Bubba the Love Sponge. This guy was wild. Adam and I were there for 'Lesbian Tuesday'. He gets women to call in and go down on each other while supposedly holding the phone in proximity to the action. He is a massive man, 250 pounds at least. He is harsh to people on the phone. 'You're just a dumb bitch,' and he hangs up on the lesbian caller. I sat there wincing and laughing the entire time. The day before was 'Redneck Monday' where he baits rednecks and gets them so pissed off that sometimes they come down to the station. The guy was a riot. He called Adam the promo man a 'Jabba the Hut bearded bitch'. He told me that he was going to put out a Best of Bubba CD at some point and he would send it to me when it came out. If it's anything like what I heard, look out.

03-15-97 Toronto Canada: Been doing press stuff every day. It's depressing but I am sticking it out. Some people try to fuck with me but it's cool. I have been keeping to myself at night. This will be a long and lonely year. I think the best thing to do is pull in and deal with it.

One of the interviewer guys showed me an article with a drawing of me and the title said 'Henry Rollins Must Be Stopped'. OK. So, come on over and stop me. I'll wait. I guess the interviewer was trying to wind me up and get a reaction out of me. Not the kind of thing that makes me stand up on my hind legs.

03-25-97 LA CA: Our new record, *Come in and Burn* came out today. I leave for band practice tomorrow morning. I have been doing press and promotion since late January. It has been a long trip. I have been all over the world doing interviews and meeting record company and retail people. I am looking forward to finally getting to the music part of all of this.

03-26-97 NYC NY: 6.22 p.m. Got to the city around two this morning. Went to band practice and we played a bunch of new stuff. My voice held out pretty well considering it was my first day. I will have to start in slow and get into it.

The guys told me they've been reading reviews of the record and they're not good. I wonder what we could possibly do to get a good review? I don't lose a great deal of sleep over what some critic thinks of what we do.

If you stick to your guns and do what you do you get slammed. I think you have to go techno or something. It seems like a band has to be a multi-genre event nowadays. We have guitar, bass, drums and me. We do our thing as good as we can. We spent well over a year working our asses off on this music and it seems that it's still not good enough for the guys who sit on their asses and make money being critics. What really matters is how we feel about the music. Music is for people, not for critics.

I am in a rented room near the practice space. I will be going to the gym soon. I don't have a good time in New York anymore. I get too many phone calls and I associate the city with lots of bad times in my life. The streets make me hostile. People fuck with me and it makes it hard to keep my cool. I hope I don't do something I regret. It's hard to take the sneers and petty bullshit from these fakes. I should attack a few of them so they will tell their friends not to fuck with the animal. On the other hand, I shouldn't care about these people who work on their hair so much. The village is hilarious.

It's only when I am in hotels that I ever watch television. If you don't watch too much TV, it's very strange when you do. Tonight's items were intense: a car show that featured new and futuristic models. The one that stuck out the most was a car that looked like an urban assault vehicle. The headlights were behind screens and it had roof lights. It looked like it should have been in a science fiction film. Machine gun turrets optional. The car company said it was a 'family car'. Photos of Michael Jackson's child are now on the cover of a magazine and commanded the highest price ever paid by the media for a photo session. He looks like a white kid. I don't see a black father in there at all. On the news, some white kids nearly beat a black kid to death in Chicago. The kid is in a coma right now. I know it is a totally generic sentiment but WHAT THE FUCK IS UP WITH THESE PEOPLE? They showed a photo of the kid, obviously before his beating. He was one big smile. Things like this upset me a lot more than they probably should.

11.28 p.m.: Workout was pretty good. Got some good sets in. That place is a trip. Whenever I go in there, the people seem to get stranger and stranger. One guy was wearing all this jewelry and looked like Vanilla Ice. Being in there makes me hostile. I see these fucking people and it makes me mad. On the bench, the bar was slippery, probably some guy's hair care products. I think that men should not be allowed to use hair care products. If they do, they should be made to wear a sign that says, 'I am a guy who spends a lot of time on his hair.'

I have to get up early and get ready for band practice. I want to fucking break shit.

03-27-97 NYC NY: 0256 hrs. Hard to get to sleep because of the time change. Watched the news for a while. I saw an ad for Folger's instant coffee. A woman pours some Folger's instant into a cup and adds boiling water and the last shot is her drinking this swill and smiling. Whenever I think of Folger's coffee I remember that Abigail Folger was one of the people killed at Sharon Tate's house in the Helter Skelter thing. Television makes me disgusted with people. Have you ever seen the ad where the waiter serves Folger's crystals to his diners and they don't know it's instant coffee. What, are they dumb as a bag of stumps?

The *Hard Copy* type shows are sad. The celebrity types are pathetic. I watched some of the half hour comedy shows. Depressing as hell. The talk shows where they get people to act like fools for the amusement or, aptly, abusement, of others are hard to watch. Good thing I like to read books.

I have done over three hundred interviews this year so far. I have traveled all over the world. I have worked hard and have had very few days to myself. I have worked very hard for the welfare of the band and I am not sure if they will ever know the extent that I have put myself on the line to make things good for all of us. It doesn't matter. It's part of it.

I might be wrong but today I sensed a bit of apathy when I told the guys about what was happening with the record. I can't tell if they are into it or not. I hope so. There has been a lot of work done on this thing.

03-27-97 NYC NY: 11.37 p.m. Band practice was better today. It's still a little sluggish. It will get better as it goes. My voice is good not great. I am hoping that it will get stronger after a few days.

The press lady read the review we got in *Entertainment Weekly*. I don't think it was all that bad. The interviewer quoted me out of context so I will have to tell the truth about him. When he interviewed me a few months ago I asked him a few questions of my own. I asked if he thought *EW* was a good magazine. He said he thought it was OK. I asked him if he would buy it on a newsstand or only read it on an airplane, he said that he would not buy it. I asked him why he took the job. He said he was interested in the money. He said he thinks he sold out. So, we're dealing with a man who doesn't like his job and who has contempt for the magazine he works for. I will be passing along this information to his magazine. I think his workmates should know. What a coward. I wonder if he calls himself a man.

The gym was pretty good tonight. Not as many jokers as last night. Depressed as usual. I don't know what it is, maybe the accumulated stress and failures of my life. Now that we are in the media eye right now I feel more self-conscious than usual.

I get confused with lyric writing when I read our press. What is a guy supposed to do? You write like you feel it and that's it right? They say I am a fake because onstage I am full on and then when I am being interviewed, I am a nice guy. Well, that's good to hear. Now I guess it's time to be that guy all the time. Fuck being nice. For me, it is an act. To be nice all the time, to be fucking civilized with what I know, with what I have been through, fuck it. Why be cool to swine? I reckon sometimes I should just be fucked to almost everyone. Especially in this town where they talk too fucking much and stare too much and get in my face. I think that I should use less restraint.

Tonight's television hilarity. A house full of people killed themselves to get their bodies taken away on a spaceship. A cult of computer operators who made websites and made a lot of money. They all poisoned themselves and died in shifts. Let's see. I am smart and rich and now I will kill myself so I can join the space brothers, whose ship is trailing behind the Hale-Bopp comet. I am in my twenties and I think now is the time to go to space and onto the next level. These people are funny like Scientologists. Hilarious like professional golfers. *Hello, I am a professional golfer. I have devoted my whole life to knocking a ball around a lawn.* How weak is that? Does anyone fuck these guys? Ladies, what the fuck are you thinking? Don't fuck golf pros! Don't give people like this an inch. On the other hand, do whatever the fuck you want. You buy so much shitty music and idolize actors and stupid musicians, why shouldn't you fuck golf pros?

I am looking forward to going on tour. I don't look forward to life like I did years ago. I will not kill myself but I don't care about having a long life. The most I could get done is listen to some music and read some books, other than that, there has been a lot of disappointment in my life. My failures in relationships and the death of my friend make me feel like life is a gyp and the game is being run by weaklings. One of the only ways I feel good is to get onstage and let it rip. I have been cool to too many people and have been burned in the process. I learn all my lessons the hard way.

03-28-97 NYC NY: 0230 hrs. There were some highlights from the press trip. I will recount them in the weeks to come. It is always a pain in the ass to deal with the silly press people of England. The NME guy was great. A fat piece of shit with nothing on his mind who immediately showed himself out to be the cruel failure in human engineering that he was. Some people should be drowned in warm water at infancy. We would end up with less like this pathetic mouth breather. He said that useless pop music was good and that 'monolithic' stuff like ours was ruining music. He said that good music was disposable and temporary. I looked at this flesh bag and saw where he was coming from. He thought his jaded cynicism was intellect. I asked him about the disposability factor of Al Green, James Brown, Aretha Franklin or Sam Cooke. He didn't have a lot to say about that. Now shouldn't you just club this guy like a baby seal? Just get it over with. His mother would have thanked me.

I'm tired of taking shit from these little mouths. I'm tired of hearing shit spewed my way by those who never get out there and get into the mix.

We put the band's video press kit on some cable channels so people other than critics and industry types could see it. I get e-mail from someone at *Spin* magazine wanting a statement about this because they're going to do an article about it on their online magazine. I could tell from the tone of the letter that she wanted me to defend myself against the allegations they were going to bring against me. OK, you have pushed me and now I will have to push back. I don't think you'll like it too much.

I have nothing to lose. I am not married. I am not in love with anyone and I do not care all that much about material possessions or my life. That makes it possible to go through the day-to-day bullshit.

7.04 p.m.: Today sucked. Lasted about three songs and then my voice fell apart. I think I overdid it the two days before. It's hard to take. It makes me want to quit. I know I have to go through another year of hoping the throat works. I'll have to be very careful. I will have to ease into it all in the coming weeks. I was bumming hard this afternoon. From the collarbone down I am ready. It's hard for me to be able to hit it so hard with the rest of my body and have to be so careful with my throat.

04-03-97 NYC NY: 7.25 p.m. Voice better and holding up well. Band practice has been fairly raging.

I will never work as hard on another record again. You're not worth it. All those interviews and waking up at the crack of dawn to go everywhere and do all the hard work is just ridiculous. Why bother when you don't notice or respond? I have been foolish. I was stupid to believe that you could measure up. I give you motherfuckers much too much. I try too hard to be the best I can be. What a waste of time.

Looking forward to the shows more than ever now. I only live to fuck you up. I will continue to punish my body to make it harder and more resistant to pain. It's not going to go like you think it's going to go. Fuck all y'all.

04-04-97 NYC NY: 0103 hrs. Good lift tonight. I like it when my shins bleed when I deadlift. Very inspiring. While I hit my work sets, Green Day was coming over the PA. It made me so aggravated to be trapped in a room full of iron and that pussy music that I pulled hard as hell. During the last set, it was Candle Box. Brutal. I pulled that one hard and slammed it down hard. My hands are a little swollen but that will go away in a few hours. I have to do an anti-heroin public service announcement in the morning and then I have the afternoon off until band practice.

My pain threshold is going farther out as I hit the heavier lifts. I must maintain a good level of pain all the time to be able to withstand the bullshit that will come with the tour. I want to go now and get into it. The waiting is hard to take. The longer I wait, the more rage-filled I become. I live to confront. The only time I feel alive is when I am defying. Age, contemporary music trends – whatever you got.

04-09-97 NYC NY: 0108 hrs. I got a phone call at band practice from a woman who works at a magazine called *Time Out*. She wanted me to make a statement about the song we did with Ru Paul and why it didn't come out. She said the word is that Dream Works was afraid that me working with a gay man would damage my 'hardcore image' and that's why the track was not used on a compilation album put together by Elektra last year. We did that song in December 1995. That's how old this is. I told her why the track didn't come out. The reason is that Dream Works didn't want another major label to put out something around the time they were trying to put out our record. I agreed with them and I still do. This is typical of a shitty magazine trying to have a go at me. I told her that I now know that she and her magazine are full of shit. She said that she was just doing her job. I told her that is what people in Nazi Germany said. I thought that was the end of it and this idiot calls me back to talk more shit. This 'article' has nothing to do with anything, just to fuck with me.

Why do people fuck with me? I told her that she should go pick on Newt Gingrich. It just so happened that Ru Paul was in the building today. I told him all about it and he thought they were full of shit as well. Fuck these people. I am tired of trying to be cool to people. I see where it gets me. I see that some people think they can fuck with me. Well, it's time to turn that one around. I will eventually catch up with the wrongdoers and they will have to deal with me on some level. Until then, I am no one's friend. Don't write me any fucking letters, don't talk to me on the fucking street. It's not going to go like you think.

So now I'm tired of writing in this fucking book. I get fucked with more than anyone I know. You go out there and kick ass and then have to take it from these little motherfuckers and tell me the mood it puts you in. The only thing I can think of is to start doing more for myself. Start keeping the money I make instead of giving it to artists so they can do their thing. All I get out of that is bills and people calling me names. If I'm going to get fucked with I might as well start putting it away so I can get out and never bother with people again. Don't wonder why I get pissed off all the time.

04-12-97 NYC NY: It's Saturday. We are days away from starting the tour. We have three shows locally this coming week, then we play on *Saturday Night Live* and then we take off for Germany. It will be a long year. Management said that tickets are going OK in Europe. That's cool. It might be that we will go back to the way it was in the beginning, when we played a lot outside of America because that's where people would come to see us.

What is on my mind is the next move to be made. If you think I am going to depend on you for my next meal you got another think coming. I have never had any faith in you and have always known I was on my own. I will never allow myself to feel betrayed by anyone. I know that people are in it for themselves and they only care about number one. That's why I always looked upfield and always went at everything with a survivalist attitude. By the time I was 21, I knew all about 'fans' and how much you can depend on them to come through when you deliver the goods. That's why I don't make records for people. I make them for myself. Otherwise you just let yourself in for a bad time.

You won't starve me. You won't make me homeless. Your reporters and critics can take their cheap shots. You can do whatever you want. You will not break me. You are welcome to try of course, I love a good challenge. I have nothing to lose that I can't lose. Some material property and that's it. You murdered my friend. The woman I wanted didn't want me, I don't have any great, overwhelming love of life, it really doesn't matter. I only live to defy you now, so let's get it on you bitches.

Much better now. I feel OK with all of the bad news but I know that the guys in the band will not take it so well. I don't depend on their gung-ho spirit. I know that they will leave and pursue different things and I don't blame them at all.

I notice that things are coming full-circle. We will soon be back in the small places. Like I said, I don't care for myself but I don't think the guys will be able to deal with it. I don't know if they like playing enough to go back to the low level of things. I don't think they will be into it. I do think that is what's on the horizon.

Don't get to the point where you're burning lean tissue and you don't have what it takes to withstand the ravages of the hellish world around you. I am hollowing myself out. I have been here before. I am good at being a dead man. The less you have, the less they can take off you. The less you appear, the less they see. A samurai on the long march.

04-15-97 Providence RI: Played pretty well tonight. I liked it better than last night. Last night was the first show of the tour. We played in New Jersey. Tonight's crowd was a little on the still side but it was a Tuesday night. I don't know if people dig the new material. Not much I can do about that at this point.

I played hard tonight and will play harder as it goes on. Pain is what rules me now. There's a lot of hostility around me. I get hostile e-mail, mean reviews, etc.

I am alone in a hotel room and I can't wait to play again tomorrow. I am tired but still thinking about the night. I love to play gigs. It's so hard. I think this is going to be a hard year for us. Best thing to do is keep to myself and stay lean. I never thought I had many friends ever but I get the feeling now that I have less. I don't know why but I sense there's a bad feeling in the air. As far as keeping my skin thick and my numbers small, I have always done this and will continue to do so. I will not be broken.

04-16-97 New Haven CT: At Toad's again. We were here a few months ago. Tickets are not going well. I was told by our road manager that tickets are not going well in Europe either. Could it be that we are now becoming obscure? It puts a strange tension on things. It makes me feel illegitimate somehow. The new album is solid. The set is good and the band is playing well but no one seems interested. It makes me wonder what this year will be like. If anything, it's going to make for a good story, if you want to read about a band going down the tubes.

The band's morale is good. I am surprised. I figured they would be all fucked up about things. Doubt if they're all that happy about it but they seem OK. They are good guys.

I'm looking forward to playing tonight. I always do. There won't be many people here tonight but we'll rock anyway. I wonder, since tickets and record sales are going so bad we will be playing all the shows this year.

I wouldn't be surprised if we can't afford to play all the shows. I can see doing shows all the way up to the European festival dates, getting off the road and then doing the Pacific Rim shows and ending it there. I don't know if we will go on or not. It's hilarious that you have to wonder if you will be able to afford to be able to work. Isn't that a pickle? Isn't that a cute thing I just wrote?

I have never had these problems to wrestle before and it's throwing me for a loop. It's time for an old dog to learn something. I don't know what the lesson is this time around. We work our asses off and do our best and that isn't good enough.

I have been doing press on the record since late last year. I spent many weeks on the road all over the world working. If I think too hard about it, I get exhausted. I live alone in a room wherever the work is and don't think about it too much. I think about women but I don't get too involved with these thoughts. I just can't see opening myself up to anyone. I have been feeling strange around people. When they talk to me, I can't seem to hear what they're saying, I just nod and stare. Also, I can't seem to remember people who I just met. I meet someone and then days later they come up to me and I just stare at them. When they remind me that I met them three days ago, I just nod. I don't know what that's about. It might be exhaustion and the never ending depression that seems to be taking permanent residence within me.

04-17-97 NYC NY: Saw Boozoo Chavis play at SOB's tonight. He was awesome. He and the band played great and they did 'Dog Hill'. I got left alone almost the whole time except for a guy asking to take my picture. I have every Boozoo record I have ever seen. I don't think there's a bad one out there.

We played well last night. I had a great time. The crowd was great except for the guy who kept spitting on me. He told me after the show that he thought I would have liked it. He was scared that I was going to hit him. I told him that I wouldn't and told him to have a good night. I guess he meant no harm. I am changing. In years past I would have hammered him without even thinking twice.

We went to NBC studios to rehearse for *Saturday Night Live*. It's like any other television show and the staff are friendly but seem jaded. We played well in rehearsal. I was walking around the hallways looking for the dressing room. I get lost immediately in places like this. I see a sign for the *Rosie O'Donnell Show*. Right at this moment, a guy comes up to me and says that if I'm interested, he can get me into her show which is taping right now. Cool guy right? I blow it immediately by telling him that I would like to gain entry to her show but I left my rifle at home and so there's no point. I think I'm a funny guy, right? The guy kind of looks at the ground and says, 'OK, sure. Well, have a good time here,' and leaves pretty bummed. Oh well. I can't help myself in situations like this. I can't stand that woman. I have seen her show and I think she's a bloated cow with no talent. I see her appeal though. She reminds a lot of mediocre people of themselves. This country has always applauded the mediocre and below average. 'Give us your poor, your semi-literate, your racist, your ignorant, your lazy – we'll put 'em in the Army, and teach 'em to smoke and kill!'

I have been enduring an especially deep depression. Tonight was really bad. I am unable to reach out to anyone, the thought of doing so repulses me and that makes me feel ashamed.

I can't wait to get on the road for real where all there is to do is play, lift and ride the pain. It's the only time when I feel remotely alright about myself. Days off and too much time on my hands in a place like NYC and all I want to do is break things and die. I don't know what to do about this.

04-18-97 NYC NY: Another day of rehearsal at NBC. We play the song over and over. Apparently Matthew Sweet was supposed to be playing on the show this week but we got the spot instead and his management was not too pleased and not especially thrilled that it was us instead. A source tells me that his management was yelling that he was a bigger artist and all. Oh brother, do people really talk like that? I don't believe that I have ever met the guy but people tell me he's cool. I am not familiar with his music. For some reason, I associate his music with women who don't fuck and men I would like to kill.

I am staying at the Paramount Hotel. Guests of SNL stay there. I would rather be downtown in my little room. I am in the Times Square neighborhood. Not a whole lot to do except be stopped by tourists and take pictures with them. Now that's my idea of a good time. The lobby is full of people posing out and being seen. People from here rip on LA residents for hanging out and being seen when they do the same thing here. It's all the same. They're all a bunch of posers. I'm in NYC, I'm going to go out and find some pizza.

04-20-97 NYC NY: 0107 hrs. We played on SNL last night. It was an interesting day and night to say the least.

They don't want band types to get lost, thrown in jail, whatever, so they kind of make you stay in the building from soundcheck to the end of the night. I was in there for hours.

I must admit, I had a bad attitude when I got there in the afternoon. I figured that Pam Anderson was going to be an idiot with no talent and a big attitude. She was pretty much the exact opposite. She was very friendly and extremely cool. It was easy to tell that she is sharp and she had her lines cold. She was at least as good if not better than most of the SNL cast. When she made jokes, they were at her own expense. I was impressed and it made me see that I was a jerk for judging her like that. As well, I figured that the Motley Crue guy would be a drag but he was actually cool to us.

We had been hoping to play two songs on the show. They run the show two times. They do a late afternoon version in front of a full audience to see how the show looks. We sat backstage and watched the show from the television that was in our room. There were parts that were really funny. They did another installment of this routine 'Goatboy' which is a guy who looks like a goat interviewing musicians from the past. On this one, they interview Pamela and Motley man as himself and then they bring out one of the cast doing a David Lee Roth impersonation. It was harsh. I hope that Dave didn't see it. The crowd went nuts. Goatboy tried to eat the hat the DLR guy was wearing, exposing his balding head and the DLR guy grabs that hat back, etc. It was brutal. People are hard on that guy.

We did two songs in the first run through. Then when it was time to do the show 'for real' we were told that we were going to do one song. I guess they didn't like us all that much. So we went out there and did our thing. I don't know how it went as those kind of things just kind of blow by and all of a sudden you're walking off and back to your room. At the end of the show, you get onstage and wave goodbye at the camera and pose out. In the earlier version of the show, I saw how the camera was going to film the scene and saw my placement with Pamela so I knew I had to do something the next time around.

When it came time to do the last bit, I grabbed a banana from catering on my way to the stage and when the camera was full on Pamela, I got next to her and peeled the banana and gave it the big oral sex show on prime time. After that was over we talked to the guy who was in the *Kids in the Hall*, I don't know his name but he's the 'I'm crushing your head!' guy. *Kids in the Hall* ruled. Meeting him was the best part of the whole ordeal. Otherwise it was a boring turn off that took too long.

04-22-97 Hamburg Germany: 0050 hrs. Got here several hours ago. Spent the day walking around, trying to stay awake. I got a good bunk on the bus which was waiting for us at the airport. Flight in was OK. No turbulence and no one talked to me. Read *A Swell Looking Babe* by Jim Thompson on the flight. Good not great.

Found some good stuff in the record store down the street and the record company people gave me some other cool stuff when I did some press in the afternoon.

Slept some and after walking around outside I am in the room waiting on sleep. In the room next to me a man coughs endlessly. He sounds lonely. He coughs abandoned planets out of his body onto the floor.

One of the interviewers asked me why I write so much about loneliness. I told her that people make me lonely because they let me down. They always fall below expectation and that's why I like them better on record and between the covers of books. It is the nature of the human experience. Being with a woman makes me lonely for a woman. I imagine that someone like me is in for a lot of disappointment. I think if you travel a lot you get lonely. It's the nature of so much movement. What these press shitheads never see is that loneliness is no bad thing for me. It's not the greatest feeling all the time but sometimes it is, absolutely. People who can't stand being alone for the smallest amount of time are boring to me. Sometimes there's nothing better than to want for what's not there. I don't like the idea of being satisfied all the time. There's times that I want nothing more than to be tired and stressed and overworked. At least it's memorable.

I went out of the hotel a little before midnight tonight. No one is on the street until I pass two guys who call out my name and pull out photo books that have pictures of me in them for me to sign and then they pull out the cameras and we do photos. How the hell they knew where we were staying is beyond me. Can't go out even late and not have someone get in my face. Everything is an event. Going places is like a Broadway play. People are a drag.

Looking forward to the shows coming up. It's good to finally be out in it and out of New York. It seems that every year we go out the guys are not on tour but merely away from home for a while. Their attitude towards life on the road has changed. It's to be expected, I guess. I turned out different than everyone I know.

04-24-97 Berlin Germany: In front of the venue waiting to drive overnight to Köln. The Hamburg show was cool. The sound was hard to deal with but I hung on. The Berlin show was a different story. It was feedback hell. My voice blew out in a few songs and the rest of the set I had to fight it. Now my voice is fucked and I'm pissed. I was blowing out left and right. When I can't hear myself and have to deal with feedback I have a bad time. It shakes my concentration and fucks me up.

Today will be a day off in Köln. I have some interview stuff but that's about it. I will work on my throat and try to keep it loose. I think I would have been OK if there wasn't so much damn noise on stage tonight. Made it a drag to play. We are doing long sets but they pass really fast. Seems like we're done before we start.

I want to have good shows more than anything. I was so happy after the Hamburg gig. I think that every show should be like that. I hated the Berlin show and wish I could do it over again.

Now I'm sitting on the bus waiting to leave. I don't feel lonely or anything. All I can think of is finding a gym in Köln and getting the onstage sound together. It's lucky for me that there's a day off now. My voice is fried. I wonder if I will be able to do all these shows. I better get my shit together. If I knew the right thing to do I would do it.

1139 hrs. Köln: We just got into the hotel. As soon as I walked in a guy I apparently met in Dublin awhile ago started talking to me. I had gotten one foot in the door and it starts. Sometimes I want to go on strike.

Today is a day off. I have to do some interview on the phone in a couple of hours and I have to find a gym and after that I have some time to myself. I would rather play of course but I have to feel lucky to have this day off for my feeble fucking throat, the bane of my existence.

04-26-97 Munich Germany: 2.30 p.m. We pulled in a few hours ago. Last night's show went pretty well. Throat held up OK. See if it stays steady for tonight. We are in a nowhere part of Munich. Luckily there's a gym around the corner from the venue so I can get a workout in soon. Will try to see what my legs can do today. Right knee in constant pain from the workout in New Haven.

I am boring and have nothing to tell. The gigs are good but eventless. They don't bother us and we don't bother them. The shows have been well attended and we have been playing well. Last night was the best one in the batch so far. I think that we'll be doing some good gigs this year. I am having a great time up there. As long as I can keep my voice hanging in there, I'll be OK.

Looks like we won't be playing in Oslo because we only sold seventy tickets and the promoter is freaking out. He says that he'll just pay us what he owes us and he'll get to skip the operating costs. We will have a day off in Stockholm. I know a good gym there so I can at least get a good workout in if nothing else. I don't want the guy's money. I don't want to get paid for a show I didn't play.

Depression keeps me at a low level. I get up for the shows and that's about it. Constant financial frustration is hard to live with. It's almost like you get punished for doing good. The more you give, the more you get screwed. I wonder what it is like for a successful band on tour to be able to have good production and all and be able to make a little money as well. It's hard to have been at this for so long and still have the tour manager have little good news to tell you. I think of all these other bands on their second album or whatever playing huge places and it somehow doesn't seem right but that's the way it is. Deal with it.

04-27-97 Munich Germany: 0036 hrs. A great crowd was there for us tonight. My throat died after three songs and the rest of the night I sounded like I was dead. I have an appointment with a doctor tomorrow when we get to Stuttgart.

Not much is going well for me these days. I am alone and my body is failing me at a critical time. All the training and work amounted to nothing. I don't see a lot to live for at this point. I hate to have thoughts like that but I do and that's it. Every day is depressing and hard to take. I'm getting tired of the stress. It's not as if I'm fighting the good fight. All I'm doing is burning myself out and for what? For nothing at all. I have spent a good deal of my life being a fool. It's hard not to tell myself that I should not be melted down for scrap metal. If you can't do the job then don't step up to the plate.

04-28-97 Paris France: 1.22 p.m. We didn't play last night and we are not playing tonight. I spent a good deal of the day at the hospital yesterday just trying to get my throat looked at. The guy finally checked me out at around soundcheck time. He hastily gave me a prescription for an antibiotic and sent me on my way. I went to soundcheck and sang two songs and had no voice. We canceled the show. I sat on the bus and watched all these people walk up and walk back to their cars as the PA was broken down and loaded back onto the trucks. Someone should shoot me.

We drove all night to Paris and we now have a night off. I feel totally worthless. I would give almost anything to be able to play every night. I am hoping it is just some kind of cold and that if I am really careful I will be able to play all the rest of the shows. I feel illegitimate being on a tour when I can't do the work. I am tired of feeling like this all the time. Every day I am filled with anxiety, wondering if I'll be able to pull off the show that night. It's nerve-wracking and no fun. I don't know what to do about it either. The voice coach says I have all the voice I have always had and all I have to do is warm up and stretch. I remember the 1994 tour and every night was like this and it sucked.

7.48 p.m.: Went to another doctor who at least seemed to have some time. He looked at my throat and said I have a nasty case of laryngitis. He sent me to the pharmacy to get some drugs. They gave me a syringe and an ampule of something. *Here ya go. Here's a needle and some crap. Shoot yourself up.* I had to have a guy come to my room and inject it in my ass cheek. Cortisone I think.

The weather is great and the sunset was beautiful. I could not live in Paris but for a couple of days at a time. It is one of the most beautiful places I have ever seen. We went to a small bar and had a sandwich and the place was ancient and cool. Waiters here have a different attitude than the ones in America. They have class and don't act as if they're doing you any favor by bringing you your order. It seems like you're on their time more than the other way around. It's cool in a way. They can do their job and not have to feel like the job of service is a lowly one. Everyone's in service one way or the other. It's the business I'm in.

04-30-97 Paris France: 5.50 p.m. Soundcheck went very well. I hope the whole gig can go that way. I just have to keep it cool and not blow out. My throat hurts a little now but I think that's OK.

We did a song on a television show last night. A lot of waiting around and one little song. After that the night was great because we went to see Nick Cave play. He was amazing as usual. He and the band are their own genre at this point. There's just no one else out there like Nick and what he does with the band stands on its own.

The high point for me was when he played 'Into My Arms' on his own. The place went nuts for every song. There was no room in the place. I had my back to the door. Paris loves the man and his band. It was great to see him there.

The first time I ever saw Nick with the Bad Seeds was summer 1984 in Bristol, UK. He was great then but nothing like the man he is now. Talk about development. There's so much depth to what he does now. It's more than a bunch of songs on a set list. Most bands I see, that's all it is, they play the songs on the set and you hear it and leave. With Nick it's much more. It's like seeing Johnny Cash. You get a sense of the whole man. Not many people pull that off these days when songs are just soundbytes – advertisements of what music could be.

11.52 p.m.: I was lying in the hotel bed this morning. I was half awake thinking about the dream I had last night. I was in a house. I wake up when a girl I know comes into my room. The first thing I notice is that the sheets are covered with blood. I ask her what happened but she ignores me. She looks strung out and her hair is all chopped up. I go out the front door and see men walking across the front lawn. For some reason this makes me angry. I go up to one of them and ask what the deal is. He's very tall and his skin was dark as coal. He ignores my anger and points to two apartments across the street that are being built. He tells me that the apartments are going to be filled with gangsters soon and the neighborhood is going to be very dangerous and he and his men are going from house to house warning people. I ask him if they were Crips and he says yes. That's the end of the dream.

After that I started thinking about girls and imagined I had a girlfriend I went out with on a regular basis. It made me laugh because in my mind I just said fuck it. I couldn't even be bothered to think about it. I like being on my own. The longer on this trail I go, the more I figure I'll always be alone. I think I am luckier than any married man. I like traveling the world alone. I hope I die in some foreign land, unnoticed.

I read a review of one of my books in one of those shitty English music magazines and the woman said that I write in that 'adjectives are for girls' type of writing or something like that and then said I was like Ernest Hemingway. Hey, I'd rather be compared to him than Anne Rice. I read the rest of the review and decided fuck all of you. You don't live in my reality and of course you and I will never see eye to eye, so fuck it. I'll always come from another planet. I'm never going to get any closer to your world than I am right now and I'm not going to make any attempts to get any closer. I'm going to do my thing and you can check it out or not. If you get something out of it, that's great, glad to have you aboard, but if you can't get to it, know that I'm not the one losing sleep over that. So fuck you review bitch, my blood pays your rent. You're the little fish underneath the shark.

05-01-97 Tilburg Holland: 11.24 p.m. Another good night for the throat. If I could have nights like this all the time, suicide would be out of the question. We are taking off on a ferry to England tonight. We are leaving in half an hour. We have a day off tomorrow and then we play in Spain and England back to back.

I have a meeting with Goldie tomorrow night. I don't know much about his music except that practically everyone I know thinks he's great. We might do a song together for a movie soundtrack. We'll see how it goes. I'd rather have the whole night off to myself but I can't see this taking too long. I have to get up early in the morning to get to the airport for Madrid. We are playing on a festival, a forty-minute set.

05-03-97 Madrid Spain: 11.33 p.m. We got here in the early afternoon. Hung out at the hotel and played a forty-minute set a few hours later. No soundcheck, rented equipment, you just get out there, do it and split. And that's what we did. For me it was a fairly eventless thing. Eight songs with no context. I thought we played alright. About as good as one does at a festival. People seemed to dig us OK. They stood there for the most part.

I had to do a press conference which was a joke. I counted nineteen walkmans in front of me. Dumb questions from idiots.

A waste of time. One thing is for sure, we don't fit into the contemporary music scene at all. I think we are getting too old for these people or something. Hey, maybe we're not good anymore. One of the only questions that kept me awake today during the press thing was the guy who asked me if I thought the *End of Silence* record was the best one I ever made. I told him I like the new one the best. It would be so easy to do that kind of stuff again. I don't know why people want things to be the same every time. If we wrote more stuff like that I would feel so stupid doing it. It would be so corny. Whatever. You do what you do and that's it.

I went into all of this knowing that it was going to be hard all the way. Hard going in and hard going out. Even at the beginning I knew that there was never going to be any quarter given. I am at the point now where people want to have a go at me and try to take me down a peg or two. What they don't know is that I got to where I am by means that would make them cry for their mothers. They will be cruel and brutal. The first ten years were good training for this. They have no idea what I am used to, what I am ready for and what I can deal with. I can see now that it's going to take all I have to withstand my future. There will be no friends at the end of the trail. Good thing I already know how to go it alone.

It's a disgusting thing to see a man come in hard and go out soft. I can see going out on your shield. I don't mind getting destroyed as long as I go out fighting. I think it's disgusting when men get soft with age or when their lifestyle changes and they cannot maintain the edge they used to have yet insist that they still have it. It's OK if you're a milkman or something but if you are a warrior then you have know that you will be going without certain things and it will hurt and you will want for these things and sometimes you will hate the way your life has played out. You can always get out but you will have to live with the shame of that. For myself I cannot. I cannot. At this point, this stand is the only thing I have. Everyone goes with their story, no matter what it is. This is mine. I'll take the shots that come with it.

I know that on the way out you will be spitting and cursing and calling me names. I am 36. I knew this as truth when I was 20. When you come with the knife, I will not be surprised. Also know that you'll leave with it stuck in your ribs. I have been awaiting your arrival for almost two decades. That's why I never get close, don't like compliments, don't feel an affinity with anyone. I'm on my own. Always have been, always will be and it's totally cool. Some music critic bitch can read these words and attempt to tear a strip off me but the truth is that if he does, it proves that he doesn't know. These people are soft. They are cautious. They are spectators. You always know what you are. I have never expected a fair shake. I have never expected equality. I have never believed in human rights or justice. I never believed that those things were options. The bottom line is, if you are living it, then you know. Otherwise you don't and everything you say is just assumption, projection and lies. For the millionth time: you go in hard, you go out hard. So?

05-04-97 London England: Almost midnight. Tonight's show in Brixton was cool but hard to pull off. First couple of songs in the monitors were so bad that my voice blew up and I had to relax and get it back. We went into 'Shame' and I could hear my voice was gone. Third song in and it was blown to bits. I almost panicked but kept it cool. I managed to get it under control and the rest of the show was OK. Now my throat hurts like hell and I am hoping I have a throat for tomorrow's work. I spent the entire gig figuring out where the sweet spots onstage were so I could hear. After I figured them out, I had a good time playing. The audience was great. About 2700 people. That's better than we have ever drawn here.

After the show I talked to TV Smith and Gaye Advert. So great to see them again. They gave me some new reissues of Adverts stuff. Can't wait to hear them. TV Smith is a huge influence on me. When I first heard his lyrics on the early Adverts singles, they really put the hook in me. I remember Ian and I buying their records just to check them out and being blown away at how great they were. I always wanted to meet

TV Smith. In 1993 he was on a festival the night after I was and I left him a note telling him that I was doing two nights at the Astoria in London and he was on the guest list. He was still in France when the shows happened but Gaye, the Adverts bass player came instead. I finally met TV in 1994. It's always so cool to see them both. He's such a great song writer. 'From writers to scientists, it's all the same, their facts to twist. I'll be hit by passing fists, but this is where I'll stay.' – TV Smith from the Adverts song 'My Place'.

I wish my throat wasn't so fragile. I don't remember if I ever had problems like that with a bad stage sound. I cringe when I think back to a few hours ago looking out at all those people with my voice all fucked up wondering how I was going to pull it off. It was horrible. I am proud of myself that I was able to get my voice calmed down so it could deliver. The throat coach has helped me greatly.

05-06-97 London UK: 0111 hrs. We did a radio show tonight. We played four songs. I sang the first two OK and then the others I was pretty bad. I am sick of not being able to do my job. I am sick of having nothing else on the brain other than my voice. I am sick of letting everyone down. I remember when I never had to be concerned about my voice and now it's all I think about.

All this makes my life torture. Should my life be torture all the time? I don't mind work. I don't mind a lot of work. I don't mind physical pain. I can't take this though. Tired of being miserable all the time. I don't like being held back by my throat.

11.38 p.m.: Did a show on BBC with some other bands. One of them was Beck. He and his band were very good but it was more slick than anything else. They were ripping off old Devo stage moves but I guess that it doesn't matter if you're not original these days. He's seen as a big deal and I think he's talented but when I hear recycled riffs and see ripped off poses and moves, I can only dig it so far. It's a put-on and I'm sure critics like him because he's meek and harmless like they are. He is what happens when you have nothing to say and have no soul. For myself, I prefer something stronger. Whatever. He and this amazing piano player from Cuba, Ruben Gonzalez, were the best things on the show. We played well. Of course my voice almost quit after the first song. Only had to do two and the fucking voice lasted about one and a half. I pulled it off but just barely. It makes me nervous to do these shows with my voice like this. I sit all day before the show wondering if I'll be able to pull it off.

05-09-97 Copenhagen Denmark: 5.15 p.m. Last two nights have been good. I have been pacing myself and it has been going alright. I've learned a lot about myself. I love to play and all I need to be happy out here is a voice that works. If I don't have that then I feel like dying. It has been 48 hours of feeling relatively good. Since I don't think about anyone on the road it allows me to be fine out here indefinitely. As long as the voice holds out, I don't care if I don't get off the road until next year. I would like nothing more than to play seven nights a week. There's nothing for me off the road. I've tried to be at home off the road and it doesn't work. I feel weak when I am in my apartment. I feel good out here. I don't feel like I am wasting my time out here.

05-10-97 Amsterdam Holland: 11.46 p.m. Throat broke tonight. I made it through most of the set. That was the 8th straight day of singing without rest. Not bad, I think. Hopefully it's getting stronger. I will have to be patient and careful. From the neck down, I am playing my ass off though and that's a lot of fun. I wish tonight could have been better.

05-12-97 Boston MA: 1111 hrs. Got here last night. I hung out with Mitch Bury of Adams Mass and went to a shitty hotel and checked out this morning. I'm now at Mitch's. He's off working and I am getting ready to go to the gym. Not much to tell. Waiting to hit the stage tomorrow. Keeping myself cool and trying to keep my voice quiet. It was hard to get used to it at first, being quiet all the time but I got used to it fast and it suits me well. I like sitting amongst people and not talking at all. It's how I should be anyway. It's better for me not to talk. I feel better when I don't talk much. I think it's like you start with one hundred points in the morning and all you can do is lose them all day. You have to see how many you can home with. When I talk, I usually lose. I say something stupid or get it wrong. I can talk easily onstage, it's off that I don't know what to do. That's pretty fucked up. David Lee Roth once told me that he stopped going to as many parties as he had been because he was usually put in the position of being the center of attention and he said he went into entertainment mode when he didn't want to and it bummed him out. I have a similar thing happen to me where I talk to keep people at bay. They think they're getting close but they're really being kept at a controlled distance.

05-19-97 Columbus OH: 0138 hrs. Got the eventless day off over with and now waiting for sleep to come in this shitty room with the broken air conditioner so I can get out of here in the morning.

I went to a shopping mall to see a movie. Waiting to go in there were people coming up to me asking me to sign stuff. I did and stared at the floor a lot so people wouldn't see my face. I saw the movie and on the way out, some guys asked me to take pictures with them and I said yes because I am trying to be a better person. I did it and all the people coming out of the movie stared at me and made me feel like a jerk. I hurried into the men's room and waited for them to pass. I went outside to see if the rest of the band guys were around so we could leave. I couldn't find the rented car that we came in so I figured they had left without me. I was walking back to the theater to call a cab when a car pulls to the curb. I stop walking, hoping that the people inside will not bother me. I am alone in a parking lot in Ohio. People have died under these circumstances.

Two males got out and slammed their doors behind them. For a second I thought I was going to get jacked. They looked young but I was still looking for the guns to come out. I asked them what they wanted as I backed up. They stopped and said that they were fans and asked me what the problem was. I told them that everywhere I go there is someone on my dick. They backed up a few steps and turned around and got back in their car. I saw that I had bummed them out. I said after them that I meant no offense but I don't think they heard me and even if they did, I bet they wouldn't believe it.

I feel bad about what I said to them. Sometimes all this makes me so mad. Every time I go somewhere it's an ordeal. I can't walk at a normal pace. I cannot go from one place to another without having to stop and talk. I'm walking in a parking lot in the middle of the Midwest and people get out of a car and have to talk to me. I don't handle these things well. I think if I were a happier person I might but I am depressed and miserable most of the time so any kind of attention close up makes me nervous. If I ever saw those guys again I would apologize.

The shows have been going pretty good. In most of the places, less people come than last time. We didn't even break a thousand people in Toronto the other night. I don't know of anything I can do to change that so I just go out there and make sure to give it all I have and that is enjoyable. I wish we had played tonight and am looking forward to getting to the venue here in town and doing it again.

I wish I could just play and not have to meet people, not have to talk about what I do with interviewers, not have to take pictures at all. I am not cut out for any of that stuff anymore.

Right now, I am exactly as I should be. Alone in a small room. Some music playing on the box. That plays like a clean line.

Alone in a small room
Some music playing on the box
I am wordless, silent
Locks on the door locked
Phone and me
Off the hook
I plead
Temporary anonymity

So far tonight, I have listened to a Freddie Hubbard record and now I'm listening to Ahmad Jamal's *The Awakening* album. Here, I cannot hurt anyone's feelings. I don't have to feel freaked out every other second with what they put me through, the horrible things they write about me, the distortions they depict. It is only when I am alone that I do not despise myself or feel claustrophobic. It gets worse with age. The miles burn it into me. All I know is I'll take this over a desk job any day. This a war on some level. Without a little conflict, what do you have? The truth is: harmony does not rock.

05-20-97 Pontiac MI: 2.53 p.m. Last night was Columbus OH. We played well and the audience was great. Now in Pontiac, MI. Brutal. Cold and gray and there's nothing around here to do. Waiting to go to a gym after soundcheck. Tickets are not doing well but what else is new?

For the amount of tickets we are selling, we should be in a van with a small crew. We are drawing less people than we did four years ago. Of course the guys wouldn't be able to deal with that. After a few weeks, I don't know how well I'd do either.

Last night I was talking to a girl who knows one of the two guys I met in the parking lot in Columbus. I wrote a note to give to them, I hope it makes a difference.

I have not been writing much. The depression and stress effectively shut down any creative will I have. When I have ideas to do something, I just sit and let them pass by. I don't have the desire to communicate with people outside of the songs. The songs are about as far as I want to go with the outside world right now.

I have been thinking of another line of work. I reckon the music has another year and then no one will want to hear from us at all and it will be time to move on to something else. I suppose the speaking dates will hold for a while and then they will dry up as well. But for right now, all I should be thinking about is the shows and playing well every night. I like having to think of these things. I like being in a band and working hard. I like going up there and giving it all I have. I like playing better every year. Too bad no one seems to be interested in attending the shows like they used to. That's the way it is in this business. You get beat in and you get beat out and in the meantime you get beat up.

7.07 p.m.: Did a phone interview with some woman at a radio station She told me that she liked my work with Robert De Niro in some movie I wasn't in. I went with it, of course. Sure, thanks a lot. It's going to be one of those years.

05-24-97 Kansas City MO: 0040 hrs. Had a great day off here. Ate good food. Got in a good workout and got a chance to check out some good books. People left me on my own for the most part. Didn't get followed around that much but enough to be relieved when night came and I was harder to recognize.

I sat in a park for hours and watched the stars and the traffic. I had a great time. For me, that's a good night off.

The weather has been good and the shows have been going well. Not many people showing up but those who do are getting one rocking set, that's for sure.

We play early today. It's a radio thing and we hit stage at two in the afternoon for fifty minutes or something. The next three shows are radio shows. No soundcheck, short sets, big stage which suits me just fine. At one of these we get to see Iggy play. I look forward to that big time.

My voice has been holding well. This makes me look forward to shows. I don't have to wonder about how the throat is going to do so now I can throw myself into the gig two hundred per cent and get off totally. We just did four straight and I could have played tonight no sweat.

So, the last few days have been good for me. I feel good when I can play with all I have. There's plenty to keep me up at night stressed and preoccupied. This is temporary. A lot of my stress comes from the deeds of others. The less people in my life, the less problems I have. No parents, no parent problems. I hear people complain all the time that they have to go see their parents and how they dread it. How they hate holidays because the family gets together. I don't have any of that. No girlfriend, no girlfriend problems. I don't remember what it was like to have one so I don't miss it most of the time but sometimes I do, what I can remember of it.

I was at the bookstore today looking through the magazines. I saw a man looking through the racks as well when his daughter came up and started nagging him that it was time to go. He said he would be there in a minute and he started looking through the magazines really fast, trying to cram it all in. Seconds later she was at him again, telling him that it was time to go. Another assuring reminder that children are definitely not in my future.

With kids, you could not play your rock music jams loud in the house whenever you wanted to. Their shit would be all over the place. Fuck that. Never going to happen. I am listening to Al Green right now. How could you listen to Al Green with kids yelling and knocking things over? You couldn't. Coltrane's music would be ruined by a house full of family. Hell, that's all I need to know. Not to say that I don't like kids. How can you not like them? I just don't want any. I like sharks too, I don't have any of them either.

I see so many men not doing what they want to do because of the relationship they are in. They check their swing. They promise themselves they'll get back to it later. They are chained to a relationship that restricts them as life goes hurtling by.

I sat outside tonight in a park. I hid in the trees so no one would bug me and took in the night air. Years ago I would have thought that it might have been good to have someone to share this with but now I see that it would be absolutely ruined by the presence of someone else. Alone is pure. I think of the times when I missed someone and it makes me sick. I miss events. Perhaps people were involved in these instances but when that experience is over, that part of your life and their life is over. You will never know that person that way again. With every breath, you are different and you never get it back. All you can do is remember and meditate upon that which has passed. The one you fell in love with is not the one you're with, only a rendering of that person. Life is a crushing disappointment when you hang onto time.

6-02-97 Portland OR: 1.35 p.m. I don't know what time we pulled in. I got up in time to see Tim McVeigh get nailed on all counts. The streets here are filled with shuffling homeless men. I see the same guys walk by every few minutes.

Shows going well. Vancouver and Seattle were cool. Whenever I am in Seattle I always wonder if I could live there. There's parts I like about it but on the other hand I get a feeling it could get pretty claustrophobic and depressing. It might be OK if you had someone to hang out with. Being a loner, I like big cities that have a way out so I can leave when I want. Seattle seems tied off.

6-12-97 San Antonio TX: A little past midnight. We started driving here last night a little under 21 hours ago. That was our day off, spent in a bus driving through desert expanse.

The shows have been going good. I have been singing well and playing hard. I don't know where it's coming from but I am hitting it hard every night. It's getting hard to keep the weight on. I have not been this light for years. We have not done this many shows without a break in a long time either. At the end of this leg it will be about sixty shows and then there's a few days off where I think I have to go and do more press in Australia. Basically we will go without stopping until September 1st. I don't mind. I'd rather be on the road than not.

6-13-97 Austin TX: 3.10 p.m. Here at Liberty Lunch. We won't be playing until 11.15. It is hot everywhere, even on the bus. Last few days the heat has been like an oven.

Playing has been good but there has not been anything interesting to write about except that every night without exception I have bad nightmares. In one, I smash a kid's face between my hands for no reason. In another I give a guy I know a bunch of money knowing that it's fake. There was another bad one last night and now I forget it. They have been the ones when I wake up wondering if it was real for a few minutes.

6-15-97 New Orleans LA: Playing almost every night without a break. I am feeling a little fatigue and my voice could use a rest but over all I am holding up well. Today is a day off. I walked around and didn't do much. The weather was hot but nice. People were in my face. I do the best I can to be cool with people but sometimes they make it hard. I don't care about days off. I would rather have played tonight. I am having a great time playing these days and we are playing pretty damn good.

Hot all the time. The summer is all around me. The depression that plagues me keeps me quiet. Depression and me, what a pair. The one constant in my life it seems, ever since I was young. I remember it when I was six. I think the first time I ever heard the word was from my mother when I asked her what was wrong with me. She was cool about it and told me to make a list of all the things that were making me feel bad. I would do it and it was helpful sometimes. I still do it from time to time. It's like trying to dissect your worst day and get to the real reason why you seek to fuck yourself up so much. I have always thought my worst enemy was myself. I often wonder what I have against myself to make myself feel the way I do. I don't like to blame others for the bad things I feel. You bring on yourself every time.

06-23-97 Chicago IL: Almost at the end of my day off in Chicago. It was a lousy one. Got here late coming in from Atlanta. Had about an hour to do things and then had to sit still and do phone work. Waited for an hour for phone interviews from Australia to come in but they didn't. They got the time wrong, I guess.

I walked around and got hassled by people and it wasn't a good time. I ate some bad Mexican food that I could barely finish. All the coffee places closed early and there was nothing to do. I have to get up early in the morning and do some radio show. Fantastic. I am an idiot.

06-24-97 Chicago IL: It's the crack of dawn and I have hardly slept. Went down the street and got a cup of coffee. Came back to the room because it's already hot outside and the place was all glass and people were looking at me. It's hard to deal with that kind of thing before a cup of coffee. I like Chicago. People are cool to me here. Always have been. It's a great place to play and I always look forward to a day off here, that's why I am so pissed off that yesterday's was so lame. Don't know when I'll get a chance to get back here again.

The other day in Atlanta I woke up in the bus in a parking lot behind the venue. I noticed a guy sitting outside. I sat inside for quite a while trying to wake up and force food down my throat. I finally left the bus, got one foot out the door and the guy starts talking to me. Apparently he had been waiting in the hot sun just for me. Why do people have to be like this? It's like getting up in the morning and finding a guy standing between you and the bathroom. He wanted to give me something he wrote. I wasn't all that nice to him but I have to say he had it coming. I feel bad that I was a little short with him. I guess I was more in disbelief than anything else. I asked him why he would sit out in the sun waiting for some fuckin' guy from a band to come out of a bus. I am the wrong guy to talk to most of the time. I just want to do the show and lift and turn myself off.

Last night people were in my face pretty much the whole time I was on the street. They were cool but sometimes I just want to walk down the street and think and not have to talk to people. I never get a chance to be that guy unless I am in a room alone.

Soon I will go down to the lobby and wait for the radio guy to pick me up. He's a funny guy and very cool to me but he knows that this is a dead record and he is doing all the work on it because he's been assigned to it and you can tell. Doesn't mean he isn't doing a good job but you can tell that he knows that radio doesn't care about it at all and all the work he's doing is pointless.

4.18 p.m.: I was warned about a guy who was going to be looking for me. I was told he was a witch and wanted me to put out his book. He told Rick that he and I met in 1981 and I would remember him. I go out to the bus and sure enough there's this guy sitting in front of the door, blocking my way.

He starts talking a mile a minute about the time we spoke in San Diego fifteen years ago and asks me if I remember, 'Come on, think back!' He pulls out a picture book about Aleister Crowley and tells me that he has fifteen people in his coven and he has his own Tarot cards or something and that I should put his book out. I told him that I didn't want to put it out. He kept asking and I kept telling him the same thing. He told me that Rick had promised to kick his ass if he saw him near me. At that moment Rick came up to us and started yelling at the guy. He fucked off with Rick dealing on him and I never saw him again. I saw some of the staff checking him out so if he comes tonight, they will be watching him.

Rick told me later that the guy threatened to call the police if he touched him. I figured if you had Satan on your side, you wouldn't have to resort to the local authorities.

06-26-97 Philadelphia PA: 0429 hrs. The night off is over. Drove here from Chicago last night. Got to the hotel at six in the evening. Right in time to walk into my room and do three phone interviews with Australia. I don't know how I am going to do interviews in the future. I am over it so bad. Bad reviews and the bullshit that these little idiots generate is like a handful of sand thrown into the wind. It just doesn't matter what they think either way. Love me, hate me, whatever. Publish your opinion and then after people have read it, they throw the paper away and move on. I am still here, they are scribbling madly away about someone else. It really doesn't matter at the end of the line. I have ceased to care. I did the interviews and don't remember what I said. They have fucked the taste right out of my mouth and I don't care at all.

Show in Chicago was great. I like playing that town a lot. Ed Coan the power lifter came to the show. I wrote him a letter a while ago and sent him the new record and he wrote back and said he liked it. I put him on the guest list and he showed up. He was dead cool. One serious athlete. I respect anyone going for something that intense. The guy lifts a lot of weight. His handshake could break your fingers. He sent me his training videos. Seeing the weight he pushes is truly amazing. It was an honor to meet him.

Wesley Willis came to the show and he was more sedate than I have ever seen him. Wesley dug the show and promised to make a song about the band for the next record. It was great to hear him say that we whipped the horse's ass with a belt. I had to meet some radio people and some radio ticket winners. It was pretty funny to see these people take in Wesley, talking nonstop and Ed, who is this bulletproof hulk of a man. Ed doesn't know who Wesley is and was regarding him curiously. It was worth a million in prizes.

Tonight was pretty good. Hung out and went to a record store. People were cool to me and pretty much left me alone. I like Philadelphia. I'm looking forward to playing the show here. It's usually a great crowd that turns up. The New York day is going to be a pain in the ass. We have to do an MTV thing that totally blows everyone's schedule. We were going to stay here tomorrow night but apparently now we have to do some bullshit to get the band to Queens to play a song and then go to soundcheck. As well, there is another bullshit phoner to do in Australia. I am told that my week off will now be taken up by me having to fly there early and do interviews. I don't see why I can't do them on the phone and get left alone for a few days. I don't think that's asking too much.

Sometimes I feel like I'm getting rolled over by a tank. Journalists give me shit so I have to talk to them more. Radio stations don't play our music so I have to go to radio stations and hang out at the crack of dawn with them for reasons I don't understand. MTV doesn't play our videos so we have to go there and play live and fuck up our whole day. I don't see the point in any of it.

06-27-97 Queens NY: 11.10 hrs. At the television studio. The show we are playing on is called 'Oddville' It features contortionists and all kinds of idiots. We are the biggest idiots of all because we will be here three hours to do one song. What a blow to the day's schedule. This was a great idea.

We got into the city at around four in the morning. I have not slept much yet. The room was cooking and I just lay there looking at the ceiling. So far, the day has not been going all that great. Someone kill me.

Just found out from Rick that we have an 8 p.m. stage time. That will kill any chances of getting a workout in. I'll be lucky to get a few hours' sleep. It's only our one show in New York, not too important.

06-28-97 Washington DC: 4.04 p.m. It's hot outside like we're in Arizona or something. No humidity but hot like an oven.

Yesterday was a long and aggravating day. We finished the stupid television show and then went to the venue. A cord needed to power the system had to be brought in and it didn't get to the place until half an hour after we were supposed to go on. The opening band didn't get to play and we got no soundcheck and we had to cut the set a few songs short because the club has a strict time limit. They want to get the live bands out and put the DJ on so they can start making money. It was such a great show too. Good sound onstage, great audience. All this would have to happen in New York.

We don't go on until late tonight. Nothing in this neighborhood to check out. I thought I would be more interested to check out my old hometown but I am not. I wish I could get a work out in but the schedule never seems to work. It's good to be out of the places where there are people who know me. Yesterday was distracting. I have no idea why people would want to talk to me after a show. I tried to find a way to sneak out of there without having to deal with anyone but couldn't do it.

06-29-97 Norfolk VA: 0330 hrs. Looks like tonight's show was the last one for America. In my opinion it should have been the first leg of at least three but no one seems to want us so off we go to Europe and points beyond.

Last night in DC and tonight were good shows. You couldn't get better crowds. I spoke to Alec MacKaye and Mark Sullivan while I was there. They seem to be holding up well. Ian is in

Australia right now The opening band, Squatweiler was great. Besides their own songs which are really good, they do a great cover of 'Hot for Teacher', which was a high point. The vocal delivery was awesome.

I didn't go looking around in the hours before the show. I just didn't feel like dealing with the place in the heat. I was going to go there today and have a day off but I will be leaving for NYC in two hours to get deposed. Getting deposed on no sleep, how great will that be? At about 5 p.m. I get out of there and have the night to myself.

I am tired but it's a joke trying to sleep when you know you have to shower and hit the deck in ninety minutes or so. So my life is fucked, what else is new? Sure have been playing well though. Wish we were playing more shows here. I feel rejected!

06-30-97 NYC NY: Late. Today was hellish. We played last night in Norfolk. Last show in America. Got to the hotel around 0230. I had to go to the airport at 0530. Got to NYC, slept for a couple of hours and then went and got deposed for the last time.

The lawyer didn't have much to ask me and the deposition didn't go longer than a few hours. A day off slaughtered so this hotshot could ask me some stupid bullshit for a couple of hours and change. I could have done something with myself.

Not much of a night off. Walked around and slept. The neighborhood I am in has nothing open past nine. I leave for Denmark tomorrow. I am depressed and frustrated. I guess it really burns me that we are done touring in America. What I mean to say is that I am burned that America is done with us. I learned some powerful lessons this summer.

07-02-97 Copenhagen Denmark: 3.07 p.m. Sitting in the domestic flight terminal. Screaming children sent me a few gates down. The air is hot and unmoving. The flight leaves in and hour and a half. The flying time is about 25 minutes. I guess the place, Odense, is about one hundred miles or so. Too bad we couldn't have just driven it.

This is the time to do what David Lee Roth suggests: go smooth. Just cool it and let the time pass quietly and coolly.

I am tired as hell but I am going to stay awake until at least ten tonight so I can get on the new time schedule. The next few days will be short festival sets. We're in good shape for this and it will feel like a vacation. We will be trapped by shitty bands whose music we will not be able to escape. Maybe we will be able to play and leave quickly.

I am looking forward to tonight. Maybe I can get outside and walk around under the stars. I like the night. I look forward to nights when I can be outside and breathe it in without getting bothered.

Wish I wasn't so burnt out but my sleeping patterns have been erratic at best. The children that are making all the noise belong to one family. One family, all that noise. Another reason not to have children, a wife, any of it. The idea of having to deal with kids on a day to day basis makes me exhausted. Never never never having kids. Kids are great but it's not the life for everyone. I think that too many people have children before they're ready and they just settle into their fate and accept it. They raise their kids in a state of compromised ambition and it rubs off on the kids.

07-06-97 Belfort France: 8.30 p.m. Another day in a muddy field. A good show though. We played early, at 5.45. We have a long drive tonight to Rimini, Italy. We have a day off there before we play. Voice holding up well and I'm having a good time playing.

The festivals get a bit depressing to do. Especially when a lot of the same bands are on the bill. Paul Weller was on the last couple of shows and I thought he was great. Better than when we saw him play a few years ago in Italy, where he was good but now I think he's even better.

I can't wait to get out of here. We are parked near the stage so when any band goes on, you can't hear anything else.

I am sitting on the bus to try and avoid as many people as possible. I had to do a short interview with some television show and the guy was a jerk and I had to endure him so I figure I've had enough of people for a while. Sometimes I just don't get along with people unless I'm acting. I just go with it so they'll move along.

07-08-97 12.24 p.m. Rimini Italy: We will be going to the venue soon. Looking forward to playing. A day off is nice and all but I'd rather be rockin'. On a day off I get too much time to myself and I get depressed.

I play all these places knowing it's likely this band will never be back there again. After ten years, it's a heartbreak. But it is the way of things. One must be ready to give it up and move on. What the next move is will be the most important decision I'll be making any time soon. It will be important to take a look and see what is happening in the music world in the next year. It might be time to do one more record and leave it. It might be a sinking ship not worth going down on.

07-09-97 Vienna Austria: 4.13 p.m. It's good to have done the Italian date and be out of there. It was a typical Italian production. We sound-checked at around 7.30. The monitors were bad, the hall sounded bad, etc. People stood and stared. A few guys flipped me off for the entire gig. I think that's some kind of punk rock thing. Whatever. We played well and that's really all that matters. A rocking four hundred people in attendance!

Tonight's show has, of course, been moved into the smaller part of this venue. Our band is in its Spinal Tap phase. We're mining that 'exclusive audience' we've been trying to cultivate over all these years. Ah yes, it feels so good to be able to enjoy the fruits of our labor! Be looking for us in the 'where are they now' bin at your local cut-out section.

Whenever someone makes a joke or remembers something from a previous tour, I try to enjoy every bit of it because I know that these are some of the last times we will all be together. I think that will be the hardest part of seeing this band go down the tubes, besides not having something to throw myself into for months at a time, will be remembering the guys and the history we have created. The fact that we will probably not be touring again not due to creative differences but due to the fact that no one wants us is a heartbreak. Makes me feel a little stupid for working so hard and eating so much shit for so many years.

It feels to me now that it was all for nothing. But, that's the way it is in this business. You get beat in and you get beat out. Especially if you play the way we do. I am not surprised. I knew at an early age that I was going to take a beating all through my life and prepared for it. I was right.

Maybe it wasn't all for nothing. I mean, who do you do it for? I had a great time and am still having a great time. I guess that's what gets to me, our audience is obviously done with us but I don't feel done. You can't have everything.

Later: Came back into the dressing room in time to see one of the biggest damn rats go hauling ass under the seats. I could hear its footsteps as it charged along, that one had some weight for sure.

We are playing in the same hall that Black Flag played with the Minutemen in 1983. I still have scars from that show. Being back on that stage immediately made me mad about that. After we were done I walked outside and I saw all the piece of shit squat punkers standing around uselessly just like the first time I was there. Just seeing them and that hall makes me want to fuck one of them up if they even look at me.

07-10-97 Vienna Austria: 1.20 a.m. Place was packed and very hot. The audience was great. It was fitting to play the place that I had played in fourteen years before. The monitors were bad but still it was a good time.

Now I'm sitting in the bus waiting to go. We don't leave for an hour or so. I'm not as depressed as I was this morning, I don't know why.

4.31 p.m. Prague Czech Republic: Looks like the place will be well attended tonight. That is surprising but good to hear. I am sitting in the backstage area waiting for it all to start.

Will have to be very careful with my voice, the last few PA's have left quite a bit to be desired. Theo says tonight's monitors will be good. We have a day off here tomorrow. I walked around here last time and it was very nice but these days I am not in the mood to check out the scenery.

Depression is hard to fight on the road. I go through long periods where I just try to get through the day to get onstage. When I'm playing, I'm alright, it's the rest of the day that is difficult. I'm so tired of feeling stressed all the time. I would like to think that there's other ways of living.

Voice is not sounding good. Last two days were hard on it. Tonight will be a test. When my throat is not doing well I'm mad at everything.

07-11-97 Prague Republic of Czech: 0107 hrs. The show was good. My voice held fine. What a great crowd. The last two nights have been great. We don't get crowds like that very often. There's something great about playing to an audience that doesn't get all types of bands coming through their town all the time. They're not jaded and have not had everything come through and blow all their circuitry. I think that's one of the things that's lame about touring these days is that so many people have already seen your dumb ass that there's nothing you can do to even make them notice you. Everyone has been raped and pillaged, captured and taken prisoner.

Now I'm back in the room. We are here until three in the afternoon and then we have a few hours to mill around and then we go to Bremen Germany to play a festival. A thirty-minute set. I don't know how many songs that is, something like five or six.

07-14-97 Frankfurt Germany: 0042 hrs. Shows have been going well. A day or two ago we played some kind of hardcore festival. It was pretty depressing but we stuck it out. Ran into Pete Steele from Type O Negative and talked to him for a while. It's funny to look at him. He's this big man, looks somewhat angry with the way his face sits on his skull. At first glance you might think he's some monster thug. Surprise. He's got a great sense of humor, extremely sharp-witted, totally cool and he could break you into little pieces – a great combination.

Tonight's show was in a suburb of Frankfurt called Neu Isenburg. It was a pretty good set. We played well. They just stood and watched for the most part but seemed to have a good time. Someone threw a lit cigarette onstage and when I held it up everyone booed the person who threw it. Blisters on my left foot made playing a little painful at times and the onstage temperature was pretty intense but it was a good time.

07-16-97 Nürnberg Germany: 0013 hrs. Played well tonight. It's the end of the four-night run in Germany. They were a pretty tight-faced bunch but alright. Very quiet between songs. I am glad that we have some time off for my voice to get a breather. We are on our way to London for a couple of days off. Looking forward to it.

07-18-97 Stratford-upon-Avon UK: 11.37 p.m. Sitting on the bus waiting to go to the hotel. We just finished playing a 65 minute festival set. I think we gave them a good one. I am glad to be out of London. It was cool but crowded with tourists and they are a pain in the ass.

The two days off did me good, if nothing else to give my voice a little rest. Didn't do a whole lot and that was a good thing too.

The audience tonight was really cool. They are usually very sharp and get the jokes. Even when I called them a bunch of names during 'Liar', they knew I was kidding with them and didn't get mad. I wish all audiences could be sharp like the British. There's really nothing like them anywhere. They just get it.

The moon was full recently which means that the depression is worse than usual. It gets to be too much sometimes. It would be so great if I could schedule my shows around the moon cycle so I wouldn't have to do shows when I am like this. It makes all things hard to do.

07-19-97 Dublin Ireland 0127 hrs. I leave the hotel in a few hours. Wondering whether I should bother sleeping or not. Show tonight was good. Great crowd. Felt very tired part way through. By the time we hit the last song I felt like I didn't have any more sap left in my bones. It is definitely time for a rest. It could also be in my head, sometimes with breaks coming up I tend to feel exhausted near the last show. But, this was 67 shows with not much of a break so I think I am entitled to feel a little burnt. Tonight's stage was on a slightly downward slope and it gave me the feeling that I was going to run off the edge.

07-20-97 En Route to LA: Started in Dublin with no sleep. Plane a couple of hours late getting off ground in London. Ten hours and change. Saw movies: *Dante's Peak*, *When We Were Kings*, *Absolute Power*. Smooth ride but boring. Ringo Starr and wife on plane. Cab back to place. Shower, laundry, shave, mail, etc.

07-29-97 Sydney Australia: Got in at around six in the morning. I must have slept quite a bit because I don't remember much of the flight at all. It's now about five in the evening and it's beautiful out. It's like fall in America. Crisp and cool. I am very affected by climate changes. Autumn weather always puts me in a good mood.

07-31-97 5.53 p.m. Sydney Australia: Back in the mix. Had a week off in LA and it was good. I did nothing. That was a new one. I sat and listened to music, read, worked out and wrote in my journal and that was about it.

Got out here two days ago. Played the first show last night in Newcastle. Never been there before. It was a good show. I fell asleep on the floor and woke up an hour before we had to go on. I shook myself out and hit it. The crowd was cool. They seemed to like us OK.

We were on our way out to the van to go back to the hotel when a couple came into the dressing room. Two hippie types who seemed cool enough. They said they had driven a long way to see us and they wanted to 'chat'. So I talked to them as I was walking with the others down the stairs to the loading dock. The guy asks if we have done anything since the *End of Silence* and I told him two albums and two tours of Australia. His girlfriend asked some stupid shit that I can't remember. She was drunk. I left them at the stage and walked to the van. My mind was on the bed waiting for me at the hotel. I was so tired. It was almost two in the morning. Out of nowhere this woman comes at me yelling that I am an asshole because I am not still there talking to her and her boyfriend. I politely explained that we are all jet lagging and tired and just want to go to sleep. She keeps on with her drunken bullshit until Melvin carried her away. I asked the guys if I had done something wrong because in these situations I no longer understand if these people are jerks or if it's something I have done. They told me that I didn't do anything wrong. I know how it comes out though. These people tell their friends that I am an asshole and that's all there is to the story.

The weather out here is amazing. It's clear and almost cold. It's like fall on the east coast of America. I was here two years ago at this time working with The Mark of Cain on their album *Ill at Ease*. What a great band. I guess we'll see them in Adelaide on Sunday.

I'm looking forward to the shows here. I have always had a good time in Australia.

This weather makes me homesick in a way. I hate to have feelings like that because they get in the way of playing. It's so strange to have weather like this in the middle of the summer. It feels like October outside. Sun sets early and nights are cold.

I got an e-mail from Ian the other day. Good to hear from him. Fugazi are about to leave for Brazil. He said that some of the towns they're going to are having problems and he's worried if they're going to be alright. I guess he'll have an adventure story to tell when and if he returns. He said that they have been working on a new record. Can't wait to hear that. I think they get better as they go. Their records are always amazing to me.

Tonight is a night off. It's Sim's birthday.

08-01-97 Sydney Australia: Up early. It's a little past nine right now. Couldn't sleep anymore. Listening to Roy Orbison's *Mystery Girl* album. David Lynch told me he checks this one out regularly. The best track Orbison ever did was the one that Glen Danzig wrote for him that's on the *Less Than Zero* soundtrack, 'Life Slips Away', that is so intense. I remember getting a letter from Glen when he did the track. I was living in a dump in Silverlake. Laura Cloud was my roommate. She shot herself in the head recently. I've never written about that time period. I'll have to get to that. That was some crazy shit back then.

We have three shows in a row. I am glad that we are getting into it now. Too many days away and I get nervous that I'll get out of the zone. That's going to make the shows in Japan strange. They will be hard in a lot of ways. There's a chance they will be the last shows we will ever do. That's going to be hard to come down from. I'll need to talk to management and see what they think. It will be interesting to see what they say about it.

I keep feeling that I want to do another *Hot Animal Machine* type record. I want to feel that excitement again and I don't think I'm going to get that out of this band as it is now. It's nobody's shortcoming or fault, it's just you do it one way for ten and a half years and then you want to do it another way. The idea of working with other people makes me excited. The idea of making another record with the guys doesn't excite me right now. The thing that is making me fearful is the loss of security that the loss of the band brings. On the other hand, I do well when my hand is forced and maybe now is the time.

The more I think about it, the more another record with the band would be hard on all of us. I know I would be frustrated as hell and I don't want to go there. Fuck the security, there would be none. I would know the whole time that I was fooling myself and that it was time to move on. I would be wrestling myself all the time and that's just no good.

Later: A little before 8 p.m. Will be heading back to the venue to play soon. Jet lag hitting me. I want to go to sleep right now. The gig is in Narrabeen. I don't think we have played there before.

Gig should be a lot of fun. It's already sold out and the place sounded good at soundcheck. I will be glad to get onstage and get this gig going. It will also be good to check out of this hotel soon. We have been here a few days now and I'm starting to feel like I am not on tour.

08-02-97 Sydney Australia: 0119 hrs. Played well tonight even though the jet lag made it hard. We went on at about 5.20 in the morning LA time. It takes a little getting used to. The crowd was great and we played our asses off. Nothing to do tonight except hit the pillow and sleep. The weather is nice and cold out. I want to go out for a little while and walk around but I just don't have the energy.

That's all I can write. Body hurts too much to concentrate. Tonight is the Sydney show.

08-03-97 Sydney Australia: 1026 hrs. Great show last night. One of the best nights I've had vocal-wise the whole year. The crowd was great as well. If we could have audiences like that every night I would never get off the road. Here they just forget to be cynical assholes and let you get on with it. Leaving for Adelaide in an hour.

I saw an interview with one of the soldiers from Hong Kong who had been serving in the British military stationed there. All of a sudden he was out of a job. After so many years of service they don't even get a British passport. The man being interviewed held up a good front but you could easily tell he was shattered. He was still in his uniform. It must be hard, after all those years of dedicated service to go out like that. They take the uniform away and leave. It's like saying that you were never really more than the help and thank you very much. What a fuckin' kick in the teeth. Sad too. You could see that he had been so proud of what he was and the service that he had provided. He gave them his life and they gave him enough belittling humiliation to last him the rest of his life. I feel a little bit like that. When this band stops playing, there will be a big hole in me. In a lot of ways I feel like a soldier. I feel like I serve people in a way. I am one of the people who brings the music. It hurts to think that you are not wanted anymore. This is a tough business. I have had a longer run than most.

Time to get ready to go to the airport.

08-04-97 Freemantle Australia: Got here several hours ago. We are by the water. There is a park down the road with lots of beautiful trees. They are huge and look like pines but have different bark.

Don't know why but I am so tired I cannot type straight. It's a little after eleven at night.

Didn't do much tonight. Ate some good but overpriced Japanese food and then went and drank some coffee until the noise and the people drove me out of the place. Now I'm back in the room and wishing I could write but I am too damn tired. All I did today was fly here and eat. Maybe my body is worn out.

08-05-97 Freemantle Australia: It's a little past seven. Will be playing soon. Looking forward to it. Soundcheck was boomy but will tighten up when people get in.

So here I am in Freemantle Australia in a hotel room. I am in a somewhat obscure part of the earth and that's my life right now. Someday it will be different. I have been thinking a lot about how the hell I am going to survive for the rest of my life when the music goes away.

I was contacted by a fellow at Warner Bros. Jane's Addiction is doing a live album and want me to do the liner notes. I just got the tapes. I have about two days to get it together. I want to do this badly. I want to do this right. I almost don't want to because I am afraid of blowing it. I hold that band in very high esteem. What if I write the liner notes and the band hates them?! Easily one of the best live bands of all time. Man, do I miss that band.

I fear the day I have nothing to work for. I lift weights because I like it but also to get ready for tour like an athlete gets ready for the season. I don't know what I would do without something like that kicking me along. I think to get things done, you need a challenge, I do at least. A warrior without a war. Pathetic.

08-06-97 Freemantle Australia: It's about one in the morning and I just got back from the gig. It was a good one but it was hard to hear onstage. Got hit with a few things, beer cans, spit, whatever. Nice bunch.

We have two show days in Melbourne coming up. Both are walking distance from the hotel so it will be easy to get out and get back to the room. I am looking forward to some good workouts and some good sleep.

08-06-97 Melbourne Australia: It's a little before 10 p.m. Got here a few hours ago. It's a night off. I didn't get much sleep last night. A drunk woman was knocking on my door last night and calling my name and it woke me up out of a good sleep and it freaked me out. I was told later that she was standing outside my door naked. Whoa, at this late stage I'm a rockstar? She must have thought I was someone else. I'm going out in a little while to walk around. The weather is so good. Cool and windy.

The parking lot of the hotel was near the water. While we were getting some gear in the van, we saw a dolphin playing around near the shore. It was amazing. I've never seen one of those up close like that.

08-07-97 Melbourne Australia: Last night was pretty uneventful. Walking around wasn't all that cool on account of people talking to me. It's constricting as hell. You turn your head to look at something and someone is on you. I stayed inside mostly and when I went out I went into places that were dingy and filled with old men and cab drivers so I wouldn't get stared at and talked to. It's a strange trip because these people are all cool and I have nothing against them, it's just hard to have people looking on at your life all the time. I think it's also because I feel depressed a lot of the time these days. I think this has been the hardest year for the depression yet. It has become such a factor in my life.

08-08-97 Melbourne Australia: Last night's show was good but tonight will be better. The stage in last night's venue was too small. It's hard to have a good time when there's no room to move. I tend to be harder on my voice when I can't move. We will be leaving to the Gold Coast in the morning.

It's a little past 8 p.m. We don't go on until 11.45. Bands go on late here, it's a beer thing. *It's a beer thing so you got to understand!* Fear of a beer planet.

08-09-97 Brisbane Australia: We got in a little while ago. It's so beautiful here. Warm and clear. It's so clean. We leave to soundcheck in a little while.

Show last night was good. Great crowd. I dedicated a song to Marius Bannister, a young man I visited in a hospital the last time the band played here. He was fighting leukemia. He died a few months after I met him. After the show a couple of his schoolmates came back and said thank you. One guy was about to cry. They had been good friends of his. I'll never forget that visit for as long as I live. 'For as long as I live'. What a strange thing to say.

I'm glad we're out of Melbourne. It was good to be there and all but it's better to keep moving as much as possible. I don't like being in the same hotel for more than two days.

For the last few days I have been concentrating on the shows and thinking about what the future will hold for me. It's hard to be sentimental when you are thinking of your survival. Feeling nostalgic is a luxury. It's what you do when you can afford to do so.

08-10-97 Gold Coast Australia: I don't know if I have seen a better looking territory than this part of Australia. The hotel overlooks the ocean. There's trees lining the coastline and I can smell them from here.

I have to go to soundcheck soon. This is the last of the Australian shows. They have been good. It's good to go out strong in places like this. I want them to have a good memory of us. So far all the shows have been good. I have been happy overall with them. We don't go on as late as we have been recently. Only 11 p.m. – luxury. Looking forward to doing gigs at a more realistic time.

08-11-97 Sydney Australia: I'm at the airport in the lounge, waiting to go to Bangkok. Thin Lizzy in the headphones guarding me from the idiots who talk endlessly. Headphones are so awesome. There are children in here and I can't hear them. I don't think you should be allowed to have children in business, first class or in any of the lounges. They should have separate places for them and the noise they make.

Last night's show was a good one. I think it was the best of the last four. We have played that place three times now. I made sure to go out hard on the last song knowing that it's safe to say that it was the last time we will ever play here. It's sad. I made sure to go out hard. I was thinking about it the whole time I was singing the last song which was 'Starve'. A good way to go out.

The record company guy came the second night. He brought two idiots with him. They could see that I was burnt but they kept talking away. Even when I started giving them half-answers, they just kept right on. Then they went and hung out, bugging the guys and as a parting shot, they all took a few extra beers for the road. I busted them on it and they just mumbled some horseshit. I bet I run into the one jerk again. I'll have a little talk with him. On the other hand, what do you expect these people to be like? As long as they do their jobs and I do mine, I guess it's just the way it is.

A drunk girl followed me back to my room. Her friends were with one of the road crew down the hall. She was wasted. She stank of alcohol and tobacco. She kept talking all kinds of shit and then she would start kissing me. She would walk around the room talking all this crazy bullshit. Finally she said that we had to visit her friend who was in someone else's room. I told her that she should go and that I was going to stay and pack.

She kept saying I had to go with her. I don't know what her problem was. Finally she split. Relief.

I had a good time after that just sitting on the balcony looking at the ocean and smelling the clean air. Fuck people. Fuck drunk women and their bullshit. I should have listened to my instinct like Joe always said to. I could have gotten out of there a lot earlier if I hadn't wasted time with these dum-dums.

An idea is cooking in my sleep-deprived brain right now. A book about Sheryl Crow. It will be the dumbest book ever written. Just sitting here, I am laughing inside. I can go so many ways with it and barely mention her at all.

I can have my imaginary dream date with SC where she whispers the lyrics to her songs in my ear as we watch the sun set on some exotic shore. We would converse only using lyrics from her songs. We would read her lyrics aloud as poetry under the moon.

I can write the absolutely worst poems about her. The dumbest odes of ever-lasting love. It will be a rave up to end all rave-ups. 'SHERYL CROW – STATUS: SUPERSTAR' will be the name of my book. My mind is reeling.

SC is going to take me to the Rock and Roll Super Highway!!! A potential book sample:

Q&A:

Q: In a life or death battle, who would win, Sheryl Crow or Bruce Lee?

A: Sheryl because she is the greatest and her clothes rock and she works with cool song writers who come up with gems like 'Everyday is a Winding Road' and 'All I Wanna Do Is Have Some Fun'. Bruce Lee just made a few movies, so what? Sheryl's videos kick *Enter the Dragon's* ass! How many Grammys did Bruce Lee ever pick up for anything he ever did? That's right. None.

Q: Who is the most influential female entertainer in America today?

a: Madonna b: Sheryl Crow c: Gloria Estafan d: Alanis Morrisette e: The Spice Girls

A: Sheryl obviously. I mean, sure, Madonna has had some influence on pop music in some parts of the world, well alright, to be fair she has had massive influence and presence all over the world on the level of the Beatles and Frank Sinatra for fifteen years but, but – SO WHAT?!! The Spice Girls are massive all over the world and have deals going in the highest of places but the answer is Sheryl because it just is, so there.

Q: If you could go to the moon with Sheryl, would you?
A: In a heart beat. We could talk about clothes and stuff all the way there and back. She wouldn't be mobbed by all her fans and we could get to know each other and tell each other all our deep and personal thoughts.

08-12-97 Bangkok Thailand: We got in a couple of hours ago. Same hotel I was at the last time. Weather is the same. Cool to see families cleaning out their woks on the street. The dogs running around. The heat and humidity are intense, even at night. It smells bad. I am sitting in a nice room at a good hotel. You see the people on the street and know that they're going home to some fucked up place.

The man who drove the van referred to himself as 'Number 74'. He wants to take us around in the van on our days off. It's all about money around here. Ken, Melvin and I walked to a 7-11 down the street to get some drinking water and a guy was on Ken with a book of women for rent. Prostitution is big around here.

The flight was 9.22.38. It was quiet and uneventful. I slept a total of an hour I bet. I had good and bad thoughts. Sometimes I cave in on myself and almost panic. I get depressed and fatalistic out of nowhere and it freaks me out. I'll be trying to get to sleep and all of a sudden it hits me and I'm on the ropes.

It's good to be out of Australia. I can't fault the place but it's just good to move onto the next episode. It's great to work with the agent Tim Pittman again. He does good for us every time. He's done every Australian tour we have ever done. It's so great to work with the same people every year. I wish they were all like Tim.

I'm beat and want to hit the sack. Not much to say about the rest of the day after yesterday's entry. Waited for the flight, got on it and sat down. Watched *Liar, Liar* and it was just boring as hell. I don't understand the appeal of Jim Carey.

08-13-97 Bangkok Thailand: A little after midnight. I am in my room in the hotel. Today was pretty interesting.

We met up with 74 in front of the hotel at ten in the morning and went out. We started the day by going to a clothes place and getting some suits made. We all got totally amazing clothes. Cheap like you wouldn't believe. We're going to look sharp. I don't know where I'll be able to use these clothes but when the time comes, I'll have 'em.

74 took us to some incredible temples. The best was the reclining Buddha. Damn thing was like a block long. It's Buddha laying on his side. A casual guy. His expression was so cool. He's kind of smiling but watchful. He's relaxed yet totally alert. We saw the Sukhothai Traimit Buddha who was five tons of pure gold. A few facts on this big gold brother: He's over 700 years old. The temple he was hanging out in was deserted in 1931. In 1955 while moving it, some of the plaster covering it broke and the workmen discovered that the damn Buddha was made of solid gold. That must have been one hell of a discovery.

The temples were really cool and beautiful. Lots of monks hanging out meditating. The statues were intense. Warriors and dogs and dragons and snakes.

We went to some government installation where they make jewelry and watched people working away. That was interesting for about forty seconds. The best part for me was the guard in front playing with his gun like he didn't know what it was for.

We went back to the clothes store to get fitted. These suits are going to be great. It will be hilarious on nights off. We will be the best dressed band you've ever seen since the Bad Seeds.

After all that was over we came back to the hotel for a little while and dropped off Chris. 74 took us to see a sex show. We paid 400 Bhats each and went in. We had ringside seats. Some women came out and danced half-heartedly to bad music and then a man and woman came out and fucked for a little while and left. After that, women came onstage one at a time doing things with their cavities. A short list of things that they did: Pulled very long lengths of string, ribbon and other things out of there. One of them gave the end of a ribbon to Melvin to pull on and I swear he must have pulled twenty feet. It was fairly astounding. A woman dropped balls into a cup. Another shot a banana and Ken caught it like a damn pro. Another one smoked two cigarettes. Let's see, what else? A woman installed a magic marker and drew Ken a swell picture of a palm tree and a shark in the water with the words 'Welcome to Thailand, Ken' on it. Three-color drawing too. I guess he'll get that one put on the fridge as soon as he gets home. I can't think of anything else they did. Wait a minute there's more, one gal opened a bottle of coke, pulled the cap out and gave it to Ken. She then had her furry little animal drain the coke. It came back later in another bottle.

Sound like a great time? For the cost of about twelve bucks we saw all of that. And there you go. I could have lived my life just fine never having seen that but what the hell.

Bangkok is the same as it was the last time. The heat is intense and the streets stink. It's cool but Bangkok is for tourists. It would be good to get out of the city and really see the place.

The fingers on the Buddhas were so beautiful and relaxed. I saw so many of them today. They all had this incredible expression that I talked about earlier. Such calm and strength. I wouldn't mind getting some of that for myself. Looking at them made me see how freaked out I am all the time. I don't know if I need to calm down but I sure could use some more something. I am wondering what it is. I think I could use some real world maturity. I spend too much time alone. I go out there and deal with 'real' people and then I run away. I don't think that hanging out with people more often will help me. I will always be bored with them for the most part. Because by and large, a good deal of people are boring.

It's gross being in a tourist type place. The sex show was so desperately stupid and sad. It was pathetic. The place was packed. If I knew what was going to happen, I would have spared myself. I could have sat and watched the river tonight but I went for that instead. It was so lame. I was stupid for going.

4.15 p.m.: We took an incredible boat ride today. We went through all these funky waterways. People living on the water in these fucked up shacks. Palm trees and sewage. It was like that scene in *Apocalypse Now* when the boat gets to Do Long bridge. In the middle of nowhere we got off the boat and checked out a small zoo that had some snakes, crocodiles, a lion, a tiger, a monkey. They did a show where the guy played around with two cobras and milked one of them. The cobras he used in the exhibition were in good shape but the ones in the tanks were underfed and listless. They had a king cobra which looked to be in pretty good condition. The translation of the King Cobra's Latin name Ophiophagus Hannah is 'King of the snake-eating snakes', and there you go. How do I know that? Did I look that up? No. It's one of the many strange facts that live in my brain.

7.14 p.m.: I am glad that we are leaving. It's a cool place and all but the whole thing gets old fast and I start to feel like a pig walking around here looking at all these people working too hard and living like shit. It's shameful to hang out amidst their poverty and luxuriate. What I spend on a trip to the record store is more money than a lot these people see in six months. The places I saw today were stinking hell holes. Sim said that Haiti was worse.

I feel like writing but I have nothing to write about. Seeing all the squalor around today made me not all that interested in seeing more of this part of the world for now. It's fascinating but so fucked up. I feel so white when I am here.

08-14-97 Frankfurt Germany: In the airport lounge waiting to get the flight to Munich. I slept at least eight hours of the 10.55.41 flight. I had a middle aisle to myself and I passed right out. I woke up a couple of times and that was about it. Nothing to remark upon about the flight.

I walked into the men's room here and the smell hit me. Clean, sterile and under control. Back in Germany.

Near Munich airport. Sitting on the bus as we get closer to the airport. It's hot and airless. These Euro busses are the worst. It's so easy to make them alright to live in but instead they make them fucked. So much of my life is fucked like this. The bus has to be hot and airless. It has to be. Why? Because.

Steve is our bus driver. He has some kind of twitch in his face. I was watching him at lunch. Outside is high eighties. Nice hot weather for a piece of shit bus that we will be sitting in hot fields in. Perfect. The limey nightmare rolls onto the continent.

It's about 2.30. We got here at around 10.30. We have to wait for the others. We had a two-hour layover in Frankfurt. Basically, we have been off the plane from Bangkok for eight hours and we're still in Germany on this shitty bus.

7.45 p.m. Somewhere near Innsbruck Austria: I have the Alps as my view. It took the driver a long time to find this place. This tour schedule is a little crazy but it should be fairly fun. It's almost all festivals. No bands I want to see. Too bad the bus is such a drag. We'll be spending enough time on the damn thing. Ten shows and it's back to the states.

08-15-97 Somewhere in Austria: Got good sleep last night. Crashed out before midnight and went until about nine this morning. Will be good to get out of this hotel. No moving air, lots of flies and mosquitoes, shitty breakfast, etc.

10.56 p.m.: The show is done. Played outdoors in an old fortress. Hung out all day to play but it was worth it. We played well and the crowd was cool even though it rained like hell right before we went on.

The Descendants were on the bill today so I ran into Bill and talked to him for a little while. He was cool as ever. Didn't see them play but we have some shows together over the next few days so I'll get a chance to check them out. I didn't have much to say to Bill but it was cool to see him all the same.

I hate to admit it but I have a lot of regret in my life. I don't know if it's regret exactly but, whatever it is, I don't like seeing people from my past. No happy memories from the Flag days. None of that is Bill's fault or anyone else's. He was one of the only guys I got along with in that band. It's just that it takes me back to where I don't want to go.

I am in the bus, the air doesn't work. It's damp and mosquito-filled outside. I'm trapped. Some lengths of time you just have to endure. The whole time, you know you're doing just that. You study each passing minute as it slips away. There's nothing like this racket to make you face yourself all the time. You get a lot of time to ponder whether you still have what it takes and you are constantly having to prove yourself. It's not easy.

I was thinking today about a valley that was once fertile and then a drought comes and the soil dries and hardens. A few years pass and all the people move away because the land can no longer support them. Then the rain comes. It rains for days on end. The place floods. But it's too late. The soil is so hard that the water cannot get through the surface and the water passes right over the valley and moves on. The skies clear and the valley is just a barren expanse of land where nothing lives.

I think that describes me. I have tried to be close to a woman and they have been really cool to me and I just can't do it. I can't break through the surface. I have become very cynical. I just don't believe it or believe in it at all. Friendship means little to me right now. If no one ever called me again I think I would be fine. I know some real swell people.

So, is there anything to do about it? Is there anything wrong with that? I notice that I have nothing to say to people so to make conversation, I just basically give them an itinerary. A girl I know called me on it recently. She was right on the money. I didn't notice until then. I talk to people to get them away from me. That's all. Rarely do I try to communicate.

What to do? Anything? I don't know. There's nothing wrong with the way I live and at the same time, it's all incredibly wrong. I am hoping that at some point I'll be in a happier place in my life than I am now. I think a lot of this bullshit has to do with things not going so well with the band this year. I have been happy with the playing. We played well tonight and I had a damn good time up there.

08-16-97 Köln Germany: Played a festival today. Right now I am at the airport Holiday Inn. We leave for Portugal in the morning. I got out of there as soon as we were done.

A girl was killed on the festival grounds yesterday. I think she got crushed. Apparently she was on drugs. That's a shame. Imagine her parents and the hell they're in right now. I don't want to think about it. Marilyn Manson went on before we did. Watched a little. Some intense shit. That guy screams a lot. Just hearing him made my throat hurt. I was told that he was swinging the mic stand at the monitor guy and tried to break the desk but they managed to get the stand out of his hands before he could. I like the thing about trying to hit the monitor man with the mic stand. I feel like doing that every night with the guy we have now. Marilyn just goes for it. More power to him.

We played alright I guess. The monitors were not good thanks to the fact that we have a monitor man who doesn't do monitors. It was too late to get anyone who was any good because they were all out on tour. Eight more shows to go on this little run. About the show. There was a ton of people and they just kind of stood there and watched. Not very inspiring. I just played well and did my best to have a good time. I would have had a better time if the monitors were better.

I hate the festival thing where you just go out there and hit it with no context at all. No one was interested in us and it was hard to get interested in them. I just went into performance mode, chopped through it, politely thanked the audience and split.

After us was Bush. I heard a little of them before I left. Sounded like Seattle around 1990. After them was Skunk Anansie and then Faith No More.

A girl I spoke to shortly in Bremen showed up in front of our bus and tried to scam tickets. Her opening line of 'I tried to call you in Austria,' was such a turn off. I just looked at her and asked why. 'So I could see about getting on the guest list.' I don't know this person and here she is scamming me. Aren't people wonderful? What else? A girl stopped me as I was walking to the backstage right after I got through playing offering me some kind of massage and whatever. Fuck these people. I don't know why I bother. I would like to get a different job. Sometimes I get sick of this shit. I always get frustrated at festivals seeing what weak bullshit people are into. There's nothing I can do about it so fuck it.

The more I think about all this shit, the more hostile I get. I went in soft and came out hard. I went into the storm and gave all. I gave it all I had and then some. What I know, they never will. That's one thing that gives me satisfaction. I sacrificed where they stood back. Knowing this makes it hard to take shit from press people and anyone else. They make lofty, sniping statements about me and they never have to pay. I have to open for bands that are so lame and so full of it. It makes me feel stupid to have wasted my time doing so many of the things that I have in the past. One last kick in the teeth. It always hurts on the way down. It has been the story of my life.

It's truths like this that make it impossible for me to have a relationship with a woman that ever goes past a certain point. I know what I know and it keeps me on the other side. Sometimes I am so full of fury and hatred I have to manually stop myself and cool out. Sometimes I don't care about anything. I have been given no reason to want to live. I worked my ass off and nothing came back but the music so I know where I'm at.

Sim was describing someone to me today and he was dead on right as he usually is. It made me think because he said that this person doesn't converse, just basically acts like he is being interviewed. I know I do that because most of the 'conversations' I have *are* interviews. I am always explaining myself to people. I have to get off that shit. I know that it is probably something that comes with the territory. Anyway, the less I talk, the better. I think it would be great to only speak professionally. Other than that, just have a few business oriented conversations like with people at the book company and then I get left alone. I don't like to talk. And to listen is torture to me most of the time.

08-17-97 Somewhere in Portugal: Portugal reminds me of Italy and Spain. In fact, Spain is right across the water from us. The drive from the airport was almost three hours, a little longer than the idiot's estimate of an hour and a half.

7.32 p.m.: Back from a good meal. We leave for the festival in a couple of hours. It is beautiful here. I wish I had more time to walk around. It's all mountains, water and blue skies.

I tried to take a nap but was unable to sleep. Will try again in a little while. I don't feel all that tired but I hardly slept last night.

When I hear all these bands at these festivals we play, I don't feel like being around this present music scene at all. I feel old and stupid amongst these hipsters. They're so weak. They disgrace the very thought of music. You get your time and then it's over. A few get to stay around longer than others but still, they have to play their greatest hits to survive. Even Eric Clapton has to play 'Layla' or the audience feels let down. He has found all these different ways to play it. What a bunch of bullshit that is. I would rather do something else than play dead like that. And that's what it is – playing dead.

08-18-97 Budapest Hungary: It took twelve hours to get here. We started out at 5.30 and drove for an hour and a half and then went from Portugal to France on a flight and then on another one to here. We got to the hotel and went to get passport photos for visas to get into Russia.

The hotel overlooks the Danube. Another great night. Last night's place was beautiful as well. We played outside around midnight under the full moon. We gave them a good one. People seemed to like us alright. About seven thousand people there.

The moon had a small star to the lower right of it. The moon was very large and bright. The air was dry and cool. I listened to a man sing with what sounded like a violin. I sat outside my room listening to this for a while before I had to go to the festival. These things are better enjoyed alone I think.

It's a night off and I can hardly walk because of the blisters on my feet. It's another hilarious kick in the teeth on the way down. It's a little before eleven and all I can do is get some writing done. I have no energy to go out and take a walk.

Sometimes I am ashamed I spent the prime of my life trying so hard to be good in front of some of the people I had to endure. At the end of the trail, there's ridicule and weakling buzzards circling overhead. That's what you get. That's alright. It makes sense. It makes all the sense in the world.

Gotta stay on my own, try to survive and lift a lot of weight. Somehow find a way to keep fighting it. Best thing to do is to work as hard as I can and keep the numbers around me as small as possible and get ready to go out hard. I am not good with people. Let me rephrase that. I am good with people as long as I keep a healthy distance and am always polite. Better off alone. Just leave them alone, man. Just leave them alone.

Too damn tired and broken to write anymore. I tell you one thing, I'm going to fuck some people up when we play tomorrow night.

08-19-97 Budapest Hungary: It's a little past four. I got some good sleep last night. I didn't do much besides eat and go out to a place next to the hotel and sit there for a while and take in the night air. It was great but I was too tired from the travel to stay out too long.

Voice is feeling good and I'm looking forward to playing tonight. Rick said that this is a ten-day festival. Bowie headlined the other night and apparently it was not one of the big selling nights. Didn't even do as well as today.

I watched an interview with Donald Trump today on CNN. He's a pretty interesting guy. He was asked what was the biggest mistake he ever made. He was hot. He said that it was when he lost focus. He said that he made the mistake of going out and enjoying life and he dropped the ball. That's intense. That's also why he is successful. He recently got divorced and said that he is better off single. There again, he was talking about the money he might have to spend on possible litigation. He will have to pay this fucking woman a ton of money. Another nail in the coffin of marriage. Fuck that shit. Getting married is so stupid. He should have saved himself all the trouble and just kept away from that agreement. She wants to get married? Get another one. Bottom line is that you shouldn't get taken out by a woman in a divorce. That is a failure. Knowing this has helped me immensely. All the times I have been fucked up with all of that relationship stuff. All that pain that fucked me up. What a waste of time. That's how I learn though. I learn by my mistakes only. Marriage? Insanity. Looks good on you, though.

On CNN right now is a thing on pro golfers. I have the sound off but it's hilarious to watch these grown men in their golf costumes jumping up and down when they make a little putt. How could you call yourself a man and do that for a living? At best it's a hobby. People are so lame.

08-20-97 Budapest Hungary: Half past midnight. Back from the gig. Had a great time playing and I know we gave them a good one. Wish we could have played longer. It was such a good time up there. There were all these people at the gate looking into the backstage area yelling every time they saw me. Some people had painted their faces red. When we got back to the hotel, there were some people waiting with cameras. The guy with a video camera was fairly insistent. They came all the way from France. They can't get into the hotel so they're just waiting outside to talk to bands on their way in I guess. I talked to them for awhile. It's only 0040 hrs. and I'm back from the whole thing with the rest of the night for me.

I am feeling pretty good. Still coming down from the gig. I need to go back out to the bus but I don't feel like dealing with the camera boys. They have to be gone by now. Here I go.

Later: They were still there but they were sulking. They look like Descendants fans to me. They have that eunuch look about them, that's why they're probably still standing around. Hopefully someone will talk to them and make their night.

Next up is a day off in Holland on my own.

08-21-97 Amsterdam Holland: Walked around a lot today. I am waiting for a Russian phone interview to come in. Hopefully I will be back out in half an hour. The weather is hot but good. Too many people on the streets. You have to know where to go in this city otherwise you get swamped with tourists.

I want to work with different people band wise. With the band as it is now, it's always a lot of waiting around for them to get through the bullshit to make it OK for them to rock out. I want to do much different music. I want to kick harder than we are now. I want to have an idea and do it and not have to discuss eight reasons why that won't work or why it is 'too rock'. The more I think about it, the more I see that it's time to do something else musically. I like them fine as people and players but I think we don't have anything more to say together musically. I think we all would be better off going separate ways.

Going to these festivals I see that it's over as far as touring. I think we have hit the wall. For example, if we went out next year it would be so lame. I don't want to be on the bills with all these weak bands. They can have it. They can have the whole thing. I'll miss the guys and the whole thing but there is a lot I won't miss either. I will not miss the depression of the last year and a half. I don't remember what it's like to breathe without stress. I don't think that any of that helps to make good art or anything else. I remember when things weren't as fucked up. I wrote more and thought more. Now all I do with my thoughts is self-medicate. I think it should be a project for me to get more happiness into my life. How the hell do you do that?

08-22-97 Amsterdam Holland: A little after midnight. I am sitting in my room.

I have only myself to blame for the situations that I put myself in. I only have myself to blame for being mad all the time. I should only be mad at myself and no one else. Getting mad at people is like getting mad at a dog for chewing up your shoes.

I don't know what to do to make myself feel better on a regular basis. I have conditioned myself to always see the worst in things and I get what I deserve. When you look for things to be bad, then you will always see just that. I am afraid of letting my guard down because when I have in the past I have always regretted it and vowed never to do it again. When people fuck with me it hurts. I don't bounce back all that well. Better than I used to, but still not as well as I should. I have been fucked with too much for too many years. All I want to do is get to the eventual bad part as soon as possible and get into the worst of it. It's the only thing that feels right, just get to the bottom line and get into the thick of it. When people call out to me on the street it wrecks any thinking I was doing, any sense of being on my own. When I go for hours without any human contact I feel fine. People cause me pain these days. I have not had a break since 1992. I have just gone and gone. I don't know what else I am supposed to do.

When people ask me how I'm doing, I always tell them that I am fine. The truth is too much work and I don't get anything out of telling someone how the fuck I am. Sometimes people call me to ask me how I am and it makes me mad. I hate to be called in my own place and have someone play that shit with me. It makes me feel weak.

6.04 p.m. Dronten Holland: At the gig site and it's been raining off and on. We are on the Delta stage with the metal and hardcore bands. All the pop bands are on the big stage. We are in the middle of nowhere with Agnostic Front. The bus electrical goes on and off like the rain and the whole bus is moist and there's no moving air. We go on in three and a half hours.

All I can hear out there is some band screaming in a language I can't understand. It's really bad, it must be THE DELTA STAGE. If you're on your way to middle age, obscurity, early death, you'll find yourself on THE DELTA STAGE.

11.25 p.m.: Gig finished. Good time. Good crowd. The stage was small and the monitors were weak but we still rocked out.

Now we wait for the gear to get packed so we can get the hell out of here. We have an overnight to Frankfurt and then a few hours before we have to be anywhere.

08-25-97 Moscow Russia: Got here a few hours ago. Flight was late boarding and sat on the ground with no air conditioning for 75 minutes. Food sucked. Took about two hours just to get the tickets straightened out.

I got out of customs and there's a television camera and crew waiting to bug me. Some idiot interviewer guy starts talking all this shit to me and I just watch and listen. We get out to the car and some woman starts hitting on me and shows me a picture of herself naked. It's getting a little strange and then the interviewer introduces her to me as his wife. Swell, huh? Finally he gets his questions out of the way and it's over with.

We went to a mafia disco for some food at around 11.30. It's now half past two. The food was pretty good and the scene in there was insane. Women stripping to Bjork, etc. Third strip place I've been to in my life if that place in Thailand is to be included. This place had a metal detector you had to go through. Armed security everywhere. What scenes I end up in from time to time. It's things like this that make it impossible to stay home for too long. There's too much going on out in the world. Constant travel will beat the shit out of you but it's worth it. I would much rather be out here, getting my brain stretched than be at home and 'content' like a house cat. I might be fucked up most of the day but at least I'm seeing it. I'll take a kick in the teeth over the bullshit that a lot of people settle for any day.

Back in the room here at the Hotel Ukraina. It's an old Stalin-era building. The view out my window overlooks the Moscow River and the White House. I can see the bridge they shelled it from.

Today's trip wore me out. It's a drag to see how shoddy things can be. As bad as things can be in America, it's still the best place in the world. I could never live here.

I was talking to the promoter Nick, who told Melvin and me about the mafia's presence here. They are in every crack and crevice, working all the angles from the top brass of the military to the executive offices of government. Of course the mafia controls the police, the easiest of all the takeovers.

The Frankfurt show was a piece of shit festival complete with bad bands and a crap PA. We played alright and had a typical German experience. They try to come off all aggro and then when you give it right back to them, which I always do, they get all bent out of shape. It was one of those nights. The fuckers tried to start right in and I just gave it right the fuck back. When I wasn't singing I was looking at them and telling them to fuck off and calling them bitches. When one would spit I would throw a water bottle into the crowd as hard as I could. They got the picture fast and cooled out. I played hard as hell though. By the end of the show they weren't playing that shit anymore. Fuck these people. They have no idea what they are fucking with. They are fucking with seventeen years of abuse onstage. They just don't know what I have seen and been through. If they had they would never bother with the bullshit that they do.

That's about it as far as the gig. A psycho chick got backstage and tried to get to me. I had just finished playing and she starts right in with the psycho-crap. Rick got her out of there. I managed to get out of there without having to deal with many people. A girl who had ridden on the bus with us the night before got kicked out of the room she thought she was going to stay in because she didn't want to fuck him so she calls my room and asks me if she can stay there. I said no because she is another nutcase and you really can't let these people get too close to you because they waste your time. That is the way to deal with most people. The big mistake people make is that they commit to others on a deep level and all they get back is a little and they are stuck with the deal. Like the guys who are married and stay on the road for long periods of time. If they want to fool around they have to deal with the fact that they are breaking their vows to their wives. Whether they care or not is a different story. But they are under contract and they have to deal with that. Why you would want to tie yourself into a deal like that is beyond me.

Moscow time has it nearly three in the morning. I am tired and the room is hot and the air doesn't move. I want to stay up and keep writing though.

08-26-97 Moscow Russia: Today was a drag. The room was hot and I didn't get a lot of sleep. I had to do a photo session. The drive there was a drag because the car had some engine trouble and would seize up and nearly die every other second and it was blazing hot and of course, the handles on the rear windows were gone so you couldn't open them. I get to the photo place and the idiot produces this large sword and a horned helmet and asks me to pose with these things. Of course, that didn't happen and he bummed out and the session was over in about five shots. Do I care?

After that we did a soundcheck at the hall and went back to the silly casino for some food and then a press conference. That was boring and the whole band had to attend and what always happens happened. The press idiots had no real questions for the band, only me so the poor guys had to sit there while I got asked boring questions.

After that was over I came back here to the room of hot, unmoving air and grabbed my stuff and went down to the gig to see a band I was told was just like us, whose singer was going for my thing. I watched a little of it. Average hardcore music with a singer in shorts wearing no shoes. Whatever.

The set was hard tonight. Strange crowd. Some spitting and beer can throwing. I don't react well to that. Didn't make me give the best performance since I was always looking for the next thing to hit stage. The place was hot and the monitors sucked.

After the set was over I got right out of there. I didn't want to talk to or meet anyone. I was tired and people pissed me off with the beer cans and spit routine. The woman who hit on me at the airport was there and had me sign the naked photo of her. Her idiotic husband hovered around me the whole time I was dealing with her. What part of this am I supposed to understand?

I am done with this place. I am looking forward to leaving. I did the show and the place sucked and I am over Russia for now. Interesting place and I am looking forward to reading more of the writers but it's not a place that I'm thinking about coming back to for awhile.

11.04 p.m. Denmark: Waiting for the ferry. We will be out of here on the way to Arhus soon. Today was all travel. It was good to get out of Moscow. We have been on planes all day and will not get to the hotel for quite a while. The day off is shot. All we'll be doing is eating bad food on the boat and getting to sleep some.

Getting out of Russia was crazy. We were in line to get our passports stamped and get onto the flight, which was leaving shortly. There was a black man ahead of us getting thoroughly hassled by the guards. They had his carry-on bags unpacked and the contents strewn all over the floor. The line wasn't moving and I figured we were going to miss our flight. I asked Alexander, our friend from the radio station who was with us what we should do. He asked Rick if he had any leftover rubles. Rick did and Alexander called a guard over and pointed to us and then gave the rubles to the guy and we were waved right through. How crass are these people?

08-27-97 Arhus Denmark: We finally got in at around three in the morning. I am in my bad room at the moment. Half of the lights don't work so it's hard to see. I had to re-rig all the lamps just so I can see what I am doing.

It's a little past three in the afternoon. I went out and had a cup of coffee and some food. It was alright except for the long looks I got from the older folks. I had to sign a few autographs. I got tired of that place and the bad coffee so I came back here hoping that the room would be better. Depressed again. Having major pain in right elbow.

08-28-97 Arhus Denmark: Got back from the show about half past midnight. It was fairly unremarkable. We played well but the monitors or the monitor man were not so good and the rug was slippery and I was sliding all over the place which makes it hard to play well but it was alright anyway. The audience was annoying at times, grabbing my ankles and pulling, putting their hands in my face, the kind of thing that makes you see why there's barriers to keep people away from you.

What made it slightly interesting was that I had played this place before in 1983 with the Minutemen. It was much nicer this time around. Back then it was dirty and the people were all belligerent. They tried to get a little of that going tonight but I wasn't having it. It's easy to stop that thing fast. You make an example of one guy and all the rest figure it out fast. I had to do it twice but they eventually got it. I will not take shit from these people ever again. I will never lose control of a crowd. Fuck these people when they fuck with the band. You have to lay down the law fast and firm otherwise they think they can get over on you.

I have to hit the sack because we have a long one in the morning. We leave here at eight and go by ferry to Copenhagen and then to the airport to go to Trondheim to play a festival. It will be a monster haul but we'll rock.

Trondheim Norway, 9 p.m.: We got here a few hours ago. It's really not much of a festival, more like a gig that is outside. Here in my airless room being battered by noise from the outdoor cafe.

We play at 11.30 and then have to leave at five to fly back to Copenhagen. Then we have a long drive and some ferries and then we arrive in Leipzig really late. After that we play one last show there and go back to America. It's going to be a long trip back. I think I go Frankfurt–Newark–LA. Fantastic.

It's cool outside but very moist and the people below me are laughing all the time. It sucks in this room. By the time I get back here it will be about two and I'll have enough time to shower and doze. No sleep till Copenhagen.

08-29-97 Trondheim Norway: It's a few minutes past two and the idiots are walking drunkenly down the street. The show was cool. It was outside and the air was great. I played my ass off and tore up my feet some more. My left foot is hurting. Right arm and right knee are flicked. I think I have tendon problems in the arm. I hope it won't slow me down on the lifting front. It doesn't hurt for most lifts. I can still deadlift, and squat, what else do you really need?

From now on I live for myself. I have been living for others for too many years. I have wasted so much time and gotten nothing in return. I will fade out these activities and start living for myself. I can't get back all the years but I can get back my life.

Basic rap up on Trondheim: We got here after an eight o'clock lobby call. We drove to the ferry and then to the airport. We flew here and went to the venue. Theo is in really bad shape. He didn't do sound at the show tonight. Peter did FOH and some guy did the monitors. At the end of the show one side kept feeding back. I got so pissed off with him, I picked up the damn thing and threw it. I called him some names and kept rocking. Earlier in the gig one guy kept throwing his coke at me and I told him after one song that I would beat his ass in front of all these people and everyone was into it. I told him that I would fuck his face up and it wouldn't even put me off my next meal. He backed off and no one threw anything after that. We leave in ninety minutes for the airport. We will be on the bus all day.

Leipzig, Germany: A little after eleven. We got here two hours ago. Today was a bit of a washout on account of I slept on and off until five in the evening and then dozed off the rest of the way. I didn't sleep the night before so there you go. Now it's late and I am fully awake. Saw Skunk Anansie on TV tonight. They were playing some festival. They had a two-woman string section. Skin sang her ass off. Seeing shit like that makes me wonder how I get along at all. It makes me see that as small as we are, we are probably bigger than we should be. I can't sing to save my life. Chalk one up for great musicianship and my winning smile.

This morning seems like days ago. We had a 5 a.m. lobby call and we went to the airport. I don't remember much of it except the sun rising on the fjords and the jokes everyone was making about Phydeaux's neck pillow and eye shades. Of course Chris knows the rap from Monty Python about the Trondheim Hammer Dance where the old ladies are thrown into the fjords. The view was amazing but I was too tired to appreciate it much. We got on the plane and then onto the bus and that was it. The rest of the day was a blur. Now I'm in my room burning out. I have called a few people's rooms but no one is there.

08-30-97 Leipzig Germany: It's a little past one. I went down to the bar and found some of the guys and hung out with them. It's good to be around them sometimes. They are some of the greatest people I know. How much I like them bugs me. I don't want to like anyone too much because it's just another thing that can get taken away from me. Now isn't that a dumb thing to think? It is but I also think it's true. Also a thing that makes me feel bad is that this will all be over so soon. Sometimes I see why people are really into their families. If I ever had one, then this was it. I don't think it's a good idea for me to attach to anyone even on a friend level. I definitely don't feel comfortable being known. I don't like the idea of anyone knowing me past a certain point. I don't think there's anything wrong with that at all. When I like the camaraderie of being with the guys, and it is great, I feel like I am being lulled into a false sense of security and that I am not staying sharp. I have such a hard trek ahead of me before I can finally rest my bones. I have to stay sharp and work hard for a long time.

6.21 p.m.: Slept long and just came back from the bar where I sat and had some coffee. I am watching a television show on African wildlife that seems to center on hyenas and vultures. I like the thing Hemingway wrote about shooting hyenas and watching them run around as they died. I forget what he said exactly, something about watching death course through their body before they went.

We hit at 10.30. I think it's going to be a good one. Corny bands on the bill. I always play well when there's corny bands

237

on the bill. My voice sounds good today and it will be fun to play outside. The other night in Norway was killin' and tonight will be good too. I imagine the gig is a piece of shit judging from the bands that are on the bill and the fact that we are headlining it. If all you can get is us to headline, then you don't have a show.

We have an 0600 lobby call. We drive to Frankfurt and then fly to Newark. It's going to be a long day. I don't mind.

08-31-97 Leipzig Germany: Back in the room. Show was alright. Boring crowd. When they play dead sometimes I over-do it and blow out but tonight I played well. Sometimes when it's the last show I have a fuck it attitude. I gave them shit right back tonight when they tried to do their tough guy routine. Someone threw a beer can on stage and I threw it at someone's head and told them to shove the empties up their ass. It was the last of the cans.

I'm watching Beck on television right now. What a load of crap. What a fucking turn off. So contrived and corny. So lame, a critic's dream. I was right about him. Now I know for sure. How trite. Fuck these people. It's good I saw that right now. It just reaffirms what I thought.

It's a little past two in the morning, we leave on the bus at six. I have to pack my shit and then I can get some sleep. Should not be too hard. We have a five-hour drive to the airport. It's going to be one long fucking time before I get to LA. I think this one is going to be one of those 24-hour travel times like getting back from Russia. I don't care as long as I'm moving.

So good to know that you tried and you still didn't stop me. Lawyers, press, all you fuckers tried and you couldn't stop me. It feels so good to know I have what it takes.

Look at what's out there. What a load of crap. Year after year.

I have about two and a half hours before we leave for the airport. I will not be able to sleep, of course, and the book I have with me is not much of a page turner so it's another boring all-nighter as we wait to go and wait and wait some more. I hate this part of the whole trip. I hate the blank time. I hate having to hang out and do nothing.

Looking at CNN. Princess Diana's boyfriend just died in a car crash. He was about to get sued by the other idiot he had just blown off. The idiot in question was interviewed by Larry King the other day and she was lining up a nice fat court case to sue him for some kind of breach of promise. She won't be suing shit now. Imagine a model trying to sue a guy because he got cold on her? *When he was fucking me, he really seemed to like me!* I am thinking about her right now. She has been woken up by the lawyer. She is mad because she won't be getting that money. She was still wearing the ring he gave her. I wonder what she'll do with it now? It's a strange turn of events. It looks like the car the two were in was trying to outrun the press shitheads that were following them. That's pretty hot that the press killed a millionaire and his driver and fucked up the bodyguard and the Princess. Now they're interviewing Tom Cruise and he is telling his tales of woe about being followed by paparazzi. Two fucking guys are dead and all they talk about is Princess Diana. Poor Tom, maybe he can get L Ron Hubbard to bring them back to life.

Wow! Breaking news! Princess Diana dead! Fuck these people. They deserve each other. Nations do not mourn when real people die.

Starting to get tired. Won't be in LA for another 26 hours. It's going to be a long day and it hasn't even started yet. Hopefully I'll get some sleep on the plane.

I switched to a British station and they are all over this shit. This is their bread and butter. This is a big deal for these shitheads. This will be bigger than the fashion guy getting whacked by the gay serial killer. How hot was the idiot married to Sting making her big speech at what's his name's funeral? All the deep breaths and drama, she's corny like her husband. How hard are the papers going to work this one? It will be bigger than OJ for at least a little while. If they search out and find the press shitheads who cut and ran, they will treat those guys like terrorists. The irony of the whole thing is that the guys who took the photos and caused the accident are employed by the same tabloids who will be covering this event. It works out quite well, don't you think? If you have no news, invent some damn it! I think it's going to be open season on those motherfuckers. They done fucked up this time! How great would it have been if a carload of press people had been killed? I would like to see the Princess alive and all those damn devils gone.

5.17 p.m. En route to LA: On the second flight. Things going well. First leg was kind of a drag because it was full of students on their first trip to Europe. The kind who applaud when the plane lands.

At one point I was looking forward to being back in my place but now I just feel like not being anywhere. It doesn't matter where I am as long as I can get some sleep and a workout. I am so sick of the noise and the people that the music world has in it. All these corny bands and all the drunks and all the depression that it puts me into. I can stand it for a while but then I need to get out of it. Being home is not always the greatest thing for me. I was all into getting back a few nights ago. But as I sit here now, I wish that I was playing tonight. I have had that feeling so many times. It always hits me when I am in the comfort of home. I want to be out there. Like Willard said in *Apocalypse Now*: 'When I was there I wanted to be here. When I was here, all I could think of was getting back into the jungle.' That's the head. No one who doesn't know can understand that. That's why I don't bother talking about it with anyone. Especially women. What a waste of time. There's nothing like doing that to really let you know you are in a different world. So many times I have been with a woman and made no connection at all. Just sex and some relief. I don't tell anyone anything deep because I know that I am on my own on that one. Why bother? Why fuck up a perfectly good thing? No one wants to know. I used to bum out on being alone. Sometimes I look at women and imagine myself with them. My mind plays out all kinds of scenes. Love and happiness, all kinds of doo wop songs, but the reality is that no one can get to me and I can't get to anyone.

I heal myself with solitude and now I wonder if that does any good at all. I wonder if it just makes me worse. On the weekends when the phone doesn't ring, I won't speak for 48 hours except for occasionally singing along with a song. I don't leave the place for days at a time.

I have done 94 shows this year already. It's been a long year and there's still four months to go. And then what? I come to the end of another year all burned out and scraped thin, wondering if I'll be able to get out there next year and do it again.

All this is getting pretty negative. End of tour bitterness welling up. It's strange when what you do for a living seems at times to only want to hurt you. At the end of a tour you are all banged up and press pricks have had their go at you and you feel like killing someone or yourself and it seems like the whole thing was for nothing and you were the biggest fool ever. That's how I feel when I come back from these things sometimes. I feel used but I have no one to blame but myself.

Last thing you want to do is take it home with you. You have to learn to let it go or it won't let you go. 'Glory's only fleeting, already gone.' You shouldn't even take it back to the hotel or the bus after it's over. You should leave it on the stage when you walk off. I try but all of this means too much to me to act like it's not my life.

09-01-97 LA CA: It's about 12.41 p.m. Got back here around ten last night. The taxi driver gave me his screenplay. Must be LA.

Listened to the Lurkers *God's Lonely Men* album. It's so great when something you liked a long time ago is still good. The room is hot as hell. It's always bad here in the summer. Played *Pet Sounds* today and am listening to *In Trance* by the Scorpions. Still sounds great.

6.38 p.m.: Checking out this Dizzy Reece CD I found in Australia. I bought it because it has Hank Mobley on it. It's called *Star Bright*. It's real good.

A month passes doing talking shows in America, burning out in my room and waiting to go.

10-11-97 LAX: About 45 minutes before departure to Tokyo. Last few days have been busy and not good for writing.

I am a little worried about these shows coming up. It would have been good if we had the chance to practice a little. I guess that's what we'll do tomorrow.

10-13-97 Tokyo Japan: Cool to be back here. I got in last night. It took about an hour and a half to get here from the airport with the traffic. It was alright with me though. I just looked out the window and knew how cool it was to be hanging out in Japan watching the sun set. You gotta keep things in perspective at all times.

We are playing tonight. It's now about ten in the morning. I am looking forward to playing the shows but I want to get them done because I have a bunch of talking shows coming up and I am geared for them and the band thing is a little strange. It's like when we played Brazil and Argentina after Europe in 1994. We got together in Buenos Aires and went for it. It was cool but lacking a little vibe-wise.

I went out with some of the guys last night even though I wanted to stay in my room and sleep. I am damn glad I did too. Might be awhile before I see these guys again. When I hang out with them, I want to go make another record with them starting as soon as we get home. Being with them makes me want to go to NY and settle in for a long stint of work. These feelings make me confused. I have to be able to separate the friendship from the work.

Then there's the reality of this. I think at this point, the band has become a place to go when you don't have an idea what to do with yourself. The last writing period was ridiculous. I think that after the initial period of settling in passed, all of a sudden we would have to deal with how much we have changed. Sim has moved to Brooklyn. Not that it would change things that much but it's easy to see that everyone is getting on with their lives. I don't think we can play any harder, any more whatever than we already have. What the fuck could we possibly do? We know each other so well that I think we fall into a trap of trying to anticipate the other's moves.

Now thinking about it, walking up those flights of stairs to the rehearsal place every day and saying hello to all the same people seems like escapism and not reality.

I think I am better off on the road. Just now sitting in my little room, I am filled with thoughts. I know that a lot of them are ridiculous. I spend a lot of time thinking about things that don't matter but all the same, I am thinking. I say this because the last time I was in LA I didn't do much thinking, didn't do much daydreaming.

The time I spent in LA was strange. I felt like I was at the end of the line and then at other times I felt good. I liked it at night when no one was there. I am a night person. If I had it my way, I would live like a vampire. I would get up in the afternoon and do my workouts in the evening. But you can't live like that if you have to have any contact with the outside world. I don't think I am there yet. The night is rich. The night heals. The night is where all things creative come from.

10-14-97 Tokyo Japan: A little after midnight. Played well tonight. I sang well. We did pretty damn good even though we had just gotten off long flights. We are booked two nights in this 1200 seater. Tonight's draw was 350. I can't imagine what the next night will be.

We went out after the show and ate at a restaurant where we all sat on mats. It was very cool. It's great to hang out with the guys. I see now that all the nights the guys were out and seeing things when I was sitting in my room or something, that I was missing out on a lot of fun. I wouldn't have gotten done all the things that I did if I hung out all the time though. You make your choice, always.

Sometimes I don't know what I should do with myself and I think that I should be more normal, until I hang out with normal people and it's so depressing. All the tragic, useless responsibility they feel the need to take on to make their lives have meaning. I think it's important to have some level of happiness in your life, otherwise, you have misery all the time and nothing at all comes from that except more misery. Like I'm one to talk.

I continually try to think of things that make me happy and what it will take to keep that happening. I have been under the weight of failure and financial strain for quite some time now. It has distorted my thoughts. It has made all the things I do a distortion and echo of that situation. It sucks.

10-15-97 Tokyo Japan: It's the day off. Last night was a good show. About the same number of people as the night before. I don't get it. There's nothing to get uptight about. It is what it is.

11.35 p.m.: Did an interview with Ozzy who also happens to be out here. He was dead cool as always. We had a great time hanging out. Of course, I always think of Joe on these occasions and how he should have been there to hang with the man.

10-16-97 Nagoya Japan: It's a little before eleven at night. We had about a hundred people in there tonight. What a damn heartbreak. I don't know what it is. I don't know what to do about it either. It hurts my feelings but it's a sign that people are tired of us. I guess it's time to pack it in or something. I just don't know and it distresses the shit out of me.

I guess I'll never get the chance here again but hey, four trips here is pretty damn cool considering where I started. I have been fortunate and am grateful.

10-17-97 Osaka Japan: I am waiting to go back to the club to do the show. It will be a good one. I like this place. I am sure no one will be there but what the hell. I am wondering if this will be the last show we will ever do. I know I have written about it before but when you see the way things are going, it makes you have to seriously consider.

I don't know that I will be doing anything different. Like with all gigs, you try your best to get through it the best you can without any blow outs.

I am leaving early in the morning and I am glad of it. I am into getting on to the next thing as soon as I can. I'll see the guys for dinner after the show and then I'll try to crash for a few hours. I have a 0630 lobby call. It's going to be Rick and myself going to Tokyo and then I have a long ass wait until I get on the flight to Perth, Australia.

It's strange doing band dates out of context like we have been here. For me, the thing was over in Leipzig and this is just a strange turn in the road. It feels like a dream. If we came here after Australia or something it would have been a different vibe but it is what it is. I don't like playing like this. It took me a gig just to remember how to do it. If we could have had a day of practice and then a day off, that would have been great.

I am very depressed right now. The bad attendance and the idea of this being it makes it hard to keep my head up. I am associating Japan with all this torment so I am looking forward to getting out of here and onto the speaking dates. I have a lot of fun on those because there's not the voice thing hanging over my head all the time. Also, it will mean that the band thing is over for the year and I can put all that stuff away and put *Come In and Burn* behind me. It will be good for me to do that. This time period has been a heartache.

Soon I will go back to the venue and sit there. Nothing to do here except think about going to the venue.

10-18-97 Osaka Japan: I have to get up in a few hours to start the flights to Australia. The show was good tonight. It's tonight that I got back in the pocket with my pacing and breathing and it was good. Now I want to play a bunch of band shows but that's over with.

I have a long layover in Tokyo where I'll write more. Now it's time to go to sleep. It was a good tour and now it's all over. I thought I would feel more than this but I don't. I don't feel anything at all.

10.27 a.m. Narita Airport, Tokyo Japan: When I went to check out this morning at 0630, there were girls waiting for me. What could they possibly want at this hour? They wanted photos. I am done with my interest in this country for now. I have found the record company types to be only into what you can do for them at all times and their kindness is forced. That's cool. I know where I stand. With the attendance at the shows, I think it's safe to say that there's no real interest in what I am doing over here. Hell of an interesting experience though and it was good to see the guys one more time.

All I know is, the Rollins Band is like a blunt instrument that we just pound away with at a wall that will not give. Another year of pounding will not help anything. In fact, I think it would be doing the exact thing that I said I would not do, which is stick around after it's time to split. This entire year has given me every indication that it's time to do something else. The thought of that is exciting.

I have to stay focused. 1998 will be hard and full of confrontation. I will have to avoid anything that will distract me. It's funny that as my life goes on, it seems to get harder to sort out. I thought it was supposed to be the other way around. I don't know if I am doing something right or wrong. I guess it's always a challenge and you have to keep rising up to meet it. I know that it's always been that way for me. I always seem to have something in my way. I also know that it's always me who put the obstacles there so I have nothing to complain about. I have a good life.